Anthropology and anthropologists

By the same author

Kalahari Village Politics
Wives for Cattle
Changing Jamaica
The Invention of Primitive Society
South Africa and the Anthropologists
The Chosen Primate

Anthropology and anthropologists

The modern British school

Third revised and enlarged edition

Adam Kuper

London and New York

First published 1973 by
Allen Lane The Penguin Press

Revised edition published 1983 by
Routledge & Kegan Paul Ltd
Reprinted 1985 (twice) and 1987

Reprinted 1989, 1990, 1991 (twice), 1993 by
Routledge
11 New Fetter Lane, London EC4P 4EE
29 West 35th Street, New York, NY 10001

Third revised and enlarged edition published 1996
by Routledge
11 New Fetter Lane, London EC4P 4EE

Simultaneously published in the USA and Canada
by Routledge
29 West 35th Street, New York, NY 10001

Reprinted 1997

© 1973, 1983, 1996 Adam Kuper

Typeset in Times by
Keystroke, Jacaranda Lodge, Wolverhampton

Printed and bound in Great Britain by
Redwood Books, Trowbridge, Wiltshire

British Library Cataloguing in Publication Data
A catalogue record for this book is available from the British Library.

Library of Congress Cataloging in Publication Data
A catalogue record for this book is available

ISBN 0–415–11895–6

For Jessica

Contents

Preface to the third edition

Two decades ago, Isaac Schapera invited me to write an account of modern British social anthropology. I had not for a moment contemplated such a project, but he is a good salesman, I was young and heedless, and I took it on. I duly reread the monographs and journals, and organized a seminar series at which several of the older generation were persuaded to reminisce. I was able to interview some of the leading actors, which compensated a little for the fact that I could not gain access to private holdings of letters, or even to the Malinowski archive that was being built up at the London School of Economics. (Evidently some of the elders in the profession planned to write their own accounts, though in the event none has appeared.)

News of the project drew a mixed response. Some of my seniors were cautious, even furtive, readier to purvey unreliable anecdotes about their contemporaries than to talk openly about themselves. Two or three were deliberately obstructive. Yet I was not prepared for the reactions that publication provoked. It was, of course, a young man's book, and the tone lacked reverence. Because it dealt with very recent events, it was bound to touch on matters that were still controversial. I appreciated that some colleagues might feel that it dealt too much in personalities. Nevertheless, I was astonished at the furious reaction of some of the older generation when they read the book (or even, in at least one case, when she had not read it, Lucy Mair remarking that it would upset her too much to read the thing, which was a pity since she had given me the best of my interviews).

Reviewing the book in *Man*, after the dust had settled a bit, Roy Willis remarked, 'His audacity in desacralising the godlike founding fathers of our discipline and presenting them as human beings, warts and all, has predictably aroused fury in some quarters: it was nonetheless a necessary and salutary action.' In truth, I had not realized how audacious I was being. Fortunately I was in the field, in Jamaica, when the book appeared in 1973. Several months later my wife and I returned, and found the atmosphere still heavily charged. Professional occasions in London were, for a while, liable to be rather awkward, although Jessica tried to clear the air by spreading a rumour that I was preparing a new edition, with fresh insults.

In retrospect, the emotional reaction had something to do with the fact that the book appeared at a moment of transition in British social anthropology. As an intellectual tradition, social anthropology can be traced back to the 1860s. In the last decades of the nineteenth century, in the hands of E. B. Tylor and J. G. Frazer, it became a specialized discourse on social and cultural evolution. At the turn of the century, Alfred Haddon and W. H. R. Rivers, both teaching at Cambridge, organized the first British ethnographic expedition and began the process of professionalization. In his theoretical writings, Rivers drew on the evolutionism of the Victorians, and on the diffusionist writings of the German geographical school, but he also anticipated, and helped to shape, some of the debates of the next generation. A. R. Radcliffe-Brown was Rivers's first student in anthropology, and he was casting his arguments in the form of a critique of Rivers twenty years after his teacher had died. Bronislaw Malinowski worked in Oceania, about which Rivers had written his masterpiece, and he once boasted that if Rivers was the Rider Haggard of anthropology, he would be its Conrad.

Yet if there were continuities, the discontinuities were more striking. Malinowski pioneered new methods of field research. Particularly under the influence of Radcliffe-Brown, Durkheimian sociology and other intellectual models replaced the evolutionist and diffusionist ideas of the older generation. Malinowski and Radcliffe-Brown were self-conscious revolutionaries. They established what amounted to a new tradition of intellectual enquiry, which came loosely to be called 'functionalist anthropology', or simply 'British social anthropology'.

The break was not so sudden or so complete that it can be dated exactly, though contemporaries had no doubt that it was real enough. Any starting-point is arbitrary. This book takes 1922 as its baseline, the year in which Rivers died and both Malinowski and Radcliffe-Brown published their first major field studies. What was at first a radical, fringe enterprise soon became an established profession, a distinctive, recognized branch of world anthropology. The generation trained by Malinowski in the 1920s and 1930s took over the leadership of the new profession after the Second World War. They were appointed to the chairs in the various old and new departments in Britain and the Commonwealth, and controlled the field for two decades. In the early 1970s, when my book appeared, they were all retiring. It was a touchy moment, particularly since, as the Belgian anthropologist Luc de Heusch perceptively observed, 'L'anthropologie sociale britannique diffère profondément de l'ethnologie française par un trait remarquable: elle a l'esprit de famille.'

Twenty years on, as I prepare this third edition, it is clear that the project initiated by Malinowski and Radcliffe-Brown underwent a crisis in the 1970s, and that my book was in the nature of an obituary notice. In the post-colonial world, a different social anthropology emerged. Some of its roots can be traced back to developments within British social anthropology in the 1960s and 1970s, for as I have tried to show, this was never a settled or completely homogeneous discourse. But there were many fresh currents. The generation that came into the discipline in the 1960s, as research students or as young lecturers, were influenced by structuralism and by the Marxist ideas of the period. Later they were impressed by what Quentin Skinner identified as the revival of grand theory in the social sciences. They took note of the changing fashions in American cultural anthropology, which was going through a transformation of its own. Some were especially influenced by feminist ideas. Others took up new specialities, notably medical anthropology, visual anthropology and cognitive anthropology.

A distinctive social anthropological discourse continued to develop, but it was transformed: and it was no longer a specifically British enterprise. Classical British social anthropology had quickly established itself in Australia, New Zealand and South Africa, and it had become a recognized speciality in some American anthropology departments, notably at the University of Chicago. After the war, social anthropology began to develop in Indian universities, and also in some African universities. French social anthropology, essentially a twin of the British neo-Durkheimian project, influenced scholars in Latin America and in West Africa. But it was especially in Europe that interest in social anthropology spread, and new departments were established. In becoming a truly cosmopolitan project, social anthropology changed fundamentally. I have described this ongoing process of transformation in a new, final chapter. For the rest, I have made a number of editorial changes, and added an appendix that notes the major recent publications on the history of British anthropology.

Adam Kuper

1   Malinowski

The magnificent title of the Functional School of Anthropology
has been bestowed by myself, in a way on myself, and to a large
extent out of my own sense of irresponsibility.

– Malinowski[1]

. . . a unique and paradoxical phenomenon – a fanatical theoretical
empiricist.

– Leach[2]

I

Malinowski has a strong claim to being the founder of the profession
of social anthropology in Britain, for he established its distinctive
apprenticeship – intensive fieldwork in an exotic community. For
the fifteen years that he spent at the London School of Economics
after his return from the Trobriand islands he was the only master
ethnographer in the country, and virtually everyone who wished to
do fieldwork in the modern fashion went to work with him.

Yet Malinowski, and many of his students, felt that he was much
more than a pioneer in method. As one of his most distinguished
students has remarked, 'he claimed to be the creator of an entirely
new academic discipline. A whole generation of his followers were
brought up to believe that social anthropology began in the Trobriand
islands in 1914.'[3] This grander reputation persists, despite the poverty
of Malinowski's explicit theoretical formulations. His ethnographic
triumph was based upon a novel perspective which is still an integral
feature of British social anthropology, however much it may have
been obscured by his attempts at formalization and his incessant
polemics. There *was* a functionalist revolution, and Malinowski was
its leader. But it did not establish functionalist theory as Malinowski
propounded it.

II

The subject-matter of anthropology was fairly clearly defined in the early twentieth century, although it was called by various names – social anthropology, cultural anthropology, or ethnology, ethnography and sociology. Its core was the study of 'primitive' or 'savage' or 'early' man, and by the last third of the nineteenth century the study of 'culture' – in Tylor's sense, embracing social organization – was clearly distinguished from the biological study of man. There was, then, a specific study concerned with 'primitive culture'. This field was conventionally considered under various heads – material culture, folklore, religion, magic, 'sociology', language, law and environment.

There was also by the early twentieth century an accepted distinction between a broadly geographical approach, which was concerned with migration, cultural diffusion and the classification of peoples and objects, and what was generally called the sociological approach, which dealt with the development of social institutions. Exponents of the former approach tended to be more descriptive and particularistic, while the sociologists were more comparative and theoretical. The distinction between them had been formalized at least as early as 1909, when, according to Radcliffe-Brown,

> A meeting of teachers from Oxford, Cambridge and London was held to discuss the terminology of our subject. We agreed to use 'ethnography' as the term for descriptive accounts of non-literate peoples. The hypothetical reconstruction of 'history' of such peoples was accepted as the task of ethnology and prehistoric archaeology. The comparative study of the institutions of primitive societies was accepted as the task of social anthropology, and this name was already preferred to 'sociology'. Frazer in 1906 had already defined social anthropology as a branch of sociology that deals with primitive peoples. Westermarck had the position of Professor of Sociology, though his work was really in the field of social anthropology.[4]

A similar distinction was made in the syllabus adopted for the newly established diploma in anthropology at Oxford in 1906. 'Cultural anthropology' was distinguished from physical anthropology, and it was considered under four heads – archaeology, technology, ethnology and sociology. The distinction between ethnology and sociology was clear. Ethnology included:

> The comparative study and classification of peoples, based upon conditions of material culture, language, and religious and social

institutions and ideas, as distinguished from physical characters. The influence of environment upon culture.

Sociology was concerned with:

The comparative study of social phenomena, with special reference to the earlier history of:
(a) Social organization (including marriage customs), government and law;
(b) moral ideas and codes;
(c) magical and religious practices and beliefs (including treatment of the dead);
(d) modes of communicating ideas by signs, articulate language, pictographs and writing.[5]

Each of these approaches to 'primitive culture' was associated also with a particular theoretical tendency. The ethnologists inclined towards diffusionism. Cultures were patchworks of traits, borrowed from others, the superior traits moving outwards from a centre like the ripples made by a stone thrown into a pond – to echo a favourite analogy of diffusionist writers. These cultural traits could be classified, on stylistic or other criteria, and their movement, or the movements of their bearers, reconstructed. Diffusionism was given a great impetus in Britain by the dramatic discoveries of Egyptian archaeology, and the development of the theory that the 'fertile crescent' was the cradle of most of the artifices of civilization – a theory propagated in the 1920s by Elliot Smith and Perry at University College London. The sociologists, on the other hand, were by and large evolutionists, though their views diverged from each other, and none any longer favoured the unilinear evolutionary schemes so fashionable in Victorian England. Speaking very generally, they tended to see cultures as systems with an interior dynamic, rather than as the products of haphazard borrowings; but they varied as to whether the dynamic element was intellectual, economic, religious, or whatever.

This is a simplified version of the situation, but it permits the immediate identification of the impact of functionalism. The functionalists took over 'sociology', but dropped the 'special reference to the earlier history of ... ' which had been the hallmark of the evolutionists. They also rejected not only diffusionism but the whole ethnological enterprise, so that for a generation the preoccupations of the ethnologists, including specific histories, were disregarded by British social anthropologists.

In the concluding pages of his first Trobriand monograph,

Argonauts of the Western Pacific (1922), Malinowski set out his own point of view with reference to the preoccupations of these major schools. He wrote:

> it seems to me that there is room for a new type of theory. The succession in time, and the influence of the previous stage upon the subsequent, is the main subject of evolutional studies, such as are practised by the classical school of British Anthropology (Tylor, Frazer, Westermarck, Hartland, Crawley). The ethnological school (Ratzel, Foy, Gräbner, W. Schmidt, Rivers, and Eliott-Smith [sic]) studies the influence of cultures by contact, infiltration and transmission. The influence of environment on cultural institutions and race is studied by anthropogeography (Ratzel and others). The influence on one another of the various aspects of an institution, the study of the social and psychological mechanism on which the institution is based, are a type of theoretical studies which has been practised up till now in a tentative way only, but I venture to foretell will come into their own sooner or later. This kind of research will pave the way and provide the material for the others.[6]

A few years later Radcliffe-Brown wrote, more directly:

> I believe that at this time the really important conflict in anthropological studies is not that between the 'evolutionists' and the 'diffusionists', nor between the various schools of the 'diffusionists', but between conjectural history on the one side and the functional study of society on the other.[7]

Nevertheless it is misleading to see functionalism triumphing over the orthodoxies of evolutionism or diffusionism. The hallmark of British anthropology in the first two decades of this century was a cautious and sceptical attitude to any grand theoretical formulation, evolutionist or diffusionist. Frazer's work was being treated with a certain derision, even at the turn of the century, in the anthropological journals; and in the hands of men like Westermarck or Marett evolutionism was only an ultimate point of reference, not a central organizing concept. It is true that the extreme Egypto-centric diffusionism of Elliot Smith and Perry was a force in the 1920s, and that even Rivers was a convert, but the theory did not gain much credence in professional circles. Indeed, Myers, as president of the Royal Anthropological Institute, had a difficult time preventing Elliot Smith's resignation in 1922 as a protest against alleged censorship of his ideas; and he wearily complained about the absurdities of the great man's evangelical fervour. Malinowski spent a good deal of time in the 1920s in debate with Elliot Smith and Perry, but this was for popular rather than professional audiences. It was as though a modern social anthropologist were to spend a lot of time in very public debate with Robert Ardrey and Desmond Morris. The functionalist oral tradition has greatly exaggerated the significance of these confrontations.

There was also the counter-influence of Durkheim and his school in Paris, which had attracted the attention of Radcliffe-Brown and Marett before the First World War, and which continued to influence the British 'social anthropologists'. Durkheim's theories were particularly influential in the study of religion, and they led away from the concerns of the diffusionists, and also of the intellectualist evolutionists, like Tylor and Frazer.

But if one were to characterize the mood of British anthropology in the first decades of this century one would have to stress the overriding concern with the accumulation of data. The ultimate goal might still be the reconstruction of culture history, or evolutionist generalization, but these interests were overlaid by a strong resurgence of British empiricism. There was a feeling that the facts which were increasingly becoming available made facile evolutionist and diffusionist schemes look rather silly. Further, these 'facts' might soon disappear, with all 'primitives'. Their collection was an urgent matter. 'In many parts of the world,' Rivers wrote in 1913, 'the death of every old man brings with it the loss of knowledge never to be replaced.'[8] One might detect incipient moves away from evolutionism or diffusionism towards some sort of functionalism; but more obviously there was a change of emphasis, away from theoretical preoccupations and towards field research. The rivalries of 'sociologists' and 'ethnologists' seemed in general less urgent than the calls of 'ethnography'.

The demand for professional fieldwork was the motive force behind the Cambridge expedition to the Torres Straits in 1898–9, organized by Haddon and including Rivers, Seligman and Myers. Rivers worked among the Todas in India in 1901–2 and in Melanesia in 1907. Seligman worked in Melanesia in 1904, among the Veddas in 1907–8 and later in the Sudan. A. R. Brown (Radcliffe-Brown) was sent by Haddon and Rivers, from Cambridge, to study the Andaman islanders in 1906–8.

There was a grave shortage of funds and of trained workers, and very little professional work involved more than a few days in any exotic area. Despite the obvious dangers, the workers had to rely upon interpreters, or bilingual informants. None the less, this represented a departure from the traditional system, whereby – as Marett described it – 'The man in the study busily propounded questions which only the man in the field could answer, and in the light of the answers that poured in from the field the study as busily revised its questions.'[9] It was now realized that the man in the field should be expert in the discipline, and that the European resident in the tropics was not generally a reliable informant. Some of these, particularly among the missionaries, had produced masterly ethnographies, but they were very much the exception; and even the best of them relied too heavily upon selected informants. Even Junod says that his information came almost entirely from three men. Two were Christians; the third 'a Bantu so deeply steeped in the obscure conceptions of a Bantu mind that he never could get rid of them and remained a heathen till his death in 1908'.[10]

It is a measure of the hunger for information that Hartland, reporting to the readers of *Man* on the meeting of the British Association for the Advancement of Science in South Africa in 1905, could write with some enthusiasm:

> specimens of several Bantu tribes were kindly brought together at the Victoria Falls by the Government of Rhodesia for anthropological study. Time was short, and only admitted of a few measurements and photographs.

And further,

> I had the pleasure of travelling a few days later with Dr. Kannemeyer of Smithfield, a gentleman who was born in Cape Colony, by descent, on the father's side German, on the mother's side French, both families having been colonists for some generations. He is in practice as a medical man. Some of the notes I made from his conversation follow. He has learned from more than one person intimately acquainted with Bushmen . . . [11]

Even the faith in the ethnographic expertise of professional anthropologists may have been rather excessive. As late as 1915, in a glowing review of Rivers's *History of Melanesian Society*, Hocart wrote:

> The idea still persists that no trustworthy material can be collected in a few hours, and that it requires a long sojourn among savages before we can understand them. This idea being based on no proof will persist in spite of all proof.[12]

Although he had spent three years in Fiji to Rivers's three days, Hocart said, he could testify to the accuracy of Rivers's material. He did not add that he was Rivers's main source on Fiji.

Rivers himself took a more perceptive line. He distinguished between what he called 'survey work' and 'intensive work'. Survey work involved visits to tribes over a wide area, in order to map distributions and identify problems requiring investigation. Rivers's own work in Melanesia was a good example of this; another was Seligman's survey of the Sudan. Intensive work was a different matter. Rivers wrote, in 1913:

> The essence of intensive work . . . is limitation in extent combined with intensity and thoroughness. A typical piece of intensive work is one in which the worker lives for a year or more among a community of perhaps four or five hundred people and studies every detail of their life and culture; in which he comes to know every member of the community personally; in which he is not content with generalized information, but studies every feature of life and custom in concrete detail and by means of the vernacular language. It is only by such work that one can realize the immense extent of the knowledge which is now awaiting the inquirer, even in places where the culture has already suffered much change. It is only by such work that it is possible to discover the incomplete and even misleading character of much of the vast mass of survey work which forms the existing material of anthropology.[13]

Since Malinowski was the first British social anthropologist, professionally trained, to carry out intensive research of this kind, it is perhaps impossible to answer the question which must suggest itself – does fieldwork of this kind inevitably demand a synchronic, functionalist perspective? Rivers might have had good grounds for doubting this, since Boas in America had done fieldwork that approached the intensive ideal and had still remained an ethnologist. Yet despite his own ethnological and diffusionist bent, Rivers pointed out that a lone ethnographer engaged in intensive work in a small community would be bound to demonstrate how the different domains of culture are interconnected – 'Thus, for instance, among peoples of rude culture a useful art is at the same time a series of religious rites, an aesthetic occupation, and an important element in the social organization.'[14] Even Marett, one of the last of the armchair anthropologists, came to stress synchronic analysis. Ironically, in a lecture in which he was concerned to salvage the reputation of Frazer from the attacks of Elliot Smith, he said:

> Some of us, indeed – and I can at least speak for myself – are so greatly preoccupied with the study of the mind of the savage as it works here and now under social conditions complicated by all the

contaminating influences of modern civilization that, while fully allowing that anthropology is purely historical in its scope, we are more immediately interested in analysing existing tendencies than in using such analysis as a key to the past.[15]

The influence of Durkheim was at work here; and of course, the most important of the evolutionists, Spencer, had recognized the place of synchronic study. Nevertheless it does seem that the intensive study of small communities was recognized to imply a commitment to synchronic analysis of a type which later came to be called functionalist. This was not necessarily seen as an approach which would displace evolutionist and diffusionist concerns, but rather as something to be added to them.

This was Malinowski's own view. He remained an evolutionist throughout his career, and like his orthodox colleagues he believed that the collection of living cultural facts would ultimately yield evolutionary laws. In the special foreword to the third edition of *The Sexual Life of Savages* Malinowski published a 'recantation from evolutionism'. He admitted that he had been concerned with origins as late as 1927, and even now he was not prepared to abandon evolutionism. Simply, he had 'grown more and more indifferent to the problems of origins'. But even this was a tempered indifference:

> My indifference to the past and to its reconstruction is therefore not a matter of tense, so to speak; the past will always be attractive to the antiquarian, and every anthropologist is an antiquarian, myself certainly so. My indifference to certain types of evolutionism is a matter of method.

Anthropologists should concentrate upon the processes 'which can still be observed in present-day stone-age communities' in order to provide a firm base for reconstruction. Once he understood how culture meets man's needs the anthropologist would be in a position to say something about the gradual evolution of institutions in response to the growing complexity of derived needs. Therefore he wrote:

> I still believe in evolution, I am still interested in origins, in the process of development, only I see more and more clearly that answers to any evolutionary questions must lead directly to the empirical study of the facts and institutions, the past development of which we wish to reconstruct.

And after completing his cycle of Trobriand monographs, with the publication of *Coral Gardens and their Magic* in 1935, he turned back to the classical problems of cultural evolutionism.

This brief review of the situation may serve as an initial perspective on the 'functionalist revolution' in British anthropology. When *Argonauts of the Western Pacific* was published in 1922 it was welcomed as a useful addition to the literature rather than as a call to revolution. This was by no means a crass response, and Malinowski's initial caution supported the reaction. The book was dedicated to Seligman and even carried a generous preface by Frazer, who remained sufficiently favourably disposed several years later to introduce Malinowski's inaugural lecture as professor at the London School of Economics. As a percipient reviewer might have remarked, the book answered a felt need. Yet at the same time the type of material Malinowski had collected, and the manner in which he presented it, did amount to a radically new view of a 'primitive culture'. Malinowski was fully conscious of this, as few others were at first; and he soon showed that the material for revolution was there.

III

A new mode of action requires a mythical charter, and Malinowski in his prime developed a personal myth which his followers passed on to later generations. It runs something like this. Malinowski, a brilliant young Polish student, becomes ill when on the point of entering a professional career in science. (His *Who's Who* entry always stressed two elements in his background – 'parentage on both sides Polish *szlachta* [landed gentry and nobility]'; and 'Ph.D. 1908 with the highest honours in the Austrian Empire [*Sub auspiciis Imperatoris*].') He is told he is too ill to continue his scientific research. In despair he decides to divert himself with an English classic, chooses *The Golden Bough*, and is at once bound in the service of Frazerian anthropology. In due course he sets off for England (after a detour in Germany) and becomes a student at the LSE. After precociously solving the problems of Australian aboriginal family organization he finds himself in Australia with an anthropological mission when the First World War erupts. He is an Austrian citizen, an enemy alien, and may be interned. Fortunately he is permitted to spend his internment in the Trobriand islands. There he passes the war inventing intensive fieldwork by participant observation, working through the vernacular, and living as one of the people, in total isolation from European contacts. After the war he returns to England, and in the face of pigheaded opposition from reactionary evolutionists and mad diffusionists he builds up a group of dedicated disciples who go forth, etc., etc. . . .

In whatever version, the myth presents the classic story of a prophet. The false start, then the illness and conversion, followed by migration; the earth-shattering calamity – no less than a world war – leading to isolation in the wilderness; the return with a message; the battle of the disciples. I have presented the outline of his career first in this form, since it brings out more profoundly than any contemporary account the messianic self-image of the man. A version of the myth is embedded in any oral account of Malinowski's 'functionalist revolution'. The myth is important to the understanding of the man and his career; but a more conventional biographical review brings out other significant, if less apocalyptic, features.

Bronislaw Malinowski was born in Cracow in 1884,[16] the son of a distinguished linguist, professor of Slavic philology at the Jagellonian University. His father pioneered the study of the Polish language and its folk dialects, and did research in folklore. Bronislaw's childhood was passed among the intellectuals of Cracow and Zakopane.

In 1902, Malinowski went up to the Jagellonian University. Concentrating initially on physics and mathematics, he turned increasingly to philosophy, and his graduating thesis, in 1908, entitled 'On the principle of the economy of thought', was a critical exposition of the positivist epistemology of Avenarius and, especially, Mach.[17] He was certainly impressed at this stage by *The Golden Bough*, but he did not immediately take up anthropology. His next move was to the University of Leipzig (where his father had studied before him), after a failure to win a scholarship that would have permitted him to proceed to his *habilitation* in Cracow.

At Leipzig Malinowski studied experimental psychology with Wundt and economic history with Bücher. Wundt clearly influenced him greatly, as he had already influenced both Durkheim and Boas. Wundt's 'folk-psychology' was concerned with culture, with 'those mental products which are created by a community of human life and are, therefore, inexplicable in terms merely of individual consciousness, since they presuppose the reciprocal action of many', a conception related to Durkheim's notion of the 'collective consciousness'.[18] Wundt objected to the tracing of the development of one cultural phenomenon in isolation, whether language, or myth, or religion, for 'the various mental expressions, particularly in their early stages, are so intertwined that they are scarcely separable from one another. Language is influenced by myth, art is a factor in myth development, and customs and usages are everywhere sustained by mythological conceptions.' He preferred to take another option, which consisted 'in taking transverse instead of longitudinal sections, that is, in regarding the main stages of the development with which folk-psychology is concerned in their sequence, and each in total interconnection of its phenomena'. This was possible, since at each evolutionary level 'there are certain ideas, emotions, and springs of action about which the various phenomena group themselves'.

The major elements of functionalism can be discerned in Wundt (and many of his students). It is perhaps even more interesting to note that Malinowski's first anthropological study, on Australian family organization, was begun before he left Leipzig for the London School of Economics in 1910.[19] At the LSE he worked under Westermarck, the man who had so definitively criticized earlier theories of 'primitive promiscuity', 'group marriage', etc. and argued for the primacy in evolutionary terms of the monogamous family. But this was also a theme of Wundt's, and Wundt and his circle were also very concerned with the Australian material – as were many of the social scientists of the day, of course. During 1912 and 1913 major publications on the Australian aborigines appeared not only from Malinowski and Radcliffe-Brown, but also from Durkheim and Freud; all, apparently, working in ignorance of each other.

At the LSE Malinowski encountered the British desire to support more ethnographic work. In 1912 Seligman, who became his patron, asked the director of the LSE for a small grant to allow Malinowski to do four months' research among Arab tribes in the Sudan. This was refused, but Malinowski continued to write, publishing *The Family among the Australian Aborigines* in 1913 (for which the university awarded him a D.Sc.), and a book in Polish on *Primitive Religion and Forms of Social Structure*. The Australian book was commended in *Man* by Radcliffe-Brown as 'by far the best example in English of scientific method in dealing with descriptions of the customs and institutions of a savage people'.[20] He delivered lectures on 'Primitive religion and social differentiation', which, like his Polish monographs, reflected a Durkheimian orientation, and in particular a close interest in Durkheim's work on Australian totemism.

Then came the break, through the intervention of Marett, who later described it in this way:

> As Recorder of Section H. of the British Association, about to visit Australia in 1914, I needed a Secretary, whose travelling expenses would be found for him. Thereupon that brilliant pupil of mine Miss M. A. Czaplicka (for whom, I hope, a special niche is reserved in the Polish Temple of Fame) besought me to assist her compatriot that he might see with his own eyes those peoples of the Antipodes about whom he had hitherto known from books

alone; and thus began a friendship which if on my part wholly delightful, soon proved for him disastrous, at least at first sight. For as our ship was on its way from West to South Australia, the War descended upon us, and Malinowski, as an Austrian subject, became technically an enemy, and who as such must be interned. Nothing, however, could have been more generous than the treatment by the Australian authorities of the young scholar, for they not only granted him a *libera custodia* so that he could explore where he chose within their vast territories, but actually supplied him with the funds to do so.[21]

In fact all enemy scientists who chose to do so were allowed to return to Europe. Malinowski was making the most of an opportunity. He might have been planning to remain in any case, for he came with two scholarships from London University and the LSE which Seligman had negotiated for him, and upon which he depended entirely for a year until the Australian funds became available.

IV

Malinowski was thirty when he began his career as an ethnographer, with six months' fieldwork in southern New Guinea. The shortcomings of his work there persuaded him of the advantages of working in the vernacular and in more immediate contact with the tribesmen. He also found he had a convenient facility for picking up the local languages. (After six months in the Trobriands he was proficient enough in the vernacular to dispense with an interpreter.) The Mailu study was no more than an apprentice's trial run, conventional enough in method and results. After a break in Australia Malinowski returned to the field, in May 1915, and partly by accident fixed on the Trobriand islands off New Guinea for his next study. Seligman had wanted him to investigate Rossel island, but his contacts there failed him. This Trobriand study provided the basis for his later reputation, and its pioneering quality is highlighted by a comparison with the earlier Mailu work. He really did invent modern fieldwork methods in the two years he spent on the Trobriand islands, in 1915–16 and 1917–18.

Malinowski wrote candidly about his fieldwork methods, but the posthumous publication of some of his field diaries provides a much more intimate view of his experiences in the Trobriands than his dissertations on method. Yet while the diaries bring out the personal stresses of the fieldwork, they also make his achievement at once more comprehensible and more admirable. As Malinowski told his students, he saw the personal diary of the fieldworker as a safety-valve, a means of channelling the personal cares and emotions of the ethnographer away from his scientific notes. The diaries deal with the private life of the fieldworker, and show Malinowski struggling with boredom, anxieties about his health, sexual deprivation, loneliness, and what Georges Mikes once called the Slav Soul. They also contain outbursts of irritation directed against the Trobrianders. They reveal that he did not achieve that separation from European contacts which he advocated. But above all they illustrate how hard he worked, and how creatively. Here is part of an entry for a good day – 20 December 1917:

> I got up at 6 (awoke at 5.30). I didn't feel very buoyant. Made the rounds of the village. Tomakapu gave me explanations concerning the sacred grove near his house. It had been raining all night; mud. Everybody was in the village. The policeman joined me at 9, I set to work with him. At 10.30 they decided to go for a *poulo* (fishing expedition) and I set out with them. *Megwa* (magical rite) in the house of Yosala Gawa. I felt again the joy of being with real *Natur-menschen*. Rode in a boat. Many observations. I learn a great deal. General *Stimmung*, style, in which I observe tabu. Technology of the hunt, which would have required weeks of research. Opened-up horizons filled me with joy. We made a cruise around this part of the lagoon – as far as Kiribi, and then to Boymapo'u. Extraordinary sight of fishes darting through the air, jumping into nets. I rowed with them. I removed my shirt and had a kind of sun bath. The water attracted me. I wanted to bathe, but somehow I did not – why? Because of my lack of energy and initiative, which has done me so much harm. Then, this began to weary me; hunger. The charm of open expanses gave way to feeling of absolute emptiness. We returned (by way of) Kaytuvi and Kwabulo . . .

His servant comes by boat with his shoes and billycans, and he returns for a late lunch.

> Then, around 5, I went to Tudaga where I took a census. I came back; the sunset was a blazing brick colour. Some natives observed a Tumadawa fish and 12 or 13 boats set off in pursuit of it. I tried to catch up with them, but I felt a bit tired.

He puts down his oars and sinks into a reverie about a romance in Australia. The entry ends on a domestic note:

> I felt poorly when I returned. Drank tea only. I chatted a bit, but without any specific aim. Enema . . . Slept well.[22]

Then there were the periods of depression and inactivity. In one entry he wrote:

> As for ethnology: I see life of the natives as utterly devoid of interest or importance, something as remote from me as the life of a dog. During the walk, I made it a point of honour to think about what I am here to do. About the need to collect many documents (i.e. texts dictated by informants, and charts of activities, maps, etc.). I have a general idea about their life and some acquaintance with their language, and if I can only somehow 'document' all this, I'll have valuable material. – Must concentrate on my ambitions and work to some purpose. Must organize the linguistic material and collect documents, find better ways of studying the life of women, *gugu'a* (implements), and system of 'social representations'. . . .[23]

The emphasis on 'documentation' here is significant. Malinowski was very concerned with the way in which his observations could be translated into systematic bodies of evidence. Rivers had developed a useful technique for the collection and recording of genealogies, but Malinowski had to develop a whole series of techniques to cope with other kinds of data.

In his research Malinowski came to the view that there were three broad kinds of data, each of which demanded specific techniques of collection and recording. First there was the outline of institutions, of customs, which he studied by what he called 'the method of statistic documentation by concrete evidence'. The aim was to build up a series of synoptic charts, in which one entered the range of customs associated with particular activities. The chart at once summarized the elements of the activity, and indicated the connection between its aspects. The data one included came from opinions and descriptions which were elicited from the people, and from the observation of actual cases. This systematic charting of activities was crucial – 'Indeed,' he wrote, 'the object of scientific training is to provide the empirical investigator with a *mental chart*, in accordance with which he can take his bearings and lay his course.'[24]

However, these charts reflected only one level of reality. The fieldworker must also observe the actualities of social action, what Malinowski called the imponderabilia of everyday life, minutely recording his observations in a special ethnographic diary. His gloss on this is of the greatest interest:

> In working out the rules and regularities of native custom, and in obtaining a precise formula for them from the collection of data and native statements, we find that this very precision is foreign

to real life, which never adheres rigidly to any rules. It must be supplemented by the observation of the manner in which a given custom is carried out, of the behaviour of the natives in obeying the rules so exactly formulated by the ethnographer, of the very exceptions which in sociological phenomena almost always occur.

A third kind of data must also be collected:

A collection of ethnographic statements, characteristic narratives, typical utterances, items of folk-lore and magical formulae has to be given as a *corpus inscriptionum*, as documents of native mentality.

These prescriptions reflect a perception of the systematic divergence between what people say about what they do, what they actually do, and what they think. It is this perception, almost certainly born partly of his field experience, which is the hallmark of Malinowski's work. Customs cohere around activities; but individuals manipulate the rules to their advantage when they can. And finally the understanding of the rule and the action must be put in the context of the way of thinking characteristic of the culture, for the ultimate goal 'of which an Ethnographer should never lose sight' is 'to grasp the native's point of view, his relation to life, to realize *his* vision of *his* world'.

This awareness of the different layers of ethnographic reality pervades Malinowski's first essay on the Trobriands, his minor masterpiece 'Baloma', published in 1916 and written during a break between his two field expeditions. He vividly describes the divergence between informants' descriptions of the solemn farewell to dead spirits and the observed reality:

When the *saka'u* was heard, everybody went quietly away – the young people in pairs, and there remained to farewell the *baloma* only five or six urchins with the drums, myself and my informant ... A more undignified performance I cannot imagine, bearing in mind that ancestral spirits were addressed! I kept at a distance so as not to influence the *ioba* – but there was little to be influenced or marred by an ethnographer's presence! The boys from six to twelve years of age sounded the beat, and then the smaller ones began to address the spirits in the words I had been previously given by my informants. They spoke with the same characteristic mixture of arrogance and shyness, with which they used to approach me, begging for tobacco, or making some facetious remark, in fact, with the typical demeanor of boys in the street, who perform some nuisance sanctioned by custom, like the proceedings on Guy Fawkes' day or similar occasions.

This essay was not simply a splendid demonstration of the dangers that anthropologists ran in trying to deduce psychological attitudes to religious events from formal descriptions. It was a vivid realization of the multi-layered character of ethnographic reality. Behind Malinowski's concern with field methods, then, there was a grasp of the complexity of social reality which amounted, almost, to a theory.

To what extent was this realization of the nature of ethnographic phenomena the product of field experience; to what extent did it derive from theoretical predispostion? I have indicated the kind of proto-functionalist awareness which Malinowski must have found even in the work of Rivers and Wundt, let alone Durkheim, who had influenced his ideas so markedly before his departure for Australia. One does not have to sift a great deal of material in order to find even more striking anticipations of his approach, in even less likely places. Marett, the office-bound don, was writing in 1912:

> I deem it, then, most important at the present juncture that some anthropologist should undertake the supplementary work of showing how, even where the regime of custom is most absolute, the individual constantly adapts himself to its injunctions, or rather adapts these to his own purposes, with more or less conscious and intelligent discrimination. The immobility of custom, I believe, is largely the effect of distance. Look more closely and you will see perpetual modification in process; and, if the underlying dynamic be partly due to physical and quasi-physical causes, such as changes in climate, movements of people following the consequent variations in the food-supply, and so forth, yet, most fundamental condition of all, there is likewise at work throughout the will to live, manifesting itself through individuals as they partly compete and partly cooperate one with the other.[25]

This could stand as the motto to any of Malinowski's Trobriand monographs. Yet the fact that Malinowski followed these prescriptions through in the field gave him a special grasp of their implications. It also provided him with material of unprecedented richness and complexity, with the result that Marett had foreseen:

> We portray the wood after a fashion. It suits our sketchy methods well enough to represent it as a dead mass of colour. But we have not sought, so far, to render the subtle values of the individual trees. Yet only by doing so can we hope to do justice to the spirit of the wood, which is a spirit of life and growth.

It was not a wood in which Frazer's sacred grove was likely to be found.

Yet, while the revolutionary nature of Malinowski's fieldwork is a more complex issue than some of his admirers have suggested, there can be no doubt that it was qualitatively different from the work of any contemporary. In an essay on Malinowski's Trobriand fieldwork,[26] Michael Young cites the testimony of a Catholic missionary, Father Baldwin, who spent thirty years in the Trobriands.

> Malinowski's research I think was as exhaustive as it could be, short of completely absorbing the Trobriand language. I was continually surprised on referring back to him, to find that his enquiry had already impinged upon some discovery that I had supposed was all my own. His analysis too was masterly. He seems to have left nothing unexplained, and his explanations are enlightening even to the people who live there.

At the same time, Malinowski was not a heroic figure in the eyes of the Trobrianders, let alone the settlers and officials.

> It was a surprise to me to find that Malinowski was mostly remembered by the natives as the champion ass at asking damnfool questions, like, do you bury the seed tuber root end or sprout end down? Like asking, do you stand the baby or the coffin on its head or on its feet? I preferred not to refer to him at all with the white people who had known him. He had made them uneasy, and they got back at him by referring to him as the anthrofoologist and his subject anthrofoology. I felt too that this was partly a reflection of native unease – they did not know what he was at. Partly again because he made of his profession a sacred cow; you had to defer, though you did not see why; and if you were a government official or a missionary, you did not appreciate the big stick from one whose infallibility was no more guaranteed than your own.

V

Despite the completion of his fieldwork, and the end of the war, Malinowski's return to the London School of Economics was delayed, first by his marriage to the daughter of an Australian professor, and then by ill health. In 1920 and again in 1922 he lectured at the School during the summer term, and in 1923 he was recognized as a teacher of social anthropology by the University of London. He turned down a chair in ethnology in Cracow, and in 1924 took up an appointment as Reader at the School. University College London had just made a similar appointment, in 'Cultural Anthropology', and

in response to questions about a suitable title for his own appointment Malinowski wrote to Beveridge, Director of the LSE:

> I suggest the title Social Anthropology, so that we are distinct from
> the U[niversity] C[ollege] people, who no doubt will insist on being
> *Cultural* since Cultural is their *mot d 'ordre*. Social will also indicate
> that our interest is mainly sociological, the School being the centre
> for sociology and all that pertains to it. Social Anthropology
> has also its good English tradition by now – I think this was the
> title under which Edward Tylor lectured in Oxford, Frazer in Liver-
> pool and this is the way in which the science of primitive culture is
> usually distinguished from Physical Anthropology. Cultural is really
> borrowed from German, where Kultur means civilisation with
> its fine shade of meaning not implied in the English Culture. The
> School needs Anthropology or Ethnology to fit into the general
> teaching of Social Science and broaden it perhaps, to supply the
> modest comparative basis for the Modern Humanism, for which
> the School in its theoretical role stands, if I understand it rightly.

In 1927 he was appointed to the first Chair in Anthropology at the
University of London (Seligman held a Chair in Ethnology). He
remained at the LSE until 1938 when he went to the United States on
sabbatical leave, only to be stranded there by the outbreak of the
Second World War. He taught at Yale, and did fieldwork on peasant
markets in Mexico. This resulted in an interesting monograph, written
with a distinguished Mexican scholar, Julio de la Fuente. Published
in Spanish, it was issued in English for the first time only in 1982, but
it exerted a profound influence on anthropology and on public policy
in Mexico. He died in New Haven in 1942, at the age of fifty-eight.

Malinowski's seven monographs on the Trobriand islands appeared
between 1922 and 1935. They constitute the overwhelming bulk of his
publications during the years he spent as a teacher in London, and his
Trobriand material also provided the core of his lectures and courses.
It was now that he built up his following, introducing students to
the fascinating Trobriand Man, compelling belief in his own role as
prophet of a new science, and despatching them around the world to
do field studies of their own. One cannot easily separate his Trobriand
writings from his success as a teacher in this period, but I shall first
attempt a brief assessment of his role as professor, before examining
the message of the Trobriand monographs.

Within the LSE Malinowski stood between Seligman, the ethnologist, and the sociologists, Westermarck, Hobhouse and Ginsberg.
From 1925 Seligman lectured on 'General Ethnology', dealing with

prehistory and the distribution of human races. Malinowski taught 'Social Anthropology', covering a variety of topics, but always with primary reference to his Trobriand material. The sociologists were concerned with the evolution of institutions. There was a good deal of interdisciplinary teaching, and Malinowski held joint seminars with the others, but he was given in effect a clear field for his own interests. He soon made use of it, building up his seminar and in time breaking his friendly personal contacts with his colleagues.

Several of his students have described these seminars. M. F. Ashley Montagu has a certain priority, however, for, as he wrote:

> In point of time I believe that I was actually the first of Malinowski's students. Evans-Pritchard arrived from Oxford a few weeks later, and Raymond Firth from New Zealand several months later. I had come to the London School of Economics from University College [London] where I had enjoyed the doubtful distinction of being the first of W. J. Perry's two students. As a gestating Child of the Sun it was late in October 1923 that I presented myself at Malinowski's office at the London School of Economics, a handsome room which at that time Malinowski shared with Professor C. G. Seligman. Malinowski received me most cordially, and I was at once enchanted. There was nothing of the stuffed shirt about him; he put you at your ease at once, and made you feel that you and he were going to have a fascinating time exploring human nature together. . . .
>
> Following some preliminary enquiries Malinowski suggested that I read Lévy-Bruhl and work up a critical paper on 'Primitive Mentality' for the first seminar of the session. I did this, and when I had presented my paper, Malinowski, in a manner so eminently characteristic of him, thanked me, and added 'I could hardly have done as well myself'. . . .
>
> In the classroom I have never experienced a more interesting or stimulating teacher. Malinowski would enter the room with a sheaf of papers in his hand, and without much formality would begin reading his typescript. After a few minutes of this, some passage which particularly interested him would cause him to stop, and looking round the class he would suddenly fire the question, 'Well, what do you think of that?' If no one answered he would call upon some student by name, or a colleague, and thus often a discussion would begin which would last for the rest of the period. . . . At almost all of Malinowski's classes there were generally present several members of the faculty, and often enough there were visitors from other colleges both at home and abroad.[27]

Malinowski would recruit people from all over to attend these seminars, and, perhaps, to be converted, and those students who did attach themselves to him soon became an integral part of his world. A Chinese student once remarked, 'Malinowski is like an Oriental teacher – he is a father to his pupils. He has us to his home; he gets us to run messages for him; sometimes we even cook for him. And we like to do these things for him.'[28] When he moved to his Tyrolean retreat in the summer some students would go with him, and spend the vacation working at the inn, walking with him, and taking part in informal seminars in the evening. But if he drew his favourite students into his family, he demanded their complete loyalty. He came increasingly to see himself as engaged in a battle for truth against the forces of darkness, and as his influence waxed he could not tolerate the mature differences of even his closest colleagues, Seligman and Westermarck.

The mood he created has been strikingly evoked by Leach:

> The fervour that Functionalism aroused among a limited intellectual circle was not based in reasoned analysis. Malinowski had many of the qualities of a prophet, he was a 'charismatic' leader and such men always express their creed in slogans . . . Prophets are conscious of their powers. Malinowski had no doubts about his own greatness; he regarded himself as a missionary, a revolutionary innovator in the field of anthropological method and ideas. Like all such revolutionaries he tended to belittle the significance of his more conservative contemporaries and their immediate predecessors. His published comments on fellow anthropologists are seldom flattering and in verbal discourse he was even more explicit; he claimed to be the creator of an entirely new academic discipline.[29]

In fact his published criticisms tended to bypass the real establishment of British anthropology – Marett, Frazer, Haddon, Myers, Seligman. They were aimed rather at Rivers, who had died in 1922, at Elliot Smith, a professor of anatomy, and at Freud or Durkheim. In discussion he was equally scathing about his powerful contemporaries, however, and virtually every idea he put forward was presented – as Fortes noted – 'in the form of an assault on the *ancien régime*'.[30] These attacks were often outrageously irresponsible. In the first pages of *Argonauts* he wrote, for example,

> It is a very far cry from the famous answer given long ago by a representative authority who, asked, what are the manners and

customs of the natives, answered, 'Customs none, manners beastly', to the position of the modern ethnographer.

Who on earth was this 'representative authority'? The footnote to the paragraph reads, 'The legendary "early authority" who found the natives only beastly and without customs is left behind by a modern writer. . . ' and he proceeds to satirize one Revd C. W. Abel of the London Missionary Society in New Guinea.[31]

Still, this was obviously heady stuff for the students. As one of them put it, 'The secret of Malinowski's charisma was that you thought you were being given an entirely new revelation that was known only to the favoured few and that solved all problems – could put right the experts in every other field.'[32] The message had its political dimension too, for if cultures were delicately attuned mechanisms for the satisfaction of human needs, then each had its value, and one tampered with it only at great risk. This had to be taught to colonial administrators and missionaries. And more generally, the theory implied a relativistic approach, a suspension of those ethnocentric judgements on other people's cultures that were such a feature of snug, bourgeois Philistines. Malinowski had the truth, and it was a truth which should urgently be propagated.

While many found him bewitching, there were others who could not bear his rudeness and intolerance, and found the overpowering personality oppressive. It is difficult to find a single objective portrait of him. Perhaps to round out this sketchy portrait it is best to listen to his own voice, in a joking exchange with Bertrand Russell. In 1930, when Russell was running an experimental school, Malinowski wrote to him:

Dear Russell,
On the occasion of my visit to your School I left my only presentable brown hat in your anteroom. I wonder whether since then it has had the privilege of enclosing the only brains in England which I ungrudgingly regard as better than mine; or whether it has been utilized in some of the juvenile experimentations in physics, technology, dramatic art, or prehistoric symbolism; or whether it naturally lapsed out of the anteroom.

If none of these events, or shall we rather call them hypotheses, holds good or took place, could you be so good as to bring it in a brown paper parcel or by some other concealed mode of transport to London and advise me on a post card where I could reclaim it? I am very sorry that my absentmindedness, which is a characteristic of high intelligence, has exposed you to all the inconvenience incidental to the event.

I do hope to see you some time soon.

Yours sincerely,
B. Malinowski

Russell's reply makes a nice contrast:

My secretary has found a presentable brown hat in my lobby which I presume is yours, indeed the mere sight of it reminds me of you. I am going to the School of Economics to give a lecture . . . and unless my memory is as bad and my intelligence as good as yours, I will leave your hat with the porter at the School of Economics, telling him to give it to you on demand.[33]

It is not surprising that a man like this should have his enemies. Those outside his circle particularly resented his presumption. The American scholar, Kluckhohn, dismissed him as 'a pretentious Messiah of the credulous',[34] and his colleague Lowie remarked, 'Malinowski is forever engaged in two favourite pastimes. Either he is battering down wide open doors; or he is petulantly deriding work that does not personally attract him.' But he added:

His intolerance of other approaches, his adolescent eagerness to shock the ethnological bourgeois – that figment of his fancy, the mere technologist or oddity-monger – must not blind us to his soundness on problems of social organization, his vital ideas on primitive law and economics.[35]

VI

Each of Malinowski's Trobriand monographs was concerned primarily with a single institutional focus – trading, family life and procreation, myth, the enforcement of norms, gardening. Although in each case he moved outwards from this centre, following various threads to show the ramifications of each activity, he never produced a single coherent statement of Trobriand 'culture' as a whole. Perhaps he could not, for despite his insistence upon interconnections he lacked the notion of a system. His monographs recall the spiritual, 'The toe bone is connected to the foot bone, The foot bone is connected to the ankle bone,' etc. – very just, but not a theory of anatomy. His own explanation for this failure is none the less reasonable enough. In a letter to his student Firth, shortly after the latter had returned from the field in 1929, Malinowski wrote:

You have, no doubt by now, already a general plan of your future work. I wonder whether you will proceed at once to a full straight-forward account of the Tikopean [*sic*] culture or whether you will do what I did – that is write it up piecemeal. I hope you will do the former, as I would do now, if I could go back ten years. I had, of course, my good reasons for proceeding as I did. One of them was, as you know, the poor health with which I had to fight at that time, and which prevented me from really taking in hand the difficult task of handling my full material. The other reason was that, at the time when I started my work, it was rather urgent to present the theoretical point of view which we now label 'functional', and which I could only do by presenting some fragments of my stuff, well placed in an extensive theoretical setting.[36]

To put it slightly differently, he was always concerned to deploy his ethnography to make critical points against what he considered to be general, or perhaps merely popular, but at any rate dangerous misconceptions about the 'primitive'. Trobriand Man was often set in a complex institutional context, but more often he was summoned on parade to controvert, by his flesh-and-blood reality, some scholarly theory.

There are three central themes in all his monographs. Firstly, aspects of culture cannot be studied in isolation; they must be under-stood in the context of their use. Secondly, one can never rely on the rules, or on an informant's description, for the social reality; people always say one thing and do another. Finally, if one understands what is really being done, and puts it in its proper context, one will be forced to recognize that while the 'savage' may be no more rational than ourselves, he is at least as reasonable. Moreover he is, as a reasonable man, manipulating the possibilities to his advantage. The Trobriander was the proof of all these statements, but similar conclu-sions must be drawn if modern ethnographic methods were followed in the study of any society. As he wrote in the Preface to *Crime and Custom in Savage Society*:

The modern anthropological explorer . . . is bound . . . to arrive at some conclusions as to whether the primitive mind differs from our own or is essentially similar; whether the savage lives constantly in a world of supernatural powers and perils, or on the contrary, has his lucid intervals as often as any one of us; whether clan-solidarity is such an overwhelming and universal force, or whether the heathen can be as self-seeking and self-interested as any Christian.

The solution of these broad problems of rationality, the force of rules, and the pursuit of self-interest was to be the basis of a universal theory of social man. The solution depended on seeing the real person whole, distinguishing his ways of thought and his feelings from his statements of norms, and both from what he actually did.

The notion that cultures were integrated wholes, which should not be torn apart for the purposes of comparative study, was not, in itself, a particularly novel point of view, akin as it was to all the earlier organic views of culture or society. It was a challenge to some of the diffusionist theories of the day, but not necessarily to a tempered diffusionism – as Malinowski pointed out in a published confrontation with Elliot Smith, all he was saying was that borrowed items were integrated into the living tissue of a culture, and so transformed in adaptation. But Malinowski's point was that cultures formed wholes because they were working units. Every custom exists to fulfil a purpose, and so all customs have a living, current meaning for members of a society. They were in sum the means which people used to satisfy their needs, and therefore they must 'hang together'. It is this kind of coherence which Malinowski stressed particularly in his Trobriand monographs. For instance, in a special foreword to the third edition of *The Sexual Life of Savages* he complained that most reviewers had missed the point:

> My object in publishing this monograph was to demonstrate the main principle of the functional method: I wanted to show that only a synthesis of facts concerning sex can give a correct idea of what sexual life means to a people.

This was not merely tautologous, because as Malinowski showed again and again in his monographs, the connections between different aspects of culture are not necessarily obvious. It might be illuminating to consider, say, boat-building in relation to magic as well as economics; and, so far as he was concerned, you could not claim to understand boat-building unless you examined all the activities associated with it.

This sense of culture as comprising a set of tools was fundamental. Beliefs, however magical, had to contain a utilitarian core; for the rest they served psychological functions. Rules and some magical and religious rites served to ensure the minimum of necessary co-operation, and to provide a plan for the realization of a task. But co-operation was not an end in itself. People were self-seeking, and co-operated only as a form of enlightened self-interest. Malinowski wrote that 'whenever the native can evade his obligations without the loss of prestige, or without the prospective loss of gain, he does

so, exactly as a civilized business man would do.'[37] Only the enlightened self-interest implied by the principle of reciprocity ensured
some sort of mutual accommodation. Where rules inhibited the
realization of satisfactions they would be broken where possible,
or convenient. One might sum up by saying that Malinowski's
perspective depended (like all sociological theories) upon a view of
human beings, the Trobriander being an exotic representation of a
universal type. Like ourselves, he was down-to-earth, reasonable,
rather unimaginative, perhaps, but able to discern his true long-term
interests. In short, he was very different from the figments of
armchair anthropologists. It is this insistence upon the living, acting,
calculating individual that gave Malinowski's monographs their
vitality, and made them such a startling, refreshing contrast to the
work of other anthropologists.

The contrast emerges clearly in his treatment of two major
contemporary themes, the Frazer/Tylor problem of magic, science
and religion; and the Westermarck/Freud problem of the central
importance of the family. Tylor and Frazer did not dispute that the
beliefs of savages made some kind of sense; but they were concerned
with what kind of sense they made. Did the savage make a radically
logical kind of sense, as Tylor believed, leading Andrew Lang
ironically to remark that 'We must ever make allowance for the savage
habit of pushing ideas to their logical conclusions, a habit which
our English characteristics make us find it difficult to understand'?[38]
Or did he make sense in terms of what was later called a logic of the
concrete, associating different things on the basis of external resemblances? This was basically the view of Frazer and of Lévy-Bruhl.
Malinowski's answer was simply that apparently irrational beliefs and
rites made sense when their *use* was appreciated. 'Thus,' he wrote,

> in his relation to nature and destiny, whether he tries to exploit
> the first or to dodge the second, primitive man recognises both the
> natural and the supernatural forces and agencies, and he tries to
> use them both for his benefit.[39]

Magic worked, for it relieved anxiety about the uncontrollable
elements of the future. With religion, it arose and functioned in situations of emotional stress, and the function of magic was 'to ritualize
man's optimism, to enhance his faith in the victory of hope over fear'.
This left room for a Frazerian analysis of the components of magical
activity, and equally for a Tylorian view of utilitarian knowledge.
These were problems which Malinowski thought rather marginal.
He once wrote:

From my own study of living myths among savages, I should say that primitive man has to a very limited extent the purely artistic or scientific interest in nature; there is little room for symbolism in his ideas and tales.[40]

The family was, to Malinowski, also basically a means – it domesticated sex and coped with the care and training of children. It was also the mould of personality, the locus of primary emotional attachments, and the nexus within which primary social emotions were formed. Thus he tended to argue in phylogenetic terms, deriving kinship institutions from the experiences of growing up within a family. He also tended to identify the family and the interests of the individual, so that familial emotions and loyalties were the mainspring of self-interest, while the demands of the broader society were often in conflict with these more natural claims. This is not very far from Freud, despite his divergences from the psychoanalysts.

To put it clearly, though crudely [he wrote], I should say that the family is always the domestic institution *par excellence*. It dominates the early life of the individual; it controls domestic co-operation; it is the stage of earliest parental cares and education. The clan, on the other hand, is never a domestic institution. Bonds of clanship develop much later in life, and though they develop out of the primary kinship of the family, this development is submitted to the one-sided distortion of matrilineal or patrilineal legal emphasis, and it functions in an entirely different sphere of interests; legal, economic, above all, ceremonial.[41]

The Trobriand islanders were matrilineal. A man inherited from his mother's brother, and exerted jural control over his sister's son. Although fathers and sons were not involved in these crucial relationships of authority and transmission of property, they nevertheless developed strong bonds of affection and mutual concern. This provided Malinowski with a major theme – the conflict between the interests of the father and the legal claims of the mother's brother. He could even demonstrate the limitations of Freud's theory of the Oedipus complex, for in the Trobriand islands boys resented not their father for his sexual enjoyment of their mother, but their mother's brother for his authority. Yet typically this insight was never embedded in a systematic consideration of Trobriand kinship, functioning rather as an example of how emotions might pull against the rules, and how people manoeuvred in order to bend the rules. It was left to his students, Audrey Richards and Meyer Fortes, to show how these differing interests in matrilineal societies formed two poles of a single system, and found concrete expression in forms of household that varied in time and space according to the strength of family or matri-lineage.[42]

Both in his writings on magic, science and religion, and in his writings on the family, Malinowski's emphasis was all on the individual and his goals. The advantages of this emphasis were great, but the price was a failure to treat beliefs, or kinship, as systems in themselves. As others have shown, systems of beliefs and ritual action may form integrated wholes, and (turning Malinowski's rhetoric against himself) they are not to be understood simply by tearing out elements and showing that these have a function. In studying kinship, Malinowski focused on the 'initial situation', the child growing up in the supposedly universal nuclear family, and gradually generalizing the sentiments for his parents on to their kin until he had created afresh a whole system of kin and clan. There was no allowance for the system as a pre-existing structure which the child learnt rather than created.

Fortes has pointed out that Malinowski was always promising a book on Trobriand kinship, and he suggests that the book was never written precisely because Malinowski could not conceive of a 'kinship system'.[43] But so far as Malinowski was concerned, *The Sexual Life of Savages* was a book on Trobriand kinship. In that book he showed that love and sex must be considered together with courtship, that this led to marriage, which produced the family, and that in the family sentiments were generated which provided the basis for relationships of kinship and clanship – 'and all these subjects, so intimately bound up with one another, constitute really one big system of kinship'. To Malinowski any set of connections constituted a system. He recognized, of course, that he had not touched the sorts of problems with which Rivers had been concerned in much of his writings. This was his perception of the issues involved:

> ... starting with the problem of sex, I was led to give a full account of the kinship system, and of its functions within the Trobriand culture. I have left out, or rather I have only briefly indicated, the linguistic aspect of the question – the ill-omened kinship nomen-clatures – a subject so wildly over-discussed, so often exaggerated in records of field-work, that one is sometimes led to suspect that it is nothing but an avenue to anthropological insanity. This aspect of kinship I have reserved for publication in a separate volume, hoping that by an overdose of terminological documenta-tion and linguistic detail I can administer a cathartic cure to social anthropology.[44]

It may have been true that the sociological study of kinship was still, in the 1920s, too much tied to a concern with kinship terminologies. Nevertheless Malinowski was not merely ignoring problems of terminology. Reviewing his early study of the Australian family, Radcliffe-Brown had tempered his praise with the criticism that 'the Australian notions relating to kinship cannot be studied without reference to what the author calls "group relationships"; in other words, the relationship systems, classes and clans.'[45] Malinowski, however, seldom attempted structural analyses, preferring to focus on the strategies of individual actors.

VII

In the Trobriand monographs things 'hang together' because in accomplishing any task the Trobriander mobilizes practical knowledge and techniques, magic and ritual, social relationships and the mechanism of reciprocity. In his more theoretical work, published during and after his great London period, he stressed a different kind of integration, which was expressed in his theory of needs and institutions. If his Trobriand work describes the horizontal integration of beliefs and activities, this theory concentrated upon a sort of vertical integration. Culture existed to satisfy needs, either biological needs or the secondary, derived needs, which arose from the acquisition of culture itself. Each need gave rise to an institution, and the institution was made up of various layers. To carry out the necessary need-satisfying activity there must be a material apparatus; this is deployed by a social unit, with its appropriate rules of organization and procedure; and the whole complex is finally legitimized by a mythical charter. This is Malinowski's own formulation, with special reference to the Frazerian problem of magic, science and religion:

> human culture is primarily founded on the biological needs of man. Following this cue, we can add that in satisfying his primary biological needs through the instrumentalities of culture, man imposes new determinants on his behaviour, that is, develops new needs. In the first place he must organize his tools, his artifacts, and his food-producing activities through the guidance of knowledge. Hence the need for primitive science.... Human action must be guided by the conviction of success.... Hence, magic.... Finally, once man develops the need of building up systems of knowledge and anticipation, he is bound to inquire into the origins of humanity, into its destinies, and into the problems of life, death,

and the universe. Hence, as a direct result of man's need to build systems and to organize knowledge, there emerges also the need for religion.[46]

The reasoning is straightforward: show me a complex of customs and I will intuitively decide which need, basic or derived (by which he means, for the most part, biological or putatively psychological) it subserves. The underlying psychological theory was an ill-considered mix of McDougall's 'instincts' and Shand's 'sentiments', each searching out an appropriate expression. It reads like a tinny echo of Marx, with its materialistic base, social structure, and ideological justification, and indeed it is not unreasonable to see the theory as an attempt to counter Marxism. The crudity of his theory could hardly be better demonstrated than in his comments on Marxist theory:

> It is one of the remarkable paradoxes of social science that while a whole school of economic metaphysics has erected the importance of material interests – which in the last instance are always food interests – into the dogma of materialistic determination of all historical process, neither anthropology nor any other serious branch of social science has devoted any serious attention to food. The anthropological foundations of Marxism or anti-Marxism are still to be laid down.[47]

Of all the triumphs of Malinowski's reductionist impulse, this must surely be the greatest, the reduction of Marxism to a sort of dietetics.

VIII

Malinowski, like all functionalists, has been accused of being indifferent on the one hand to the historical development of societies, and on the other to the radical changes that have affected all tribal cultures in this century. At a theoretical level, it is true, he was not concerned with problems of history, except in the guise of diffusionism or evolutionism. However, his later London years saw him becoming more and more engaged with the social problems of colonial countries, and much of his writing in the late 1920s and early 1930s was concerned with what he called 'culture change'. This was due in part to his missionary zeal, and his determination to take the functionalist gospel to colonial officials, some of whom were drawn into his seminars while on leave. In part, his new interest came with the foundation in the late 1920s of the International Institute of African Languages and Cultures, which was committed to applied studies and which supported the research of his students in the African colonies. But, as perhaps was inevitable in his case, these new interests were crystallized by direct observation. In 1934 he attended a conference in South Africa. He then spent several months visiting students in the field in South and East Africa, including Hilda Beemer (Kuper) in Swaziland and Audrey Richards among the Bemba. In 1938 he wrote:

> As soon as the 'plane crosses the border between Nilotic and Bantu peoples, it becomes obvious that it is a transformed Africa over which we are moving. Among the Baganda the houses are new, square, built on the European pattern; even from above, the dress and equipment of the natives spell Manchester and Birmingham. Roads and churches, motor-cars and lorries, proclaim that we are in a world of change in which two factors are working together and producing a new type of culture, related both to Europe and Africa, yet not a mere copy of either.[48]

And in the slums of Johannesburg he found what he took to be a symbol of the new situation, the illicit brew *skokiaan*, blended from all sorts of noxious ingredients, including methylated spirits and calcium carbide, a potent, quickly maturing, easily-hidden spirit. As he wrote, 'in the general puritanic drive against native beer – itself an entirely innocuous drink – and the police control by which it was enforced, the native was driven to invent *skokiaan* and its peers'.[49]

Malinowski argued that the ethnographer in Africa should consider three distinct cultural realities: the living 'traditional culture', a shrinking area; the intrusive European culture; and, above all, the expanding band in-between, the *tertium quid*, in which a new syncretic culture was emerging, the culture of the mining camp and the urban slumyard, symbolized by the illicit *skokiaan*. This was not quite a diffusionist view, for the elements taken from the traditional and colonial cultures were transformed by their blending in a heady brew. But like diffusionism, it was essentially an unsociological point of view. In the collection of essays on the problem to which Malinowski contributed the introductory review, from which I have been quoting, Meyer Fortes and Isaac Schapera both argued that the social field should be considered as a unity, and that the focus should be upon the system of social relations encompassing villagers, migrant labourers, colonial administrators and missionaries. As Radcliffe-Brown observed, in 1940:

> The study of composite societies, the description and analysis of the processes of change in them, is a complex and difficult task. The attempt to simplify it by considering the process as being one in

which two or more 'cultures' interact, which is the method suggested by Malinowski ... is simply a way of avoiding the reality. For what is happening in South Africa, for example, is not the interaction of British culture, Afrikander (or Boer) culture, Hottentot culture, various Bantu cultures and Indian culture, but the interaction of individuals and groups within an established social structure which is itself in process of change. What is happening in a Transkeian tribe, for example, can only be described by recognising that the tribe has been incorporated into a wide political and economic structural system.[50]

Whatever his contemporaries may have felt about the adequacy of Malinowski's 'cultural' approach to colonial societies, his characteristic determination to embrace the realities as he observed them, and to accept the consequences, is remarkable. The implications were certainly radical:

The anthropologist [Malinowski wrote] is now faced with the tragic situation which has often been bewailed in lecture-rooms and in print, even by the present writer. Just as we have reached a certain academic status and developed our methods and theories, our subject-matter threatens to disappear. In some parts of the world it has been wiped out – as in Tasmania, the eastern states of America, and certain islands of the Pacific. Instead, however, of lamenting the inevitable, we must face the new, more complex and difficult task which history has set before us, the task that is of building new methods and new principles of research in order to reclaim the 'anthropological no-man's-land' and take up 'the new branch of anthropology ... the anthropology of the changing native'.[51]

He even came to castigate himself for having falsely obscured the realities of change in the Trobriand islands. In an appendix to his final monograph on the Trobrianders, *Coral Gardens and their Magic*, which appeared in 1935, he wrote: 'The empirical facts which the ethnographer has before him in the Trobriands nowadays are not natives unaffected by European influences but natives to a considerable extent transformed by these influences.' He now believed that this recognition should guide the fieldworker, but he admitted that he had failed to take it into account while he was in the Trobriand islands, concluding, 'This perhaps is the most serious shortcoming of my whole anthropological research in Melanesia.'[52]

This was a remarkable admission. Malinowski came to *see* ethnographic reality as not 'savage cultures' but rather colonial cultures in a process of rapid change. His ethnographic masterpieces did not embody this insight, and they served as a potent example of how tribal cultures might be described as if they were 'untouched'. Further, his theory of culture change was so unsatisfactory that the impetus he gave to the study of colonial realities was gravely impaired. Malinowski might have revolutionized the British social anthropologists' conception of their proper subject-matter, but this radical change of paradigm was not accomplished.

IX

The Malinowskian revolution transformed the relationship between the ethnographer and the theorist. To be crude and schematic, but not altogether misleading, before the First World War the relationship between theory and ethnography (and theorist and ethnographer) was as master to servant. 'The man in the study busily propounded questions,' Marett explained in 1927, 'which only the man in the field could answer, and in the light of the answers that poured in from the field the study as busily revised its questions.'[53] Marett's image was of the metropolitan scientist who was in correspondence with a missionary, explorer or district administrator in the tropics. Unsophisticated about theory but wise in local ways, the old Africa hand collected museum specimens for metropolitan museums and submitted answers to the queries of the scholars.

Even the few ethnographers based in universities and museums were essentially providing a service to the theorists. From the 1890s, professional anthropologists had begun to do fieldwork themselves, but they still respected the basic division of labour. The fieldworker produced facts, the sociologist or ethnologist inserted them in a comparative framework and produced explanations. A new theory was needed before the ethnographer could, as it were, appropriate the surplus value of his labour and so transform his social status.

It was Malinowski who put theory into the field. Ernest Gellner noted that the Malinowskians 'insist that anthropology differs from "mere" ethnography by also having theory; on investigation of this theory, called Functionalism, it turns out to be in large part the doctrine that anthropology should be nothing but ethnography. Or rather – good ethnography.'[54] The functionalists insisted that understanding and explanation required an insider's view of a culture, which only the properly equipped fieldworker could deliver. It followed that only the ethnographer could be a theorist – but perhaps only of the society he or she had studied. Possibly each society required its own theory, meta-theory being restricted to very generalized and usually banal statements.

Functionalists did very often deliver richer ethnographies, more reliable materials, than their predecessors had, on the whole, produced, but their very success raised a new problem. The better the ethnographies, the more difficult comparison became. The more the ethnographers stressed the inner character of a culture, the intertwining of its institutions and philosophy, the more problematic was the move to comparison and generalization. Functionalist field studies might be necessary for the establishment of a scientific anthropology, but at the same time they undermined the prospects for the success of such an enterprise by making comparison impractical.

Malinowski himself proposed two solutions to the problem of comparison and generalization. A framework for generalization was provided by the theory that he named 'functionalism'. This states that institutions have a biological rationale. Each institution contributes to the satisfaction of basic human needs, or provides the means whereby these primary needs-serving institutions operate. One could therefore compare institutions that performed the same function in different societies. This crude utilitarian theory had few takers. It could not explain cultural variation, and it did not allow for cultural influences upon 'human needs'. As early as 1930, Lord Raglan had asked ironically, 'Does Professor Malinowski really believe that subincision was invented to detach boys from their mother's apron strings?'[55]

Malinowski's other strategy was to present the Trobrianders as prototypical 'savages' (his term) if not, indeed, representatives of all humanity. A weakness in this strategy has been identified by Edmund Leach, who commented that Malinowski treated the Trobrianders

> as *both* unique *and* universal. On the one hand, he argues as if the Trobriand political economy was a completely closed system which could be completely understood without any reference to the cultural practices of peoples in neighbouring islands; on the other, in his more popular works, he wrote of the Trobrianders as if they were the archetype primitive society, so that what he had observed to be the case in Omarakana must be equally true wherever primitive people are to be found.[56]

The analysis of an isolated and integrated society may well suggest general conclusions that apply elsewhere. Malinowski's account of Trobriand exchange, for instance, was to become the basis of general theories of exchange in the hands of Mauss and Polanyi, but only after they had compared Trobriand practices with systems of exchange elsewhere. However, Malinowski did not usually attempt to generalize, preferring to deploy his Trobriand ethnography for critical purposes. The actual behaviour of Trobriand Islanders could be shown to invalidate the grand theories of Freud, McDougall, Durkheim and others. Ernest Gellner has remarked that the early functionalist studies were sometimes most interesting precisely when they were designed to criticize general theories.[57] Yet this was to accept a diminished role for ethnography. The ethnographer could hope at best to find exceptions to some generalization. The Trobrianders might well be the odd men out, exceptions to some metropolitan theory that generalized current western practices to the world; but were they typical of anything in themselves? Looking for a more promising theoretical partner for functionalist ethnography, young scholars now began to turn to the comparative sociology of A. R. Radcliffe-Brown.

In 1957, Malinowski's successor at the LSE, Raymond Firth, collected a series of essays by former students of Malinowski on aspects of his work.[58] By this stage, few were prepared any longer to defend his theories. Clearly, Malinowski's great contribution was as an exemplar of ethnographic method. Yet his method carried a theoretical and even a moral charge. The ethnographer had to grasp the actor's point of view. If successful, the common humanity of Trobrianders and Europeans would be revealed. He passed on to his students an invaluable awareness of the tension which is always there between what people say and what they do, between individual interests and the social order, and directed their attention to the actor rather than the role, to the boasting, hypocritical, earthy, reasonable human being who could be found equally in Omarakana, Warsaw or London: brothers and sisters all, beneath the skin. 'What is the deepest essence of my investigations?', he wrote in his diary in 1917, in the Trobriand islands. 'To discover what are his main passions, the motives for his conduct, his aims ... His essential, deepest way of thinking. At this point we are confronted with our own problems: What is essential in ourselves?'[59]

2   Radcliffe-Brown

I have been described on more than one occasion as belonging to something called the 'Functional School of Social Anthropology' and even as being its leader, or one of its leaders. This Functional School does not really exist; it is a myth invented by Professor Malinowski . . . There is no place in natural science for 'schools' in this sense, and I regard social anthropology as a branch of natural science. . . . I conceive of social anthropology as the theoretical natural science of human society, that is, the investigation of social phenomena by methods essentially similar to those used in the physical and biological sciences. I am quite willing to call the subject 'comparative sociology', if anyone so wishes.

– Radcliffe-Brown[1]

I

Malinowski brought a new realism to social anthropology, with his lively awareness of the flesh-and-blood interests behind custom, and his radically new mode of observation. Radcliffe-Brown introduced the intellectual discipline of French sociology, and constructed a more rigorous battery of concepts to order the ethnographic materials. He also established several new centres for the science. Three years Malinowski's senior, he survived him by eleven years and took over the leadership of British social anthropology from him in the late 1930s.

Some saw Radcliffe-Brown as the classic to Malinowski's romantic, but he too was a man of extremes, obsessed by his message; like Malinowski, egotistical and dogmatic. Both men had pretensions to aristocratic, even superman, status (and I think it not insignificant that both were valetudinarians). Both saw themselves as prophets of a new science, a promising branch of the established natural sciences.

Malinowski had enjoyed a high-level advanced scientific training, and he flirted with advanced Viennese positivism. Radcliffe-Brown had been diverted from the natural sciences at an early stage by Rivers, but he remained faithful to the canons of the natural sciences as they were at the turn of the century.

Both were also influenced at an early stage by Durkheim, but only Radcliffe-Brown remained a faithful disciple of the *Année* school. He had fallen under the influence of Durkheim's sociological theories before the First World War, and the productive years of his career were dedicated to the application of this theory to the discoveries of the ethnographers, an enterprise he shared for much of his life with Durkheim's nephew, Mauss.

II

Alfred Reginald Brown was born at Sparkbrook, Birmingham, in 1881. When he was five his father died, leaving his mother penniless. She worked as a 'companion', while her mother looked after the children. 'Rex' was a scholar at King Edward's School in Birmingham, but he left school before he was eighteen for a job in the Birmingham library. His elder brother, Herbert, encouraged him to study further, and supported him while he did a year of pre-medical science at Birmingham University. He then won an Exhibition at Trinity College, Cambridge, and in 1902 he began to read for the Moral Sciences tripos. His brother, now established in South Africa, continued to give him financial support, in part from the proceeds of a wound gratuity, deriving from the Anglo-Boer war.[2]

Brown had wished to take the Natural Sciences tripos at Cambridge, but his tutor insisted that he was better advised to read Mental and Moral Sciences. Here his teachers included Myers and Rivers, both medical psychologists and veterans of the Torres Straits expedition, Cambridge's pioneering venture in anthropological field research. The course covered psychology and philosophy, including the philosophy of science, which was taught in part by A. N. Whitehead. In 1904 he took a first, and became Rivers's first pupil in anthropology.

Cambridge was enjoying its greatest modern period at the turn of the century. Brown was in the university of Moore, Russell, Whitehead, D'Arcy Thompson, Sedgwick and Keynes. Great advances were being consolidated in the natural sciences, and at the same time there were the first stirrings of a novel, still intensely private, culture, francophile, personal, élitist but not without a social conscience, the culture which was later to emerge from its charming adolescence into the neurotic maturity of 'Bloomsbury'. Bertrand Russell, who also read Moral Sciences, and was a fellow of Trinity, spanned the Victorian Cambridge of Moore and the Edwardian Cambridge of Keynes and Lytton Strachey. He has identified the essential spirit of the place at that time as one of intellectual honesty:

> This virtue certainly existed not only among my friends, but among my teachers. I cannot remember any instance of a teacher resenting it when one of his pupils showed him to be in error, though I can remember quite a number of occasions on which pupils succeeded in performing this feat.[3]

Rivers had the virtues of contemporary Cambridge, and Brown was fortunate in his teacher. As a Cambridge man of his day, he later concluded that Rivers was fundamentally in error.[4]

Guided by Rivers and Haddon, Brown made a study of the Andaman islands from 1906 to 1908. His report won him a fellowship at Trinity College, which he held from 1908 to 1914, though during this period he also taught occasionally at the London School of Economics.

His initial Andaman report was concerned with problems of ethnology, and it reflected the diffusionist proclivities of Rivers. However, he was soon converted to a Durkheimian view of sociology. A preliminary essay by Durkheim, which foreshadowed the argument of *The Elementary Forms of the Religious Life*, made a considerable impact in England at this time. In Cambridge the classicist Jane Harrison immediately adopted the new point of view, and Marett at Oxford thought (erroneously) that he discerned a fundamental similarity to his own position.[5] In 1909–10 Brown gave a series of lectures at the LSE and at Cambridge in which he advanced the essentially Durkheimian point of view that he was to maintain for the rest of his life.[6] In 1913 he delivered a similar series of lectures in his home town, Birmingham, which were reported in the local press. After reading the programme of these lectures, Durkheim wrote to him: 'It has brought me a new proof of the understanding which reigns between us on the general conception of our science.'[7]

Radcliffe-Brown never published a record of his conversion but he did remark that his switch from the ethnological interests of Rivers and Haddon was quite sudden. Conversion to a new paradigm is usually rapid and not, in detail, a matter of logical analysis, and in turning to Durkheim he was part of a fairly widespread movement in Britain at the time. The episode parallels the reception of Lévi-Strauss's structuralism in Britain in the 1960s. At the same time one can appreciate what the conversion offered: scientific method, the conviction that social life was orderly and susceptible to rigorous analysis, a certain detachment from individual passions, and a fashionable French panache. Like Kropotkin's anarchism, to which Brown had been attracted as a student, Durkheim's sociology was, at least implicitly, radical. In short Brown's devotion to the natural sciences and his Utopian anarchism were both provided for in a new creed that was at once scientific, humanitarian, in a mass sort of way, and, very important, French.

III

We are fortunate to possess a perceptive portrait of Brown in his Cambridge years. He made friends with a student slightly junior to him, E. L. Grant Watson, who read Natural Sciences but later became a novelist and something of a mystic. Watson accompanied Brown on his first Australian field expedition, and described him in his autobiography, *But to What Purpose*. He recalled:

Towards the end of the first term in my fourth year I met A. R. Brown, who was recently returned from the Andaman Islands, where he had been studying the social organization of the islanders. He was now planning an expedition to North-West Australia, and it was mooted that I might possibly go with him as Zoologist to the expedition. Brown, Anarchy Brown, as he was then called, for he had been a declared Anarchist, had a peculiar reputation at Trinity. In spite of his having passed all examinations with distinction and being a Scholar and Fellow of the college, there were many of the erudite who looked on him with suspicion. He was too dramatic a personality to fit easily into the conservative life of a college. He often made wild statements, he was brilliantly informed on *all* subjects. That, of course, told against him, and then he had lived as a primitive autocrat, exercising a beneficent but completely authoritarian sway over the simple Andamanese, who had not been in a position to criticise his grand gestures. He was in fact a bit of a superman, and one who strove, more consistently than any other man I have met, to live consciously and according to a set plan dictated by his reason and will. It is true that he sometimes lapsed from his high standard, and was led by his inventive genius to fabricate the stories he told, and often it was not difficult to see this invention in process. This made the scholarly and conscientious distrustful of him, but I have every reason to believe that these extravagances, which he allowed himself in talk, never once found their way into his published work.[8]

Watson seems to have been one of the few men whom Brown took into his confidence:

> He expounded to me some of his philosophy. One must cultivate style. He dressed like a Paris *savant*, faultlessly. He aspired to be conscious of every gesture; had even thought out the best position in which to sleep. Not on the back, not wholly on the side, and not like a foetus. He pictured himself even in sleep.

Watson describes how 'He made, in fact, no least effort towards people who seemed to him superfluous. They might talk to him, expecting an answer, but his eye would be fixed on the distance, and no reply would be forthcoming.' And he comments, 'This, I think, was all part of his system of using his time to the best advantage.' In fact, Watson wrote, 'I have never known a man be more ruthless, and can well understand the exasperated women who found cause to hate him, and who so often declared that he was "no gentleman"' – despite his handsome appearance, and elegant dress.

But Watson's conclusion is a dubious one – 'he was as unaffected by traditions as any man might be, whose contention was that everything should be judged and acted on from a self-made rational foundation.' On the contrary, his style and his later conduct reveal a determination to adopt the manner of an English aristocrat, rather romantically conceived. In 1926 he changed his name by deed-poll to Radcliffe-Brown, incorporating his mother's name, and in his long exile in South Africa, Australia and the United States he played the rather archaic part of the eccentric English nobleman abroad, even affecting a cloak and opera hat on inappropriate occasions in the egalitarian milieu of Sydney in the 1920s.

It is tempting to trace the roots of his later manner in the deprivations of his childhood and, perhaps, his uncertainty as a young man in the rather awesome Cambridge of his day, but such speculation can have no firm basis. Nevertheless one may discern a connection between the way in which he presented himself, and saw himself, and the theoretical position he adopted in his writing. His work has a glacial clarity, and his concern was always with the formal situation, the rules and the rituals. He lacked completely Malinowski's interest in individual motivation and strategy. His detachment was a source of strength too, for it gave a controlled power to his analyses of social systems, which Malinowski never achieved.

IV

Radcliffe-Brown's first field study, in the Andaman islands, was in his view characterized by unusual methodological rigour, but it belongs firmly in the pre-Malinowski era of fieldwork. The same is true of his work among the Australian aborigines, in 1910–12, which was survey work of the kind practised by Rivers or Seligman. But the results of his work, which formed his earliest publications, demonstrated his analytical powers, and constitute an important contribution to the subject.

Most of Radcliffe-Brown's work in the Andaman islands was done on the Grand Andaman, this for reasons of linguistic difficulty. He camped for three months in the Little Andaman and made a great effort to learn the language, finally giving up in despair. In the Great Andaman he worked at first in Hindustani, which was generally, if imperfectly, understood by the younger adults, and after a time to some extent in the local dialects. However, he found that he only made substantial progress in the latter part of his stay, when he discovered an intelligent, English-speaking informant. The contrast with Malinowski's work in the Trobriands is striking. Even his methods of data collection were inadequate. His teacher Rivers had developed the genealogical method, but Radcliffe-Brown confessed: 'I collected a number of genealogies from the natives, but unfortunately my own inexperience in the use of the genealogical method, and my consequent inability to surmount the difficulties with which I met, made this branch of my investigations a failure.'[9]

The Andamans had a population of under 1,300, and by the time of Radcliffe-Brown's study they had already been sadly affected by epidemics of measles and syphilis, following the establishment of a penal colony and European settlement. In Radcliffe-Brown's view, 'What is really of interest to the ethnologist is the social organization of these tribes as it existed before the European occupation of the islands.'[10] Therefore direct observation was of little use, and he had to depend on the memories of informants. He suggests that they could report 'What was the constitution of the islands in former times', but later, describing the kinship system, he confessed: 'It would not be safe, however, to base any arguments of importance to sociology on the above description of the Andamanese system of relationship alone.' As he explained:

> The difficulty of being really sure on these matters is due (1) to the fact that the breaking-up of the old local organisation has produced many changes in their customs, and (2) to the difficulty of

questioning the natives on matters connected with relationships when they have no words in their language to denote any but the simplest relationships.[11]

By the time his monograph was published in 1922 its real importance to Radcliffe-Brown was as an example of analytic method; so far as the fieldwork went, he was content to describe it as an apprentice study, and he relied heavily on the ethnographic reports of a former resident on the islands, E. H. Man, while dissenting from his speculative interpretations. He had gone into the field an ethnologist, and his initial aim, reflected in his first report, was to reconstruct the history of the Andamans and of the Negritos in general. Later he was converted to the Durkheimian view that the meaning and purpose of customs should be analysed in their contemporary context, and it was this that he set out to demonstrate in the book.

Radcliffe-Brown divided 'customs' into three types – techniques, rules of behaviour, and what he called ceremonial customs, on which he concentrated his attention. Ceremonial customs included those collective actions conventionally performed on occasions of changes in the course of social life. Their purpose, as he believed, was the expression of collective sentiments relating to such changes. In the first part of the book he described a series of such customs, mainly ceremonies and myths. The latter part of his study was concerned with their interpretation.

Interpretation should be concerned with meaning and purpose, for 'Every custom and belief of a primitive society plays some determinate part in the social life of the community, just as every organ of a living body plays some part in the general life of the organism.'[12] The purpose of ceremonials was the expression, and therefore the maintenance and transmission, of the sentiments by which the conduct of the individual is regulated in conformity with the needs of the society.[13] To appreciate how this works one must plumb the meaning of the custom. This is done by taking into account the explanations of the members of the society, and secondly, by comparing the different contexts in which a custom appears, so abstracting its essential significance.[14]

A good example of this contextual method is his analysis of the place of formal weeping in various Andamanese ceremonies. The Andamanese weep if friends or relatives meet after long separation; at peace-making ceremonies; when a man returns to his friends after a period of mourning; after a death; after the exhumation of a corpse; at a marriage; and at various stages of an initiation ceremony. The connection between these occurrences of ceremonial weeping lies, he argued, in the fact that they all mark situations 'in which social relations that have been interrupted are about to be renewed, and the rite serves as a ceremony of aggregation'.[15] The theory of the function of these ceremonial customs is taken straight from Durkheim, and applied rather mechanically. There is no whiff of that reality which Malinowski had insisted upon in 'Baloma', and which future fieldworkers were regularly to find in the casual, apparently impious, performance of sacred ceremonies.

V

When Radcliffe-Brown went out to Australia in 1910 he took Grant Watson with him, so that we have a vivid description of the expedition, which is very revealing of Radcliffe-Brown's character and methods, and in general helpful in understanding the field conditions of the time. There were two other members of the expedition, Mrs Daisy Bates, an amateur ethnographer and philanthropist, whom Radcliffe-Brown took on in a show of sexual egalitarianism, but with whom he soon quarrelled; and a Swedish sailor, Olsen, who came as a servant. The party was put on a sound financial footing by a gift from a sheep-farmer, who heard Radcliffe-Brown lecture on the purpose of the expedition.

The expedition's first destination was the site of a corroboree east of Sandstone, and the party was just settling down to 'the main business of our task, which was to tabulate facts pertaining to the four-class marriage system',[16] when they were interrupted by a police raid. Radcliffe-Brown kept cool, upbraiding the posse for their un-bridled behaviour, and even, it transpired, sheltering the miscreants for whom the police were searching. However, after this incident the Aborigines were unwilling to continue their ceremonies. Radcliffe-Brown decided to leave, and after a row abandoned poor Mrs Bates on her own. He took the rest of his party to Bernier island, the site of a lock-up hospital for Aborigines infected with venereal disease. The occupants had mostly been kidnapped and forcibly removed there, but the party spent several months on the island pursuing with these unfortunate informants their researches into the traditional Aboriginal marriage systems. After a year in the field Watson left, and Radcliffe-Brown went on with Olsen to study other Aboriginal communities settled around mission stations along the Gascoyne river.

In Australia he practised 'survey and salvage' ethnography, which suffers by comparison with the type of field study that Malinowski was soon to carry out in the Trobriands. As one of his Australian students pointed out, there were still functioning tribes available for study in Australia, and because he did not go to them Radcliffe-Brown was reduced to the study of formal structures – 'he could not observe how this ideal and logical structure worked. It was form without content.'[17] On the other hand, in his reports, beginning in 1912 and culminating in the famous essay, 'The social organisation of Australian tribes', published in 1930–1, he brought the complex Australian material into some kind of order.

Radcliffe-Brown's central concern in his Australian work was with the system of kinship and marriage, something he had not treated with great authority in his Andaman study. The orthodox view of the day was that the division of the Australian tribes into two, four or eight 'classes' was the basis for the regulation of their extremely complicated marriage system. Radcliffe-Brown decided that this was not the case, and that marriages were regulated rather by the kinship system working independently of the division into 'classes'. He identified two main types of Australian system. In the Kariera-type systems marriage is with a woman who falls into the category 'mother's brother's daughter'. In the Aranda-type systems it is with a woman in the category 'mother's mother's brother's daughter's daughter'. Radcliffe-Brown argued that this reflected the existence of two 'descent lines' in Kariera systems, as opposed to four in the Aranda systems.

As a modern authority has pointed out, Radcliffe-Brown's assumption that the marriage systems and class systems varied independently 'is presumably false, for while he shows that neither uniquely determines the other, his own evidence suggests that incompatible marriage and class systems never co-exist within the same society'.[18] Half a century of new field studies have exposed further weaknesses. Yet while his models have been recast, the Australian studies stand as a remarkable synthesis, and they mark a significant advance in our understanding of the intractable problems of Australian social organization.

VI

Radcliffe-Brown returned briefly to England (and his newly married wife) in 1913, when he delivered the lectures in Birmingham which aroused Durkheim's enthusiasm. In 1914 he found himself once again in Australia, at that fateful meeting of Section H of the British Association for the Advancement of Science at which

Malinowski served as secretary. When war broke out Malinowski took the opportunity to undertake fieldwork. Radcliffe-Brown became a school-master in Sydney, and was later appointed Director of Education in the Kingdom of Tonga, a post in which he served, evidently without great pleasure or profit, between 1916 and 1919.

Immediately after the war, the Great Flu reached Tonga. Radcliffe-Brown became ill, and on medical advice he left to join his brother in Johannesburg. Here he held some minor museum and academic appointments. Then came a breakthrough. Haddon had been lobbying from Cambridge for the institution of anthropological studies in South Africa, and in 1921 Radcliffe-Brown was appointed to establish the subject at the University of Cape Town. Almost forty years old, he now entered a new phase in his career. Fieldwork was behind him. From now on he was concerned with teaching, writing, and the development of theory. Practically all his important publications appeared after this first appointment to a professorship.

In Cape Town Radcliffe-Brown established a School of African Studies, organized around the new anthropology department. In addition to his teaching and administrative duties he had some impact on government thinking, mounting special 'applied anthropology' courses for administrators of the tribal areas, and giving many successful public lectures, which were often fully covered by the press. He did not, however, make specific recommendations for reform, and in general his message was hardly contentious:

> The one great problem on which the future welfare of South Africa depends is that of finding some social and political system in which the natives and the whites may live together without conflict; and the successful solution of that problem would certainly seem to require a thorough knowledge of the native civilization between which and our own we need to establish some sort of harmonious relation.[19]

He argued, now and for the rest of his career, that the anthropologist's job was simply to provide a scientific appraisal of the situation which the administrator faced; he should not attempt to advocate any particular policy.

In 1926 he returned to Australia, to take up a new chair at Sydney, the first chair to be established in anthropology in Australia. (This post was secured for him by that distinguished Sydney alumnus, the anatomist Elliot Smith, whose extreme diffusionist theories Radcliffe-Brown considered so ludicrous.) Once again he built up an undergraduate programme, and mounted special offerings for colonial officers and missionaries (which, however, were generally thought to be much too theoretical, and which suffered also from his total lack of interest in Papua and New Guinea, territories he never even visited). With the help of substantial government grants he also established research projects on the Aborigines, and started a new journal, *Oceania*.

Despite all this activity, Radcliffe-Brown's tenure of the Sydney chair was in the end only just short of disastrous. He began under the most promising auspices, but his overbearing ways and political maladroitness alienated his supporters. In a period of growing financial stringency he turned the state governments against his schemes, and when he left Sydney in 1931 the department and all the subsidiary activities he had initiated were on the point of collapse. Firth took over to supervise the dissolution, but he and his successor, Elkin, managed to re-establish the department and most of its programmes. On the credit side, Radcliffe-Brown trained a few students, and organized a little – surprisingly little – research. Perhaps his most enduring contribution was the essay 'The social organisation of the Australian tribes', which provided a jumping-off point for the researches of the next generation.

After another brief visit to England, Radcliffe-Brown went on to Chicago in 1931. Here he was free of administrative duties, and was treated with exaggerated respect by his talented coterie of students. Outside this circle he aroused considerable antagonism, by his manner rather than his ideas, although there were many who found his generalizing 'natural science' approach unsympathetic. American anthropology was in a creative and transitional phase. The main trends were on the one hand a development of Boas's historical, diffusionist approach, and, on the other, a movement towards 'culture and personality' studies, influenced by developments in psychology, particularly psychoanalysis and gestalt theory. The work of those whom Radcliffe-Brown influenced showed the impact of his sociological perspective, which was new within the American anthropological tradition. Eggan, Tax and Warner came to represent a Radcliffe-Brownian theoretical school, centred in Chicago. It was always something of an anomaly within American anthropology, but the distinctive contribution of the school has been widely acknowledged.

In 1937 Radcliffe-Brown was appointed to the first established chair in social anthropology at Oxford, so that he returned to England shortly before Malinowski finally left. His inaugural lecture rehearsed his familiar views concerning the distinction between historical and sociological studies, and the superiority of the latter in anthropology. It had a tepid reception, and he never made an impact on the wider community of the university. Within the small world of British anthropology, however, his presence was of the utmost importance. He took Malinowski's place at the head of the profession, and at one time or another the members of his department included (as staff or as students) some of the leading figures of the next generation.

To those who worked with him at the time, Radcliffe-Brown was the leader of a long overdue challenge to Malinowski, but some of Malinowski's more constant followers regarded Radcliffe-Brown as little more than a figure-head for the rebellious young men, E. E. Evans-Pritchard and Meyer Fortes. It is true that some among the new generation of fieldworkers were already turning to a more structural sociology in the 1930s, before Radcliffe-Brown's return to Britain; but although this was in part a direct response to the complexity of their field material, and the analytical weaknesses of Malinowski's theory, the influence of Radcliffe-Brown can be traced as well. He had trained a number of the students who later came to Malinowski for their fieldwork – Schapera, Hogbin and Stanner, for example. Moreover his brief visit to the country in 1931 had brought his work to the attention of some of the young anthropologists. Evans-Pritchard fêted him, and propagated his reputation. Of course, the commerce between Radcliffe-Brown and younger men of the calibre of Evans-Pritchard and Fortes was never a one-way business. Nevertheless one must recognize that Radcliffe-Brown had a very direct and personal impact upon British anthropology, particularly after 1937. This may be measured by the violence of Evans-Pritchard's later repudiation of his central dogmas, and by Fortes's no less impassioned defence.

During the war Radcliffe-Brown served as President of the Royal Anthropological Institute, and he spent two years on a British Council mission in São Paulo. Immediately after the war he retired from the Oxford chair, which he vacated reluctantly in 1946. He remained a man of influence in the profession after his formal retirement, and continued teaching for some years, holding positions in Cambridge, London, Manchester, Grahamstown and Alexandria. He died in London in 1955. Raymond Firth recalls visiting him in hospital a year before his death and asking whether he could bring him something to read. Radcliffe-Brown answered that he was interested only in reading about theoretical advances in social anthropology.[20]

VII

The sociology of Durkheim was the most important influence on Radcliffe-Brown's mature thinking, but he also remained an evolutionist in the tradition of Spencer. Cultures (later societies) were like organisms, and therefore they should be studied by the methods of the natural sciences. Like organisms, they evolved in the direction of increasing diversity and complexity. Evolution in this sense was sharply distinguished from progress, for evolution was a natural process, while progress implied an evaluation of a moral process. Many so-called evolutionists, including Morgan and Frazer, were really rather woolly-minded apostles of progress.

The organic analogy should not, of course, be taken too literally. As Radcliffe-Brown once remarked, 'Societies are not organisms; they do not experience parturition nor death.'[21] The thrust of his argument was really to insist upon the use of methods parallel to those used by the 'natural sciences', and in particular, biology and zoology.

Despite the initial talk of 'culture' and 'psychological' explanation, his orientation from about 1910 was definitely sociological. Sociology to him meant the sort of work carried out by Durkheim, and, he sometimes added, Steinmetz and Westermarck, but certainly not the general run of social survey and reportage that passed for sociology in the USA. He was apparently unaware of the work of Weber and Simmel, but their theories only became widely known in Britain in the 1940s.

Durkheim had begun with an insistence that social facts should be treated as objective phenomena. They could be explained in terms of other social facts. A social fact (exemplified by a grammatical usage, a taboo, a ceremony, a courteous gesture) was characterized by its external and coercive nature. It was prior to any individual, and exercised a constraint upon his behaviour. One could not understand a mode of sacrifice, or a dietary custom, in terms of the psychological make-up of any individual. The custom existed before his birth and would endure after his death. Nor did he freely choose to adopt it, any more than he could freely choose to create a new language in which to communicate with his fellows. These 'social facts', in a sense external to individuals and exerting a force upon them, should also not be reduced to other kinds of reality, as Malinowski liked to do. The set of social facts with which the analyst was concerned must be treated as forming a system, and the meaning and purpose of a custom could be understood only by relating it to the total set of relevant social facts. Finally, the search for speculative 'origins' must be abandoned. The 'contemporary origin', the function of an institution, must be found in its present use.

In Durkheim's view, society was essentially a moral order. Increasingly in his later work he concentrated upon what he called the 'collective consciousness', the values and norms of a society. These were embedded in the individual's consciousness through the process of socialization. In 'primitive societies' this socially conditioned sphere of individual consciousness was predominant, while in societies with complex systems of division of labour the area of individuality was greater.

The persistence of the social order depended upon the maintenance of sentiments of solidarity. In 'primitive societies' one found a series of similar local groups, and these groups and their members were mutually replaceable. The group could segment without altering the form and function of the local units, and individuals could be born or die without changing the social order. In societies of this kind – segmental societies – social solidarity was based upon the recognition of mutual resemblance. In societies which enjoyed a complex division of labour, and, therefore, were of larger scale, and more highly centralized, the solidarity of the members derived from their sense of mutual dependence. In all societies the forms of social grouping determined the social consciousness of their members, and the forms of consciousness were maintained and invigorated by being re-enacted in symbolic rituals. It is not only ritual in the usual sense which had this effect. Even crime was necessary to society, since by dramatizing deviance and retribution it strengthened the sentiments which supported the moral order.

Such a brief résumé is unavoidably distorted. One cannot easily convey the sweep of Durkheim's thought, which was developed in a series of powerful monographs dealing with particular topics. Moreover Durkheim was not working alone. The group he built up around the *Année Sociologique* included such great names as Mauss, Granet, Hubert, Halbwachs and Hertz, and in their journal they worked out their ideas in a co-operative fashion. Even some French scholars outside this group, including Lévy-Bruhl and the neglected master Van Gennep, contributed to the same broad enterprise.

The First World War destroyed this magnificent nursery of sociology. Some of Durkheim's most brilliant students, including his son, were killed in action; and Durkheim himself died in 1917. Only his nephew Mauss survived long to carry on the tradition. The war interrupted the plans for fieldwork which the *Année* group had been developing. It was many years before another cadre was built up, and when it emerged it dedicated itself to field research. As Lévi-Strauss reported in 1947, 'The younger generation of French sociologists, which came to maturity around 1930, have over the last fifteen years almost completely renounced theoretical work – though doubtless only temporarily – in order to fill this gap.'[22]

And so after the First World War Mauss and Radcliffe-Brown were left to work parallel with each other to develop Durkheimian sociology. One may summarize the development from Durkheim to Mauss and Radcliffe-Brown by saying simply that Malinowski's studies of the Trobriand islands had intervened. Curiously, these influenced Mauss more than they did Radcliffe-Brown, and Malinowski himself soon turned away from Durkheim's preoccupations and ideas.

But I have exaggerated the unity of Durkheim's legacy. One may distinguish at least two divergent threads, one of which Mauss followed, while Radcliffe-Brown took up the other. Firstly there was the study of social relationships, 'social morphology', as exemplified in the *Division of Labour in Society*; secondly the study of societies as moral systems, the view which dominates *Suicide* and *The Elementary Forms of the Religious Life*, and which led Durkheim and Mauss to anticipate many future developments in their essay *Primitive Classification*. Both approaches may be found in the work of Radcliffe-Brown and Mauss, and it is arguable that they are not divergent but rather complementary perspectives. However, Radcliffe-Brown turned more to the study of social relations, while Mauss continued to develop the study of cosmological notions.

Mauss lived to endure the Nazi occupation of Paris, which ended his active career. This was the period when Radcliffe-Brown's students and followers finally succeeded in joining his theory to the Malinowskian tradition of holistic fieldwork. The two world wars had a calamitous impact on French sociology, but by a series of chances they did not greatly disturb the development of social anthropology in Britain. These accidents secured the predominance of British social anthropology for a generation.

VIII

The only extended statement of Radcliffe-Brown's theoretical position that has been published is the transcript of a seminar he gave at the University of Chicago in 1937. This circulated widely for many years in typescript, but was published only after Radcliffe-Brown's death, under the title *A Natural Science of Society*. The seminar was a response to a series of lectures by a leading psychologist, who claimed that all social sciences must begin and end with individual psychology. Radcliffe-Brown was moved to formulate in detail his own vision of comparative sociology as the master social science. The only substantial statements published in his lifetime were two essays, on the concept of function (1935) and on social structure (1940), and the introduction to his collected essays, *Structure and Function in Primitive Society* (1952). However, he repeatedly made declarations of faith, usually as preliminaries to particular analyses, and it is relatively easy to abstract the central features of the theoretical position he maintained at least from the 1920s onwards, and probably earlier.

The object of study was the social system or social process. These were systems 'of real relations of connectedness between individuals', or more properly, between individuals occupying social roles, between 'persons'. This constituted the 'social structure', which was not an abstraction. It 'consists of the sum total of all the social relationships of all individuals at a given moment in time. Although it cannot, naturally be seen in its entirety at any one moment, we can observe it; all of the phenomenal reality is there.'[23] But while this was what the fieldworker observed, he described something different, the 'structural form', that is the normal pattern of relationships which he abstracted from the flux of observed reality. Radcliffe-Brown is often criticized for his refusal to recognize that 'social structure' is an abstraction, and it is tempting to reply that his notion of 'structural form' corresponds to what is today generally termed the 'social structure'. This is true to a certain extent, but even the 'structural form' was a generalized description rather than a model. As he once wrote to Lévi-Strauss:

> I use the term 'social structure' in a sense so different from yours as to make discussion so difficult as to be unlikely to be profitable. While for you, social structure has nothing to do with reality but with models that are built up, I regard the social structure as a reality. When I pick up a particular sea shell on the beach, I recognize it as having a particular structure. I may find other shells of the same species which have a similar structure, so that I can say there is a form of structure characteristic of the species. By examining a number of different species, I may be able to recognize a certain general structural form or principle, that of a helix, which could be expressed by means of logarithmic equation. I take it that the equation is what you mean by 'model'. I examine a local group of Australian aborigines and find an arrangement of persons in a certain number of families. This, I call the social structure of that

particular group at that moment of time. Another local group has a structure that is in important ways similar to that of the first. By examining a representative sample of local groups in one region, I can describe a certain form of structure.

I am not sure whether by 'model' you mean the structural form itself or my description of it. The structural form itself may be discovered by observation, including statistical observation, but cannot be experimented on.[24]

The structural form is explicit in 'social usages', or norms, which are generally recognized as binding and which are widely observed. They therefore have the characteristics of Durkheim's 'social facts', but once again Radcliffe-Brown insisted that they were not deduced but observed. A social usage or norm 'is not established by the anthropologist . . . it is characterized by what people say about rules in a given society and what they do about them.'[25]

Having abstracted the social form of a number of societies, one proceeds to comparison and classification, which is the basis of proper scientific procedure. One can then pose the fundamental questions of social morphology, 'How many different kinds of societies are there, and in what respects do they differ from one another? What is the range of variation, and, more important, what common characteristics are there discoverable by analysis which are characteristic of all human societies?'[26]

Despite the significance Radcliffe-Brown attached to comparison, there is a certain ambiguity about the procedures he advocated. He often proceeded as though one should always in the first instance compare societies that are culturally or ethnically related – the various Andamanese groups, the Australian tribes, the Southern Bantu groups. The goal often seems to have been to uncover the general characteristics of the 'culture area', to strip away local variations from (say) the typical Andamanese form, and at times Radcliffe-Brown seems to retain elements of diffusionist method. At other times the goal was rather to understand peculiarities and variations by comparison with better-known or more readily understood examples. Finally, he was never clear as to the units of comparison. He sometimes wrote as though one could compare the structural forms of total social systems, but at other times he suggested that it was possible to compare only sub-systems, such as kinship or political systems.

In any case the ultimate goal was not in doubt. This was to formulate generalizations about the common features of all human societies. These generalizations would constitute social laws.

Radcliffe-Brown argued that although social structures were in flux, social forms were comparatively stable. New members of the society are born, the old chief dies and is replaced, people marry, divorce and remarry; but the same social usages persist. The stability of the structural form depends upon the integration of its parts, and the performance by these parts of particular tasks which are necessary for the maintenance of the form. These are the 'functions' of the parts of the system. Laws of social statics would be statements about the needs which had to be met if social forms were to persist.

The basic need of all societies was what Radcliffe-Brown called 'coaptation', the mutual adjustment of the interests of the members of the society. This necessitates some standardization of behaviour, and it is here that 'culture' comes in, for culture is the realm of learnt ways of feeling, thinking and behaving. Ultimately coaptation requires the standardization of beliefs and sentiments, which are kept alive through rituals and symbols. But this area of social life – corresponding to Durkheim's 'collective consciousness' – could not be studied in isolation, as Malinowski and most American anthropologists believed.

> You cannot have a science of culture. You can study culture only as a characteristic of a social system ... if you study culture, you are always studying the acts of behaviour of a specific set of persons who are linked together in a social structure.[27]

Having established taxonomies and formulated the laws of social statics, that is, the laws of persistence of social forms, he faced a third set of problems. These were concerned with the manner in which societies change their type – with what Spencer had called problems of social dynamics. Radcliffe-Brown believed that these problems were logically secondary to problems of continuity. The laws of social change would be deduced from the laws of social continuity. He never devoted serious attention to them.

The conclusions of these investigations are disappointing. The fundamental laws of social statics turn out to be statements of this sort:

> There have to be as part of the social coaptation of any given society a certain common set of ways of feeling and a certain common set of ways of thinking.[28]
>
> There must be a certain degree of functional consistency amongst the constituent parts of the social system. (Functional inconsistency 'exists whenever two aspects of the social system produce a conflict which can only be resolved by some change in the system itself'.)

To this law of the necessity of a certain degree of functional consistency we may add a second, which is a special instance of the first. Any human social life requires the establishment of a social structure consisting of a network of relations between individuals and groups of individuals. These relations all involve certain rights and duties which need to be defined in such a way that conflicts of rights can be resolved without destroying the structure. It is this need that is met by the establishment of systems of justice and legal institutions.[29]

Explanation consists in showing how a social usage fulfils one of these basic functions, upon which the maintenance of stable social forms depends. Thus a ritual sustains sentiments of social solidarity. These sentiments must be maintained in order to make people play their appointed parts – that is, they sustain the degree of coaptivity upon which the system depends. This sort of argument is often plausible enough, but it does not seem to lead anywhere. Ultimately it is tautologous. If you have to start off knowing what are the basic functions upon which society depends, you have settled the important questions before even beginning to sort out the details. Criticisms of this sort are routinely made of all the varieties of structural functionalism (but since Radcliffe-Brown was one of the clearest writers in this tradition, he is perhaps most open to criticism).

In any case, Radcliffe-Brown's actual procedure was usually far superior to his prescription. Again and again his papers start with some banal statement about societies being like organisms, which should therefore be studied in pseudo-physiological terms, etc.; but he then proceeds to develop particular analyses as examples of what he means, and these analyses are generally original and illuminating. This is because he was not merely a functionalist; in the jargon of a later generation, he was also a structuralist. That is, he was concerned with the relationships between social relationships of different kinds. In exploring these he allowed himself intuitive leaps that often yielded insights which have still to be superseded. His best work is concerned with 'totemism', and with kinship – that is, with special cases of cosmology and social organization. These were to be two of the central topics of the new structuralism which came into fashion after his death.

IX

'Totemism', broadly defined as an aspect of the way in which people conceive of the relationship between the social and the natural world, was a classical issue in British anthropology, and it was one of Radcliffe-Brown's preoccupations from the time of his Andaman study. In totemism a specific group within a society adopts a ritual attitude towards a particular natural species or object. Durkheim had argued that certain groups are the objects of sentiments of attachment. These sentiments must be collectively expressed in ritual and symbolism if they are to be maintained, and one obvious way of symbolizing the social group was with reference to natural species. Radcliffe-Brown accepted this argument as far as it went – 'it is a normal procedure that the sentiment of attachment to a group shall be expressed in some formalised collective behaviour having reference to an object that represents the group itself'.[30]

But Durkheim failed to examine the next question – why are natural species generally selected as totems? Characteristically, Radcliffe-Brown insisted that this question must be placed in the context of a broader problem, the ritual relationships between people and natural species in all, including non-totemic, societies. He recalled his study of the Andaman islanders, who lacked totems but expressed 'ritual attitudes' to a range of natural species. His initial conclusion was that species important to the livelihood of the group are given 'ritual value'.

This crude statement was subsequently elaborated. Totemism was 'a mechanism by which a system of social solidarities is established between men and nature'.[31] It is a way of bringing the natural world within the social or moral order. Totemism was therefore not only a mode of symbolizing social groups; it was also a way of domesticating nature. In this sense totemism was a prototype of religion, for the essence of religion is the conception of the universe as a social, that is, a moral order.

The method is characteristic. The particular problem is set in a broad context. One then states the fundamental laws which determine a kind of activity – e.g. groups must express sentiments of solidarity, through rituals, which employ symbols. Or, human beings must be able to see nature as somehow part of the same moral order as society ... The particular phenomenon under consideration is then related to these broad generalizations. This constitutes explanation.

The other element of the method is comparison, and it was in a later essay on the comparative method that Radcliffe-Brown elaborated his argument. It had presumably become clear to him that totems are not generally selected because of their importance as food, and he now explored the problem of why specific species were selected to symbolize particular group relationships. He observed that in some tribes in New South Wales there was a division of the society into two exogamous moieties. The moieties were named respectively after the eaglehawk and crow, and eaglehawk men married crow women, and vice versa. He observed that parallels could be found elsewhere: the Haida of north-west America also have a division into two matrilineal moieties, and these are named after the eagle and the raven. In Australia there were many examples of exogamous moieties being named after pairs of birds, and these birds tended to be linked also in myths. Moreover, one could find in Australia other kinds of dual divisions, including endogamous moieties, or even alternating generations, which were similarly named after pairs of birds – and not only birds, but sometimes after pairs of animals, such as two species of kangaroo, or the bat and the treecreeper.

Further, where these divisions are found, the two birds or animals in question are usually represented in myths as being opponents in some sort of conflict. Radcliffe-Brown continued:

> A comparative study therefore reveals to us the fact that the Australian ideas about the eaglehawk and the crow are only a particular instance of a widespread phenomenon. First, these tales interpret the resemblances and differences of animal species in terms of social relationships of friendship and antagonism as they are known in the social life of human beings. Secondly, natural species are placed in pairs of opposites. They can only be so regarded if there is some respect in which they resemble each other. Thus eaglehawk and crow resemble each other in being the two prominent meat-eating birds (. . . and the Australian aborigine thinks of himself as a meat-eater).
>
> We can now answer the question 'Why eaglehawk and crow?' by saying that these are selected as representing a certain kind of relationship which we may call one of 'opposition'.
>
> The Australian idea of what is here called 'opposition' is a particular application of that association by contrariety that is a universal feature of human thinking, so that we think by pairs of contraries, upwards and downwards, strong and weak, black and white. But the Australian conception of 'opposition' combines the idea of a pair of contraries with that of a pair of opponents. In the tales about eaglehawk and crow the two birds are opponents in the sense of being antagonists.[32]

A comparative study of moieties shows that they too are seen as locked in a mixture of rivalry and alliance, at once paired and opposed. This is the sort of relationship which is often expressed in formalized 'joking'. It is therefore appropriate that they should be symbolized by two linked natural species, which are in turn represented as being in some sense contraries, and also competitors.

Lévi-Strauss has seized upon this last development of Radcliffe-Brown's theory of totemism, and suggested that it represented a departure for him and, incidentally, an approach to a structural linguistic mode of argument.[33] In fact Radcliffe-Brown's notion of opposition did include the linguistic level of binary contrasts, but it applied more particularly to a social opposition between groups, which was expressed in some form of conflict. Nevertheless in this theory the structuralist dimension of Radcliffe-Brown's thought may be clearly discerned, side by side with the insistence upon function.

X

Radcliffe-Brown saw a system of kinship and marriage as a set of interrelated social usages which were based upon the recognition of certain biological relationships for social purposes. The systems included the kinship terminology, the actual networks of relationships between kin, the set of rights, duties and usages associated with particular kinship roles, and the beliefs and ritual practices associated with kinship, including, for example, beliefs about procreation, or the veneration of ancestors.

In investigating a kinship system he concentrated upon two of its aspects: (i) the usages governing the relationships between kin; and (ii) the terms used in addressing kin, and referring to them. The kinship terminology had a certain priority, both in logic and with respect to method. This was because 'The actual social relation between a person and his relative, as defined by rights and duties or socially approved attitudes and modes of behaviour is then to a greater or lesser extent fixed by the category to which the relative belongs.'[34] At the same time he would not grant one part of the kinship system priority in causal terms. Rivers had argued that the form of the marriage rules determined the terminology. This was unacceptable. The marriage regulations and the terminology were necessarily consistent, but there were no grounds for arguing that one or the other came first, or determined the other.

Societies such as the Andaman islanders and the Australian Aborigines were organized by the principles of kinship and residence, and residential groups were themselves informed by the principles of the kinship system. Therefore in societies of this sort the study of social structure meant essentially the study of the kinship system. The hub of the kinship system was the family, but there were various possible ways of treating kin outside the circle of the family. Broadly the option was to classify them together with members of the family, as happened in the 'classificatory' kinship systems which Morgan had identified; or members of the family could be distinguished from other relatives, as was the practice among the Eskimo and in contemporary Europe. Radcliffe-Brown concentrated upon the logic of 'classificatory' systems of kinship terminology.

Every classificatory system operated with some combination of three basic principles. First of all, brothers and sisters shared a feeling of solidarity, and they were treated as a unit by outsiders. This generated the principle of 'the unity of the sibling group', which influenced the categorization of relatives. For example, in some South African tribes I call my mother *mma*, extend the same term to her sisters, and even call her brother *malume*, or literally 'mother male'.

Secondly, societies operating classificatory kinship terminologies commonly also had lineages – that is, there were solidary groups formed by the descendants in one line (traced through males only or females only) of a single ancestor. The members of the lineage, like siblings, shared a sense of unity; and outsiders treated the lineage as a unit. This gave rise to 'the principle of the unity of the lineage group', which explained further peculiar features of classificatory kinship systems. For example, among the patrilineal Fox Indians I call all the men of my mother's lineage 'mother's brother' and all the women 'mother's sister', regardless of generation. This is because I belong to a different lineage (my father's), and so, to me, they are all alike members of another corporate group, to which I am linked through my mother.

Thirdly, Radcliffe-Brown defined a generation principle. In all kinship systems members of consecutive generations are distanced from each other, for reasons which go back to the necessity for transmitting culture and socializing new members of the society, functions that demand discipline and control. But members of alternate generations (grandparents and grandchildren) tend to be 'merged'. Their relationships are easy and egalitarian, and in many societies there is a notion that the grandchild replaces the grandparent in the social system. These generational combinations and oppositions may also be reflected in the terms used for the classification of kin. Indeed some kinship systems, the 'Hawaiian' systems, classify relatives on the basis of generation alone.

These three principles, then, reflecting underlying social conditions of great generality, inform the various systems of kinship terminology. The approach developed by Radcliffe-Brown contrasted sharply with the classical method, whereby kinship terminologies were regarded as fossils, pertaining to a vanished system of kinship. For example, it might be suggested that in those societies where the term 'father' is applied to a large number of men, this reflected an earlier period of promiscuity when one could not be sure who one's father really was. Radcliffe-Brown rejected all such speculative explanations. The terminology made sense in terms of the contemporary kinship system.

But while the study of the terminology was the best approach to the understanding of kinship systems, the systems were essentially systems of social relationships, and these were patterned by the kinds of solidarity and opposition that governed all social relationships. Radcliffe-Brown's most interesting analysis of these principles came in his discussion of 'joking relationships', a problem to which he returned again and again in his work.

One of the classic examples of joking relationships was provided by Junod in his report on the Thonga of Mozambique, and this was an example which stimulated Radcliffe-Brown's first essay on the problem. Among the Thonga there is a relaxed and friendly relationship between a man and his mother's father –

> However should a child take too much liberty with his kokwana, the old man will say to him: 'Go and play with your malume (mother's brother)'. The malume, indeed, for his uterine nephew, is quite different from any other relative. No respect at all is necessary towards him! 'You go to *bombela* in his village; you do what you please. You take all the food you want without asking permission. If you are ill, he will take special care of you and sacrifice for you ... When the mupsyana goes to his maternal uncle, accompanied by his comrades who scent a good meal, the wives of the malume (mother's brother) call him: "Come along, husband! Look here, your malume has hidden some food in the back part of the hut ... behind the large basket. Go and take it". The boy steals the food, runs away with it and eats it to the last bite with his friends. The malume comes back and is angry. But when he hears that the trick has been played by his mupsyana, he shrugs his shoulders ... When another day the nephew comes again, the malume says: "You have killed us the other day by famine!" – "Is there any more food handy that I may do it again?" answers the boy.'

Sometimes the malume (mother's brother) himself points to one of his wives and says to the ntukulu: 'This is your wife. Let her treat you well!' This woman much enjoys the situation, which she finds quite entertaining. She makes a feast for the ntukulu and calls him nkata, husband. It goes so far that sometimes the nephew says to the uncle: 'Please make haste and die that I may have your wife'. – 'Do you intend killing me with a gun?' says the malume ... But all this talking is mere joke.[35]

What is the explanation of this extraordinary behaviour – 'joking', as it came to be called in the literature, characterized by the breaking of even the fundamental conventions governing the use of food and sex, and by insults which would not be tolerated in any other situation? This sort of behaviour is to be found in a number of societies, between individuals and also, as Radcliffe-Brown recognized, between groups. Characteristically for his time, Junod explained the Thonga customs in terms of a conjecture about prehistoric Thonga society. He suggested that although they were now patrilineal, the Thonga had formerly been 'matriarchal'. The customs which subsisted in the relationship between mother's brother and sister's son were the relics of a former age, when both would have been members of the same corporate group, and a boy would have succeeded to the position of his mother's brother.

In his first essay on the problem, published in 1924, Radcliffe-Brown was concerned only with this relationship between mother's brother and sister's son. He dismissed of Junod's unsupported historical conjectures, and insisted that the explanation must be found in the contemporary situation. Among the Thonga a man is disciplined and controlled by his father. His mother by contrast is a loving and tolerant figure. The sentiments he feels towards his mother are extended as he grows up to her siblings, including her brother who is regarded and treated as a 'male mother'. The mother's father is similarly regarded as a tolerant and permissive figure, and indeed all the men of the mother's lineage will be grouped together and treated in similar fashion. Even the ancestor spirits on the mother's side will be regarded as more kindly and forgiving than those on the father's side.

This sort of explanation was often invoked by Malinowski, and it has come to be known as an 'extensionist' hypothesis, since it argues from relationships within the family to relationships with more distant kin, and assumes that as a child grows up he actually extends the sentiments he has developed for his parents to their siblings. The weaknesses of the argument are numerous. It is sufficient for the moment to note that it assumes that every child builds up the customary relationship with his mother's brother from scratch; and it fails to account for the tolerance of the mother's brother to his demanding sister's son. (Evans-Pritchard tried to salvage Radcliffe-Brown's argument by offering an ingenious solution to that problem.[36])

Later, Radcliffe-Brown took a different tack. Instead of arguing in terms of the extension of sentiments, he placed the problem – and more broadly the whole question of joking relationships – in the context of the range of possible forms of 'alliance'. Social relationships were divided into those between members of one corporate group, and those between members of different groups. The latter were further sub-divided. Some depended upon common membership of a political community. Others were contractual relationships. Finally there were relationships of 'alliance' or 'consociation' between individuals or groups which were otherwise socially separated. Such relationships of consociation were in turn classified into four types: (i) based on intermarriage; (ii) based on the exchange of goods or services; (iii) based on blood-brotherhood or a similar institution; and (iv) those which were in the form of joking relationships. A joking relationship was therefore identified as one of a limited range of possible relationships between members of socially separated groups. It might be found in isolation, or together with one of the other forms of consociation.

That might set the relationship in its proper context, but why was it expressed in *joking*? To understand this one must examine the whole range of etiquette regulating behaviour in kinship roles. The general types of behaviour associated with kinship may be classed in two sets of oppositions: respect *v.* familiarity, and joking *v.* avoidance. Respect typifies relationships with parents, familiarity relationships with siblings. Joking and avoidance are characteristic of relationships with certain kin and affines who do not belong to your lineage. They are extreme forms of familiarity and respect. Joking is most commonly found in the relationships between cross-cousins; avoidance is more typical of relationships between members of successive generations, particularly between men and women and their parents-in-law. But joking and avoidance serve a similar purpose: both protect the delicate relationship between people who are joined in one set of ties, but divided by others – for example, between members of different lineages who are allied in marriage. As Radcliffe-Brown recalled:

> I once asked an Australian native why he had to avoid his mother-in-law, and his reply was, 'Because she is my best friend in the world; she has given me my wife.' The mutual respect between

son-in-law and parents-in-law is a mode of friendship. It prevents conflict that might arise through divergence of interest.[37]

The analysis then concludes with a generalization. Both joking and avoidance are 'modes of organizing a definite and stable system of social behaviour in which conjunctive and disjunctive components ... are maintained and combined'.[38]

Here again the analysis concludes with a statement of function, but its enduring value derives from the preceding statement of the structural forms in which 'alliance' appears. At this level the analysis joins up with his analysis of totemism, particularly the relationships of the eaglehawk/crow type, between moieties that exchange women and are united in their opposition. (It has also been remarked that although he did not cite Freud, the theory of joking relationships is congruent with Freud's famous theory of the joke.)

XI

Radcliffe-Brown's list of publications is not large, considering his reputation and the impact which his ideas had in social anthropology. Much of it consists of occasional essays, and a striking feature is the recurrent statements of policy, the manifestos of his comparative sociology. In these he set out the place of social anthropology among the social sciences, and prescribed its proper methods and goals. The first of these, published in 1923, marked his appointment to the chair of social anthropology at Cape Town. The last to appear in his lifetime, a note in *Nature*, in 1944, rehearsed similar themes, and these were stressed once more in the uncompleted manuscript of a textbook on which he was working at the time of his death. One may discern minor shifts in his position, notably a new conceptual emphasis on 'social structure' rather than 'culture' after about 1930, but he maintained a remarkably consistent position for most of his professional life.

His primary concern was always to distinguish social anthropology – or comparative sociology, which he equated with the sociology of the *Année* school – from ethnology. Ethnology was a real force in Britain until the late 1920s, and it continued for much longer to be the central interest of American anthropologists. Radcliffe-Brown's first objection was that the ethnologists argued from inadequate evidence. They were not strictly historians, since the societies with which they were concerned lacked a historical consciousness, and their history was undocumented. Like the eighteenth-century Scottish savants, the ethnologists were engaged in 'conjectural history', a completely unscientific enterprise.

Not, he stressed, that he had anything against history. Proper history might illuminate social studies. But – and this was his second and perhaps more important argument – one could always analyse societies from an ahistorical point of view. A study of the British Parliament would conventionally begin by tracing its development over a long period of time, perhaps for a millennium. But it would be quite possible to write an enlightening study of Parliament which dealt only with its contemporary structure and role. This apparently platitudinous statement was not without significance. Both common sense and scholarship in Europe and America were imbued with a historical point of view. The question normally posed was, how did this come to be ... ? It took an act of imagination to grasp the new question which Durkheim was asking – what does this mean, and what are its concomitants? – and to recognize that it could be answered without first dealing with the historical question.

Although Radcliffe-Brown always identified the pseudo-historical point of view as the main threat, he was concerned to defend the integrity of social anthropology on other fronts as well. Like Durkheim, he was ambivalent about psychology. Social facts could not be explained in terms of individual psychology, but it was possible that some forms of psychology might assist sociology. Like Malinowski, he was for some years an advocate of Shand's theory of sentiments, but while Malinowski later proclaimed himself a behaviourist, Radcliffe-Brown simply dropped his psychological assumptions – or left them implicit. He argued that the new sociology should maintain a guarded but neighbourly relationship with psychology. Their relationship should be rather like that between physics and chemistry, which also studied a single reality with different methods and in terms of different theories. Unlike Malinowski, he never experimented with psychoanalytical theory.

The battle in the latter part of his life was extended to Malinowski and those American anthropologists who, like Malinowski, were urging the development of a 'science of culture'. These writers treated social relations as a part of the total configuration of behaviour with which they were concerned, but by no means as the primary part. Nor did they regard social relations as constituting a distinct system, which should not be reduced to other kinds of relations. This was the crux of the dispute. The differences between Malinowski and Radcliffe-Brown which developed particularly in the 1930s were perhaps in part a matter of 'politics'; but there was also an important and growing divergence on matters of theory.

After his retirement Radcliffe-Brown – stung by being grouped with Malinowski as a 'functionalist' – charted the history of their differences. When Malinowski had first come to Britain, in 1910, he had shown Radcliffe-Brown a paper he had written on the Australian Aborigines which contained a Durkheimian point of view on social function. In 1914, at the historic meeting of Section H of the British Association in Australia, 'We had many lengthy discussions on anthropology and the aims and methods of field research, and we reached fairly complete agreement.'[39] But then in the late 1920s Malinowski began to propagate a theory of 'functional anthropology' that dealt with a whole range of non-social functions. In the 1930s he was increasingly inclined to explain social facts with reference to biological or culturally derived needs. 'He had gradually come to think of the subject as concerned not with the social relations and interactions of human beings but with "culture".' In contrast, Radcliffe-Brown always shared the view of Durkheim, a view 'concerned not with biological functions but with social functions, not with the abstract biological "individual", but with the concrete "persons" of a particular society. It cannot be expressed in terms of culture.'[40] Indeed, he later wrote, 'As a consistent opponent of Malinowski's functionalism I may be called an anti-functionalist.'[41]

Radcliffe-Brown would sometimes concede that ethnology, or psychology, or cultural anthropology might be able to develop their own valid frameworks for the analysis of custom, but he was sceptical. However, his main concern was to establish the boundaries of the pursuit he considered to be the most promising, and to maintain it against all challenges.

The outstanding feature of Radcliffe-Brown's mature work is its single-mindedness. Again and again he set out his vision of sociology as a sort of natural science, and therefore as opposed to conjectural reconstructions. He kept returning to the same problems – totemism and ancestor worship; kinship terminologies, the avunculate and joking relationships; and law. His strength lay in his clarity, his certitude and his dedication. These enabled him to win disciples.

XII

So few people were involved in British social anthropology before the Second World War that one can be schematic about the history of the interwar period without serious distortion. The 1920s saw the challenge to the classical historical approach, and the acceptance of intensive fieldwork by participant observation as the basis of a career in anthropology. The 1930s was the decade of Malinowski and the

London School of Economics. At this time it seemed possible that anthropology in Britain and the United States might make a similar shift in concert, in the direction of a synchronic approach. In 1930 Boas, the leading American ethnologist, wrote:

> If we knew the whole biological, geographical and cultural setting of a society completely, and if we understood in detail the ways of reacting of the members of the society as a whole to these conditions, we should not need historical knowledge of the origin of the society to understand its behaviour. . . . An error of modern anthropology, as I see it, lies in the over-emphasis on historical reconstruction, the importance of which should not be minimized, as against a penetrating study of the individual under the stress of the culture in which he lives.

As an American follower of Radcliffe-Brown, Fred Eggan remarked, 'some of Boas's students came to believe that "they had known it all the time" '.[42] But the American anthropologists went in a different direction, towards a psychological interpretation of culture, with gestalt psychology, learning theory and psychoanalysis coming together in the well-known studies of Margaret Mead and Ruth Benedict; or towards a new evolutionism. The real split between the American and British traditions came with the dominance of Radcliffe-Brown in British anthropology after his return to Oxford in 1937, and Malinowski's subsequent departure for the United States. The 1940s in Britain was the decade of Radcliffe-Brown, Oxford, and a sociological structuralism.

I cannot help speculating as to what would have happened if Malinowski had remained in London, and Radcliffe-Brown had stayed in Chicago; or, indeed, if both had been working in Britain in the 1930s and 1940s. The question highlights the importance at this period of the chance movements of a couple of individuals between the small number of powerful posts which existed. Yet there are indications that even in the 1930s the new generation of British anthropologists was moving towards sociology, in their search for analytical frameworks that would help them interpret the rich material they had brought back from the field. One sees this in the contributions of Fortes and Schapera to the symposium on culture change in Africa, which appeared in 1938, and in some of the monographs produced by Malinowski's students – sporadically in Firth's *We the Tikopia* (1936) and more consistently in Schapera's *Handbook of Tswana Law and Custom* (1938) and Hogbin's *Law and Order in Polynesia* (1934), to which Malinowski contributed a fiery introduction, restating his fundamental tenets in order to strengthen the reader against the heresies to follow.

But even this brief list includes several scholars who had been exposed to Radcliffe-Brown's teaching in Sydney or Cape Town. There can be little doubt that he did provide a more productive framework for analysis than did Malinowski, although he and Malinowski both had to the full the weaknesses of their strengths. Both men died in the middle of the twentieth century, but while the centenary of Radcliffe-Brown's death was not marked, Malinowski's centenary was celebrated in London, Cracow and Yale. Today, it is Malinowski's contribution that can be seen to have endured.

3   The 1930s and 1940s – from function to structure

My hunch is that at least some of the difference between the work of Malinowski and that of Radcliffe-Brown could be correlated with their personalities. Radcliffe-Brown, in sharp contrast to Malinowski, seemed to be more aloof from life, modern or tribal, and without close family ties. . . . Again, compared to Malinowski, his relations with men seemed to be easier than those with women. Also, Radcliffe-Brown had disciples in the real sense of the word. Malinowski's students learned from him, but they also argued, talked back, and made jokes about him. He wanted loyalty (you had to be on his side) but not reverence . . . Radcliffe-Brown, on the other hand, gathered about him a group of worshipping young disciples. I never heard any of them snipe or ridicule him. Today, some of these British anthropologists, now middle-aged, seem to belong to an ancestor cult.[1]

– Hortense Powdermaker

I

Almost all the first generation of anthropology students in the functionalist era passed through Malinowski's seminars. Even those who were attached to other universities made a point of attending. For the decade after 1924 this was the only school which counted. The seminar included all interested students, whatever their status, various members of the faculty, academic visitors from other departments and from abroad (including, for a while, C. K. Ogden and Talcott Parsons), administrators and missionaries on home leave from the colonies and, periodically, bewildered amateurs, some of whom might even be recruited into the profession and sent off to do fieldwork in some exotic spot.

There was no formal teaching. The participants in the seminar came expecting to be stimulated by the discussion rather than by formal contributions; and particularly by Malinowski's interventions. As the first students went out into the field and returned, the range of material available increased, and the theoretical notions were stretched, questioned, vindicated and, occasionally, relinquished, though seldom by Malinowski himself. All the major monographs of the period show the imprint of these discussions. Perhaps as much as his ideas Malinowski's personality imposed itself – enthusiastic, irreverent, supremely confident.

The new anthropology, established by a Pole at the academically unconventional London School of Economics, attracted an unusual collection of students. Foreigners predominated, often experts in other fields who had been brought in as fairly mature scholars. They came from diverse backgrounds, but they were a small group and formed a tightly-knit professional cadre. As late as 1939 there were only about twenty professional social anthropologists, in the modern sense, in the British Commonwealth, and most of them had spent some time with Malinowski. These features of the profession are significant, for they facilitated the interchange of ideas, and the concerted shifts to new points of view.

The American Hortense Powdermaker, a trade union organizer, arrived at the LSE in 1925. She wrote:

> During my first year at the LSE only three graduate students were in anthropology. The first two were E. E. Evans-Pritchard and Raymond Firth. Isaac Schapera came the second year and we were soon joined by Audrey Richards, Edith Clarke, the late Jack Driberg, Camilla Wedgwood, and Gordon and Elizabeth Brown. Strong personal bonds developed between us and with Malinowski; it was a sort of family with the usual ambivalences. The atmosphere was in the European tradition: a master and his students, some in accord and others in opposition.[2]

Evans-Pritchard was the only British native of the three men. Firth was a New Zealander, and Schapera was the first of a long line of South African recruits, many of them Jewish. He had been a student of Radcliffe-Brown in Cape Town, and when he completed his masters degree, Radcliffe-Brown advised him to choose between studying further under Malinowski in London or Lowie in the United States. He considered them to be at that time the only two other men in the world who were competent to train social anthropologists.

The high proportion of women among the early students of Malinowski is noteworthy; like the foreigners, they were a marginal group being drawn into this fledgling enterprise. Many of them became professional anthropologists, and Audrey Richards, a natural scientist from Cambridge, very soon became a leading figure.

The first organized group on a research grant were the initial set of Rockefeller research fellows of the new International African Institute. These were Fortes, Nadel and Hofstra, who joined Malinowski's seminar in the early 1930s, and whom he termed collectively 'the Mandarins'. Fortes – another South African Jew – already had a doctorate in psychology, and had worked for some years in the East London child guidance clinic. Hofstra, a Dutchman, was to return to academic life in the Netherlands. Nadel had the most romantic background. By the age of thirty he had taken a doctorate in psychology and philosophy at the University of Vienna, and was an accomplished musician. He had published studies on the philosophy of music, including a book on musical typology, and a biography of Busoni, produced programmes of exotic music for Radio Vienna, and toured Czechoslovakia with his own opera company.[3]

There is a perceptible generation gap between these students, who attended the seminars during the initial Malinowskian decade, and those who went to the LSE during the last few years of his regime. The first group of students were all specialists in other fields who had been converted to anthropology (with the exception of Schapera). The next group started younger, on the whole, and included a larger proportion who had been trained in anthropology at the undergraduate level. Some came from South Africa, where Schapera and Winifred Hoernlé preached the new gospel. In 1930 Schapera, after returning to South Africa, replaced Mrs Hoernlé for a year at the University of the Witwatersrand in Johannesburg. His first class included Max Gluckman, Ellen Hellman and Hilda (Beemer) Kuper. Eileen (Jensen) Krige was preparing for fieldwork. All of them went on to study with Malinowski and became professional anthropologists. There was a similar migration from Australia, after Radcliffe-Brown had established the department of anthropology at Sydney.

II

Malinowski's dominance lasted roughly from 1924 to 1938. It was superseded by a sociological movement, led by Radcliffe-Brown. The shift is evident in the monographs of the period. There is a period of 'functionalist' studies in the 1930s; then a period of transition; and, after 1940, a wave of neo-Radcliffe-Brownian studies. There is a time-lag between the emergence of a new theoretical consensus and its public appearance in monographs. This is inevitable, given the length of time which elapses between the departure of the ethnographer for the field and the publication of a book. There is therefore some overlap, but the phases I have distinguished may nevertheless be identified with some precision.

A second shift at this time was not entirely the result of initiatives within the profession. This was the move from the Pacific to Africa. Anthropologists now began to study large-scale societies, which were often difficult to demarcate geographically, and which had complex political institutions. These new interests were to have a distinct influence upon theoretical developments, particularly after the publication of *African Political Systems* in 1940.

But beneath all this there remained the Malinowskian emphasis on fieldwork by participant observation. This became the hallmark of British social anthropology. The rules were clear: one had to spend at least a year, preferably two, in the field, working as soon as possible in the vernacular, living apart from other Europeans and to some extent as a member of the community one was studying; and above all the anthropologist had to make a psychological transference – 'they' had to become 'we'. Of course, not everyone kept all the rules. Indeed it is now clear that Malinowski himself did not. However, as Hortense Powdermaker recently remarked, the guidelines which he laid down for his students represented an ideal:

> His students, like followers and new converts in general, may have lived up to the tenets of the myth more than did the medicine man who gave them to us. I, for one, have always been grateful. We were all, probably, more successful because of the myth than we would have been without it.[4]

III

The monographs of the 1930s which are usually called 'functionalist' might more precisely be termed Malinowskian. They reflected his interests, even when the authors differed from him on particular points. They dealt with family life, with economic activities, and with magic. They were not particularly concerned with kinship systems, with politics, or with religion. Malinowski's example also permeated the presentation. The authors often included a typical biography – a development from the old-fashioned catch-all 'life history' presentation – and this helped them to integrate their descriptive material in a coherent but non-structural fashion. Individual misbehaviour was generally stressed, and the reader was introduced to particular characters, and offered evocative descriptions to give life to the culture. The monographs moved from a particular institution along the whole gamut of the culture, achieving a thematic integration, if not a more analytical coherence.

The best-known monographs in this genre are Firth's *We the Tikopia* (1936), Richards's *Land, Labour and Diet in Northern Rhodesia* (1939), and Schapera's *Married Life in an African Tribe* (1940). Fortune's *Sorcerers of Dobu*, published in 1932, dealt with the ethnographic region Malinowski had made his own, and, although he cannot be considered in the usual sense a student of Malinowski, this book is a good example of the kind Malinowski's students were writing. Studies of this sort continued to appear well into the 1940s, particularly in the outposts of the anthropological world, and they typified the work being done in Britain in the 1930s.

Both *We the Tikopia* and *Married Life in an African Tribe* were primarily concerned with the family. Like Malinowski in the *Sexual Life of Savages*, their authors presented the family in terms of its 'functions', mainly procreation and socialization, and worked out from there to the implications of these processes for other aspects of the social situation. These are long, discursive books, and would soon seem old-fashioned and undisciplined in their manner. *We the Tikopia* runs to almost 600 pages, and because there is not a theoretical framework of any substance, one wonders almost why Firth stopped when he did. The authors did not abstract. Principles of social organization were shown immanent in concrete activities, rather than as forming systems which could be comprehended. There is no notion of a kinship system in these early monographs of Firth and Schapera, or of an economic system in Richards's *Land, Labour and Diet in Northern Rhodesia*.

The weaknesses were recognized. Firth has written of the late 1930s: 'The basic problem raised by the functional theory of anthropology in its less sophisticated form – if everything is related to everything else, where does the description stop? – was much before the writers of the period.'[5] The problem in fact was how to distinguish analytical relevance from empirical connection. What was lacking was a theory which would specify what was relevant and what peripheral to the resolution of a particular problem, or to the understanding of an event. For example, Firth spent seven fascinating pages in *We the Tikopia* on sexual themes in conversation, humour and stories (in addition to a very valuable section on indecency). One of the Tikopian tales he related was of a woman who tempted her husband's penis outside their house and threw it into the sea. She would scoop it up whenever she wanted sexual gratification, but one day her son came along, took the penis for a sea-slug, and shot it dead with his arrow. Now this Tikopian Oedipus story may be relevant to all sorts of theoretical problems, but it was included only because it dealt with married couples and sex and so was connected to the theme (and presumably because it was entertaining in itself). It did not relate to an overriding issue, but rather raised an irrelevant little problem of its own – something that might better have been treated in a separate paper. Just as the descriptions threw up these disconnected little problems, which gave the monographs a spurious theoretical content, so the material lent itself to moralizing, in the absence of a pervasive theoretical concern. Thus Schapera gave point to his descriptions by showing what a mess the missionaries were making of traditional Tswana morality, and Richards argued the point that the Bemba were not idle, as the colonists thought, but rather undernourished.

The fieldworker searching for criteria for abstraction and selection was conscious of the absence of helpful theoretical orientations. This was the central issue in the anthropology of the late 1930s. In 1937 Radcliffe-Brown was setting out his views at length in Chicago, but the experimental works of this period were not exclusively socio-logical in their interests, although in their emphasis upon frameworks for abstraction they had a marked structural tone. In 1936 Bateson published *Naven*. In 1937 Evans-Pritchard's first book appeared, *Witchcraft, Oracles and Magic among the Azande*. Radcliffe-Brown's students in Chicago produced a collection of essays, *Social Anthropology of North American Tribes*, and one of the most brilliant, Lloyd Warner, who became a sociologist, published a sociological study of the Australian Murngin, *A Black Civilization*.

IV

Bateson was a Cambridge natural scientist, and he related that 'Dr Haddon first made me an anthropologist, telling me in a railway train between Cambridge and King's Lynn that he would train me and send me to New Guinea.'[6] But Haddon (and Marett at Oxford) had got into the habit of sending their students to be trained by Malinowski for fieldwork. While Bateson found Malinowski's notion of function unacceptably ambiguous, he saw the possibilities of his adaptive theory of culture. 'This method of approach is probably sound,' he wrote, 'and its careful investigation might give a coherent system of anthropology allied to systems of economics based upon "calculating man".'[7] This was the direction in which Firth later developed the theory. Bateson also came under Radcliffe-Brown's influence, and the master accepted his views to such an extent that he usually referred the question of the relation between culture and structural form to Bateson's analysis in *Naven*. Finally, Bateson was influenced by Margaret Mead, whom he married, and from whom he learnt the new American theories of culture and personality.

Naven opened with the problem of selection and abstraction. The first chapter began:

> If it were possible adequately to present the whole of a culture, stressing every aspect exactly as appears in the culture itself, no single detail would appear bizarre or strange or arbitrary to the reader, but rather the details would all appear natural and reasonable as they do to the natives who have lived all their lives within the culture.[8]

But this was not a practical solution. Malinowski and Doughty might in their different ways approach it, but some sort of abstraction was inescapable. Yet the process of selection and abstraction should not be allowed to impoverish the interpretation. The anthropologist must convey in their proper proportion not only the structural factors but also the emotional tone of the life, which Bateson called the ethos. *Naven* was an experiment with methods of analysis – 'it is an attempt at synthesis, a study of the ways in which data can be fitted together, and the fitting together of data is what I mean by "explanation".'[9]

Bateson distinguished structure in Radcliffe-Brown's sense, meaning a pattern of relationships between persons, and what he called cultural structure, the relations between the premises of a culture, which form a coherent logical scheme. There was also a third system, of relationships between the emotional needs of individuals and the details of cultural behaviour, and between these and the emotional emphases of the culture as a whole. All three frameworks could and should be used to organize the data. But as Bateson developed his argument he came to realize that the various analytical concepts were not somehow inherent in the observed data, as Malinowski and Radcliffe-Brown tended to believe. They were 'labels merely for points of view adopted either by the scientist or by the native'. As he later wrote:

> The final climax of the book is the discovery, described in the epilogue – and achieved only a few days before the book went to

press – of what looks like a truism today: that ethos, eidos, sociology, economics, cultural structure, social structure, and all the rest of these words refer only to scientists' ways of putting the jigsaw puzzle together.[10]

The problem on which Bateson experimented was posed by a bizarre New Guinea ceremony, called *naven*, which was mounted from time to time by a man for a sister's child who had done something praiseworthy. The ceremony involved transvesticism and other dramatic reversals of normal behaviour. For example, the mother's brother of the person being honoured dressed in grotesque female attire, offered his buttocks to his sister's son, and acted the female role in a fantastic similitude of copulation with his wife. This was a classical sort of anthropological problem – an apparently absurd ritual which invited the question, what sense does this make? Bateson's 'explanation' involved the abstraction of data along the three dimensions of social relationships, cultural assumptions and emotional content. Each of these sets of data was shown to make sense – sociological, logical and psychological sense respectively; and each element in the ceremony was dissected and set in each of these perspectives.

The analysis was richly suggestive, and-contained many seminal ideas, such as the notion of 'schismogenesis', basically a rule that oppositions are continually and dialectically heightened once begun. Bateson himself later developed this idea in his 'double-bind' theory of schizophrenia, which was adopted by R. D. Laing. It reappeared in a slightly different form within anthropology, in Evans-Pritchard's analysis of Nuer feuding and in Gluckman's analyses of conflict.

Nevertheless Bateson's book did not 'catch on' among the anthropologists. Partly, perhaps, this was because he was isolated from the British social anthropologists, since he went from New Guinea to the United States, where he married Margaret Mead. But more fundamentally, he did not convince because his empirical basis was questionable. He admitted frankly the ethnographic weakness of *Naven*:

> It is clear that I have contributed but little to our store of anthropological facts and the information about Iatmul culture which I have used in the various chapters does no more than illustrate my methods. Even for purposes of illustration my supply of facts is meagre, and I certainly cannot claim that my facts have demonstrated the truth of any theory.[11]

This was too much for the British empiricists.

V

Like *Naven*, Evans-Pritchard's *Witchcraft, Oracles and Magic among the Azande* was an attempt to make sense of the bizarre, but where Bateson teased out all the aspects of the institution he studied, like some more systematic and analytical Malinowski, Evans-Pritchard was concerned only with the set of premises of the culture, with what Bateson had called the 'eidos'. His problem was one of rationality – 'Is Zande thought so different from ours that we can only describe their speech and actions without comprehending them, or is it essentially like our own though expressed in an idiom to which we are unaccustomed?'[12]

This kind of question had been food and drink to anthropologists for a generation. Malinowski had developed a theory of magical behaviour which asserted that mystical acts make sense in much the same way as more mundane technical procedures – they are attempts to shape the future, to cope with the unforeseeable accidents which may ruin the most carefully-tended garden, to set at rest the anxiety of the person who has done all that could be done in the usual way to ensure success in an enterprise, but still knows very well that success is uncertain. But beliefs in witchcraft posed a special problem, since accusations of witchcraft transformed social relations.

Only Fortune had previously published a monograph on witch and sorcery beliefs, on the basis of a professional field study. This was *Sorcerers of Dobu*, which appeared in 1932. In Dobu, as among the Azande, 'Death is caused by witchcraft, sorcery, poisoning, suicide, or by actual assault. There is no concept of accident.'[13] The Dobuans believe that mystical assaults are motivated by jealousy:

> Jealousy of possession is the keynote to the culture. In social organization this jealousy is found in a conflict between the kin and the marital groupings. In gardening this jealousy obtains between gardeners. All illness and disease and death are attributed to jealousy and provoke recrimination.[14]

Similar motives of jealousy, associated with tense social relationships, have since been found to be a feature of witchcraft and sorcery accusations in many societies. Evans-Pritchard, however, concentrated upon another aspect of the problem, at once more specific and more general – how can rational people actually believe this sort of thing?

Witchcraft, Oracles and Magic analysed four complexes of mystical belief and action among the Zande of the Sudan involving witchcraft, witchdoctors, oracles and magic. These beliefs are related to each other, and constitute a single, comprehensible and self-sustaining system. In Evans-Pritchard's view, they were mystical as distinct from empirical modes of belief and action because they depended upon objectively false assumptions about the existence of certain supernatural phenomena.

Among the Zande, witches are believed to inherit witchcraft, that is, an actual substance, found in their bodies and identified if necessary by post-mortem examination. None the less, one cannot be sure who is a witch. Witchcraft may be dormant. One may even be an unconscious witch oneself. In addition to possessing this material substance of witchcraft, the witch is associated with certain inauspicious and even inhuman familiars and practices. The power to do evil working through the witch cannot operate at a distance, so witches are sought only among neighbours. Equally they are not believed to be political superiors or inferiors.

Evans-Pritchard argued that the point about the belief in these mystical agents of harm is that it provides at once an explanation of misfortune and a means of combating it. Any misfortune may be related to witchcraft, and a serious misfortune generally is. That is not to say that the Zande neglect proximate physical causes. Cutting one's foot causes a sore, but the sore will fester, despite cleansing, only if you are bewitched. As he later wrote:

> At first sight it looks absurd to hold that if termites have gnawed away the supports of a granary and it falls on a man sitting in the shade beneath and kills him, this is an act of witchcraft; but the Azande do not suppose, any more than we would, that the collapse of the granary is not the immediate cause of death. What they say is that it would not have collapsed at a particular moment when a particular man was sitting under it unless the man had been bewitched. Why should it not have fallen at a different moment or when a different man was sitting under it? It is easy to account for the collapse of the granary. That was due to termites and the weight of millet in it. It is also easy to account for the man being under it. He was there for shade in the heat of the day. But why did these two chains of events coincide at a certain point in space and time? We say that the coincidence was chance. The Azande explain it by witchcraft. Witchcraft and the granary operating together killed the man.[15]

One cannot combat chance, but witches are vulnerable to certain kinds of counteraction. Thus witchcraft not only explains misfortune, it also provides one with the possibility of redress. It 'is [firstly] a function of misfortune, and, secondly, it is a function of personal relations'.[16] 'Witchcraft is the socially relevant cause, since it is the only one which allows intervention and determines social behaviour.'[17] As among the Dobuans, one seeks the agent of one's misfortunes among one's enemies. The witch is using an illegitimate means to remedy an unjustifiable grudge. 'Every misfortune supposes witchcraft, and every enmity suggests its author.'[18]

Having suffered a misfortune, one may consult a witchdoctor, who divines the witch – often with the unwitting guidance of the sufferer. Witchdoctors are commoners with special knowledge of certain medicines, and they are not regarded as being completely reliable. The Zande defend more particularly upon oracles, which are often controlled by the politically powerful. The most important of these is the poison oracle. A special poison (normally procured in the Congo) is given to a chicken. A question is then put to it, and the question is answered by the life or death of the chicken. The princes own the most powerful poison oracles, and these are normally consulted in cases involving witches and those quasi-witches, adulterers.

Oracles are also used to regulate everyday activities, much as the Romans relied upon auguries. Evans-Pritchard related that:

> I always kept a supply of poison for the use of my household and neighbours and we regulated our affairs in accordance with the oracles' decisions. I may remark that I found this as satisfactory a way of running my home and affairs as any other I know of. Among Azande it is the only satisfactory way of life because it is the only way of life they understand, and it furnishes the only arguments by which they are wholly convinced and silenced.[19]

Finally there is magic, which may be used in healing or in vengeance. Evans-Pritchard did not believe that the Zande medicines were in general efficacious. Most of them are magical means of combating the mystical cause of some physical ailment. In addition to healing, one may use vengeance magic to seek out the witch and kill him or her. Vengeance magic is aggressive, but it can only kill malefactors, and so it is essentially just, good magic.

There is also evil magic that can be used to harm those who have not harmed you; and the Zande believe that its use is restricted to 'sorcerers'. In Zande eyes the difference between witch and sorcerer is that one uses medicines, while the other has an innate power to harm. This is not a vital distinction. 'Both alike are enemies of men, and Azande class them together. Witchcraft and sorcery are opposed to, and opposed by, good magic.'[20] Since most misfortunes are attributed to witchcraft, Evans-Pritchard argued, rather weakly, that 'The concept of sorcery appears to be redundant, a fact that invites historical explanation.'[21]

Witchcraft, witchdoctors, oracles and magic are interlocked elements in a single process. 'Thus,' Evans-Pritchard wrote, 'death evokes the notion of witchcraft; oracles are consulted to determine the course of vengeance; magic is made to attain it; oracles decide when magic has executed vengeance; and its magical task being ended, the medicine is destroyed.'[22]

The book reads as though it is addressed to a sceptic, whom Evans-Pritchard is trying to persuade that these beliefs are in some way reasonable. Several arguments were developed to this effect. First of all, Evans-Pritchard described how easily he himself adopted these ways of thinking and acting. Secondly, he pointed out that they are not articulated in the abstract, or arranged into a developed theory, but are simply invoked piecemeal in specific situations. Hence the Zande can ignore some inconsistencies. But his most powerful argument, repeated at length and in various ways, was that, given the initial premise that harm can be caused by mystical agencies, the notion that ill luck took the form of a person, an evildoer, then the rest of the beliefs follow logically enough. Moreover they are constantly reinforced by experience. Somebody becomes ill, hence witches are active. Oracles confirm this. Vengeance magic is made. Somebody in the neighbourhood dies, and the oracle confirms that he was the witch.

Evans-Pritchard also asked whether or not there are sceptics among the Zande; whether or not there are contradictions and inconsistencies which force them to recognize the absurdity of their assumptions. For example, he pointed out, oracles are sometimes questioned twice about the same matter and give inconsistent answers. In this case the Zande explain that the oracle has been interfered with by another mystical power. The failure therefore actually strengthens their belief in the whole complex of assumptions. Even experiment is possible within the mystical framework. A Zande may test an oracle by posing a ridiculous problem:

> Poison oracle, you tell the fowl I am going to fetch the sun. If I will bring it back, kill the fowl. If a great crowd will collect today to see the sun in the centre of my homestead; if I will put the sun on the ground and people will see it there, kill the fowl. If it is untrue, if I will not bring back the sun, spare the fowl.[23]

And if it fails the test, they simply resort to another oracle. Zande will agree quite readily that some witchdoctors are quacks, and that some oracles can be – and are – manipulated. But this does not disturb their general beliefs any more than our scepticism about individual doctors or particular remedies shakes our faith in 'medicine'.

Therefore, Evans-Pritchard concluded:

> I hope that I have persuaded the reader of one thing, namely the intellectual consistency of Zande notions. They only appear inconsistent when ranged like lifeless museum objects. When we see how an individual uses them we may say that they are mystical but we cannot say that his use of them is illogical or even that it is uncritical. I had no difficulty in using Zande notions as Azande themselves use them. Once the idiom is learnt the rest is easy, for in Zandeland one mystical idea follows on another as reasonably as one common-sense idea follows on another in our own society.[24]

But the monograph had a more combative purpose as well. Evans-Pritchard saw it as in part a challenge to Malinowski, and as an example of the type of abstract argument which anthropologists should aim to develop. In the introduction to the book, he wrote:

> If any one were to urge that in discussing magic I have made a partial abstraction of the activities with which it is associated, I would reply that I am dealing with only some of its relations. It would be grotesque to describe Zande economic life in a book on Zande magic, oracles, and witchcraft, since agriculture, hunting, and collecting are not functions of these beliefs and rites, but the beliefs and rites are functions of agriculture, hunting and collecting.[25]

This evoked Malinowski's penchant for relating magic to every activity with which it was associated, and his dogma that one cannot understand a custom except by describing all its concomitants. Further, in this passage he pointedly used 'function' in the mathematical sense of something being a 'function of' something else, and not in Malinowski's utilitarian sense.

None the less the book in many ways reflected the theories of Malinowski, and even an earlier orthodoxy. The problem of rationality was the problem of Tylor, Frazer and Lévy-Bruhl; and the institutional focus was typically Malinowskian, if the method of abstraction was not. Moreover, at the heart of the book was an opposition between mystical and empirical beliefs and activities: an opposition which Evans-Pritchard took over from Frazer and Malinowski. He showed that the Zande do not make this contrast, and that they believe mystical forces operate in much the same way as physical forces, but he retained the category opposition in his analysis. This weakened his critique of Malinowski's theory of magic. He wrote, for example,

> we shall not understand Zande magic, and the differences between ritual behaviour and empirical behaviour in the lives of Azande, unless we realize that its main purpose is to combat other mystical powers rather than to produce changes favourable to man in the objective world.[26]

It would have been more interesting to examine the total Zande theory of causation, without this extraneous dichotomy between 'mystical' and 'objective' forces. However, the dichotomy was implicit in the rationalist theme of the whole enterprise – to show 'us' that although 'they' believe in magic, they are still capable of logical thought.

The Zande book stimulated a number of later studies. The analysis of the closed system of thought was generally taken for granted, but the subsidiary arguments of the book became the central themes of later studies. The key was Evans-Pritchard's remark that witchcraft provided the 'socially relevant cause' of misfortune. The book was not concerned merely to explain apparently irrational beliefs, it was also, very consciously, a model of abstraction. Evans-Pritchard wrote, many years later,

> Abstraction can mean several different things. It can mean treating only a part of social life for particular and limited problems of investigation, taking the rest into consideration only in so far as it is relevant to these problems, or it can mean structural analysis through the integration of abstractions from social life.[27]

He identified the first approach with the work of Malinowski and anthropologists like Margaret Mead in America. The structural method was the radical feature of *Witchcraft, Oracles and Magic*. It was developed to an even more severe level of abstract discourse in his second book, *The Nuer*, which was published in 1940.

VI

The experiments in abstraction by Bateson and Evans-Pritchard produced two of the most worthwhile monographs in social anthropology, but the reaction to Malinowski was soon channelled in another direction. In 1937, the year in which *Witchcraft, Oracles and Magic* appeared, Radcliffe-Brown took up the first chair in social anthropology at Oxford. Evans-Pritchard and Fortes worked in his department, and together they developed a type of analysis new to British anthropology. This was concerned with the social structure, and dealt mainly with kinship and political systems. If one is seeking to identify the models for this work, one must look to the studies of the Chicago students of Radcliffe-Brown, but these were without the political dimension that came to be characteristic of the Oxford school; and they lacked the firm basis of Malinowskian fieldwork in functioning societies.

It is a measure of the narrow institutional basis of social anthropology in Britain at that time that, when Radcliffe-Brown came to Oxford, his only teaching colleague was Evans-Pritchard, who had joined Marett two years previously as Research-Lecturer in African Sociology on a salary of £300 per annum. Fortes joined the department from 1939 to 1941, with the insecure title of 'Acting research lecturer in African Sociology'. Even after the war, when Evans-Pritchard took over the department in 1946, his staff consisted of himself, Fortes (by then a reader) and a secretary-librarian.

There were by now four centres of social anthropology in England – at the London School of Economics, University College London, Cambridge and Oxford. But social anthropology in the modern sense had been firmly established only at the LSE. In 1937, Oxford was taken over, and in due course – though only after the war – the other two departments were captured. Since the number of scholars and institutions involved was so tiny, the concentration of Radcliffe-Brown, Evans-Pritchard and Fortes in Oxford was of the greatest importance. This was particularly so at a time when anthropology at the London School of Economics was entering a period of relative decline, following Malinowski's departure in 1938.

The new balance of power was only briefly significant, for the war soon intervened. Anthropologists were dispersed, most of them engaged in specialized services connected with intelligence and administration. But the brief partnership of Radcliffe-Brown, Evans-Pritchard and Fortes at Oxford produced a series of studies, dealing mainly with politics and kinship, which established a new paradigm. After the war, British social anthropology picked up where they had left off.

In 1940 three major works in political anthropology appeared from this group. These were *African Political Systems*, edited by Fortes and Evans-Pritchard, and with a preface by Radcliffe-Brown, and two monographs by Evans-Pritchard, *The Nuer*, and *The Political System of the Anuak*, both of which dealt with societies lacking centralized government, in what was then the Anglo-Egyptian Sudan. These studies were followed by others, which explored further aspects of segmentary political systems, and which also analysed the person-to-person relationships of kinship within such societies. Although these were mainly written before and during the war, they appeared immediately afterwards – Fortes's two monographs on the Tallensi in 1945 and 1949; Evans-Pritchard's study of the Sanusi of Cyrenaica in 1949, and his book on Nuer kinship in 1951. These studies must be considered together. They form a coherent set, and they established the new paradigm that was to guide British social anthropology throughout the 1950s.

If these studies are to be appreciated in their historical context, it must be remembered that they dealt with relatively novel problems which were thrown up by the new wave of research in Africa. Seligman had carried out survey work in the Sudan, but the first modern studies in Africa, by participant observation, were carried out by Evans-Pritchard, Schapera and Richards. Evans-Pritchard's field-work in the Sudan and Kenya was carried out between 1926 and 1938. Schapera spent forty-five months with various Tswana tribes between 1929 and 1943. In 1930 Audrey Richards went out to study the Bemba, and then, with the first studies financed by the International African Institute, a number of others followed in the 1930s.

These fieldworkers were confronted not with tiny, bounded island populations, but with comparatively huge, extended, dispersed tribes and nations. It was quickly apparent that the sorts of social controls which writers on Oceania had identified – reciprocal obligations, exchanges, magical controls – formed only a small part of the governmental mechanisms of these societies. Their analysis was particularly urgent, since the colonial authorities were much concerned with the methods by which such peoples could most effectively be administered, and to the extent that Lugard's principle of indirect rule was adopted, some accommodation had to be made to 'traditional' forms of government. The most acute problem was posed by societies that lacked centralized political institutions, and it was in the study of these societies – which included Evans-Pritchard's Nuer (though not the Azande), and Fortes's Tallensi (though not the Ashanti) – that social anthropology was to make perhaps its most original contribution to the social sciences and to political philosophy.

These considerations directed attention to the political system and social control. At the same time, the way in which these problems were worked out was modulated by theoretical developments within the discipline. Above all, there was the influence of Radcliffe-Brown.

Evans-Pritchard became a fervent advocate of his ideas. In 1937, writing from his field-camp among the Kenya Luo, he contributed a programmatic statement to a symposium on the social sciences. Criticizing the Malinowskians, he wrote: 'The present habit of anthropologists, of generalizing from the facts of a single isolated society, is contrary to the methods of inductive logic which have been found necessary in the natural sciences.' The discipline had for its aim 'a comparison of all types of societies in order to discover general tendencies and functional relationships that are common to human societies as a whole.'[28] This was Radcliffe-Brown's programme, stated in very similar terms. *African Political Systems* must also be seen as one of the first attempts at the comparison, classification and generalization that Radcliffe-Brown advocated.

VII

Yet these books also represented a departure from Radcliffe-Brown's position – the difference in tone, definition and emphasis between Radcliffe-Brown's preface to *African Political Systems* and the introduction by Evans-Pritchard and Fortes has often been commented upon. The new emphasis was, in a phrase, upon the lineage as a part of the system of political relationships, rather than as a mode of organizing personal relationships, which was Radcliffe-Brown's primary conception. The term 'social structure' came to connote the structure of relationships between groups and, in Fortes's work, offices, rather than between persons.

In the introduction to *African Political Systems*, the editors distinguished two types of African polity – the centralized, pyramidal structure, exemplified by the Zulu, Tswana and others, and the 'stateless societies'. The latter were sub-divided into the band-type systems, such as that of the Bushmen, where (the editors mistakenly believed) the political system was coincident with the kinship system, as Radcliffe-Brown had argued was true of the Australian Aborigines; and the systems based upon segmentary lineages. The editors particularly emphasized the segmentary lineage systems, and one effect of *African Political Systems* was to divert attention from the many stateless political systems in Africa that were not organized in terms of kinship or lineage.

The emphasis in this seminal work was distinctly odd. Evans-Pritchard later explained:

the tentative typology Professor Fortes and I put forward ... was intended to be no more than a convenient start towards a more detailed classification of types of African society, in which the absence or presence of forms of descent groups and of state institutions were two criteria.[29]

The presence or absence of state institutions was an obvious enough criterion, dictated as much by classical philosophy and anthropology as by the difficulties of colonial administration. But why should the presence or absence of descent groups be selected as a primary criterion for the classification of political systems? It is difficult to believe that it would be as readily selected today.

The emphasis upon the segmentary lineage systems had several sources. First of all, Durkheim had defined a broad class of segmentary societies, which were presumed to be typical of primitive societies, and which were thought to be based upon divisions of clan and territory. His analysis of the principle of 'mechanical solidarity' which integrated such societies provided a model for the perception of social systems like those of the Nuer and the Tallensi.

Secondly, classical anthropologists (notably Morgan and Maine) had argued that the great distinction to be understood was between 'primitive' stateless systems, based on kinship, and the state, based on territory. The evolutionary stage which intervened between these two conditions was characterized by a combination of the principles of kinship and territory – 'blood and soil'. Fortes and Evans-Pritchard simply took over this evolutionist classification and, as it were, stood it on its side. They did not present it as a classification of political systems in time, but rather in space.

Thirdly and perhaps most important, there was the accident that both Fortes and Evans-Pritchard had chanced to study 'stateless' societies and were engaged, together, in analysing their material. *African Political Systems* set up a general classification, but the implications of their thinking were most clearly seen in their analyses of segmentary lineage-based systems, and in particular in *The Nuer*, the most important and influential anthropological monograph of the period.

VIII

When Evans-Pritchard studied the Nuer, in a series of relatively brief field-trips in the 1930s, they numbered about 200,000 people scattered over an area of 30,000 square miles in the southern Sudan. The Nuer were just recovering from a brutal 'pacification' programme, which had involved bombing their herds of cattle and hanging their prophets, and were in no mood to welcome white visitors. In these inauspicious circumstances Evans-Pritchard carried out the most influential field study of his generation.

The Nuer begins with a long discussion of Nuer pastoralism and the ecological setting of Nuer society. The Nuer practise agriculture and fishing as well as pastoralism, and all the aspects of their mixed economy are necessary to making a living, but above all they like to see themselves as cattle people. They place supreme value upon their cattle, even identifying a man personally in terms of his finest ox. Evans-Pritchard remarked that when one tries to understand a Nuer affair, the best rule is *cherchez la vache*. Cattle provide a wide range of the people's needs, and the Nuer must adjust his life to the requirements of his herds.

The year is divided into two distinct seasons, the rains, from May to October, and the dry season, from November to April. The wet season is spent in the inland villages, and the main economic activity is agriculture. The dry season is spent at riverside camps, for water is scarce in the uplands, and the pastures become barren. At the camps fishing, collecting and hunting supplement the pastoral yield. In both these sorts of settlement people are closely interdependent, and 'one may speak of a common economy of these communities, which are . . . the smallest political groups in Nuerland and in which are taken for granted ties of kinship, affinity, age-sets, and so forth.'[30]

The problem of making a living in this environment sets various constraints upon the Nuer modes of social organization. Social relationships must transcend the village boundaries, for the people must be free to move between villages and camps; the ecological conditions will not permit communities to flourish except between certain demographic limits; the simple technology concentrates the symbolism of social relationships in a few highly charged objects – particularly cattle. Yet Evans-Pritchard insisted that such constraints could not explain the structural relationships between Nuer groups. These must be understood in terms of structural principles.

The argument now moved on to another plane altogether, the plane of 'social values', which Radcliffe-Brown always emphasized, and which, he said, was another way of talking about 'interests'. The famous third chapter of *The Nuer* explored the people's notions of time and space, and it formed a bridge between the introductory chapters on cattle and ecology and the main section of the book, which was concerned with territorial and lineage relationships. It was here that Evans-Pritchard developed his idea of what might be called social relativity, borrowing concepts like 'fission and fusion', and the relativity of time and space from the fashionable discoveries of physics.

The Nuer do not have an abstract notion of time, as something that passes, can be wasted, measured, etc. They perceive time in terms of physical changes, or social relationships. 'Oecological time', as Evans-Pritchard called it, was related to natural cycles, like the seasons or the phases of the day. It was not rigidly divided into units, but rather one period passed imperceptibly into another. Moreover, it had a social referent. The rainy season, or season of village life, is called *tot*. But the Nuer do not say, it is *tot*, therefore we must move to the upland villages; rather, they say we are in the villages, therefore it is *tot*.

'Structural time', in contrast, was not an abstraction from the Nuer relationship to the environment, but rather a way of conceptualizing the periodicity of social relationships, and the social development of the individual. The units are births, deaths, marriages; or, for people in less intimate contact, such events as the succession of age-sets. Structural time was also a way of conceiving of lineage relationships. The social distance between a man and his agnate, for example, could be thought of in terms of the distance in time separating them from their common ancestor. If this was great, they were distantly related; and the shorter the time gap, the closer the relationship between them.

Similarly, the Nuer are not concerned to measure the objective distance in space between two places. They are more concerned, on the one hand, with the practical distance – influenced by such factors as the nature of the intervening terrain, the existence of hostile groups on the way, etc. On the other hand, they measure social distance:

> A Nuer village may be equidistant from two other villages, but if one of these belongs to a different tribe and the other belongs to the same tribe it may be said to be structurally more distant from the first than from the second.[31]

Now because these notions of time and space are not based upon objective measurement, but depend largely upon structural relationships, they vary relative to the social relationships defining any situation. Evans-Pritchard made this point most clearly with reference to the Nuer notion of 'home', *cieng*:

> What does a Nuer mean when he says, 'I am a man of such-and-such a *cieng*'? *Cieng* means 'home', but its precise significance varies with the situation in which it is spoken. If one meets an

Englishman in Germany and asks him where his home is, he may reply that it is England. If one meets the same man in London and asks him the same question he will tell one that his home is in Oxfordshire, whereas if one meets him in that county he will tell one the name of the town or village in which he lives. If questioned in his town or village he will mention his particular street, and if questioned in his street he will indicate his house. So it is with the Nuer. A Nuer met outside Nuerland says that his home is *cieng Nath*, Nuerland. . . . If one asks him in his tribe what is his *cieng*, he will name his village or tribal section according to the context. . . . If asked in his village he will mention the name of his hamlet or indicate his homestead or the end of the village in which his homestead is situated. . . . The variations in the meaning of the word *cieng* are not due to the inconsistencies of language, but to the relativity of the group-values to which it refers.[32]

The thrust of the argument was to show that Nuer notions of time and space were a function of their social and economic values. Moreover, the social referents of these notions were not fixed, but varied with the social context in which they were formulated. In this way the analysis of these notions bridged the earlier ecological and economic analysis, and the political analysis which was to come. Firstly, the economic and physical conditions constrained the kinds of political and organizational responses which were possible. Secondly, Nuer values made a connection between ecological relationships of time and space and the structural relationships between groups. Indeed the rest of the book was primarily concerned with demonstrating the way in which group relationships were conceptualized in territorial, spatial terms, and in terms of lineage relationships, based on a genealogy stretching back in time.

Political relationships in Nuerland are basically territorial relationships. The tribe is the largest political community, within which homicide should be settled by the payment of blood-wealth rather than vengeance. The tribal territory is divided into local units, which are again divided and sub-divided. At every descending level of segmentation the group is more cohesive and tends more readily to co-operate and to settle disputes amicably. The segments operate only in opposition to other like segments. If a man in one village killed a man in another, the two villages would mobilize to settle the debt. If a man in one of these villages killed a man in another district, the two villages would unite with other villages in their district against the villages of the other district. Evans-Pritchard termed these processes of division and coalition 'fission and fusion'. He wrote, 'fission and fusion in political groups are two aspects of the same segmentary principle, and the Nuer tribe and its divisions are to be understood as an equilibrium between these two contradictory, yet complementary, tendencies.'[33] Alternatively, the structure could be understood as a balance of power at every level of organization.

The structure was expressed most fully in the blood-feud. While feuds were quickly settled between neighbours in the community of the village, who could not afford to set up a cycle of vengeance and counter-vengeance in the small co-operative group, they often led to violent confrontations when they involved members of more distant sections of the tribe. But any feud within the tribe could be settled by mediation and the payment of blood-wealth. This mediation was usually through the good offices of a 'leopard-skin chief', a member of a hereditary group of mediators, respected but effectively powerless. Evans-Pritchard's explanation recalls Radcliffe-Brown's analyses of opposition and conjunction:

> A feud has little significance unless there are social relations of some kind which can be broken off and resumed, and, at the same time, these relations necessitate eventual settlement if there is not to be complete cleavage. The function of the feud, viewed in this way, is, therefore, to maintain the structural equilibrium between opposed tribal segments which are, nevertheless, politically fused in relation to larger units.[34]

These territorial, political relationships were conceptualized in terms of the lineage idiom. Every tribe had a dominant clan, and the clan was segmented into smaller patrilineal units – maximal, minor and minimal lineages. Everyone in the clan would claim patrilineal descent from the founding ancestor, A. Two of A's sons (perhaps), B and C would be the founding ancestors of maximal lineages. Each maximal lineage would in turn segment into minor lineages, and these into minimal lineages, with reference to a particular pivotal ancestor at an appropriate level of the genealogy. In some contexts, all members of the clan would identify themselves as A's as against members of another clan. In other contexts, members of minor lineages D and E might unite as B's against members of minor lineages F and G, who were C's, and so on, creating a pattern of fission and fusion, but one mapped in lineage terms rather than territorial terms.

This lineage framework, according to Evans-Pritchard, worked at a level of values rather than crude demography. Members of one village might belong to various descent groups, and the members of the minimal lineage segment of the dominant clan might be scattered, perhaps constituting only a minority of the inhabitants of a particular village. Nevertheless, when discussing their relationship with outsiders the villagers would identify themselves with the minimal lineage of the dominant clan, and use the clan's genealogy to express these relationships. Every level of lineage formation corresponds to a level of territorial grouping, from the clan, which provided the identity of the tribe, to the minimal lineage, with a depth of only three to five generations, which provided the core of village unity.

The lineage system worked in terms of genealogical time, the territorial system in terms of structural space. But the lineage framework provided a way of talking about the territorial system:

> The system of lineages of the dominant clan is a conceptual skeleton on which the local communities are built up into an organization of related parts, or, as we would prefer to state it, a system of values linking tribal segments and providing the idiom in which their relations can be expressed and directed.[35]

In this way the values of agnatic relationship lent cohesion to the system. 'In the absence of a chief or king, who might symbolize a tribe, its unity is expressed in the idiom of lineage and clan affiliation.'[36] Because the lineage system was in practice a function of the territorial system, 'the lineages are in number and structural position strictly limited and controlled by the system of territorial segmentation.'[37] It was accordingly often necessary to manipulate genealogies in order to adjust to the political realities, and so the 'lineage structure is twisted into the form of the political structure'.[38]

IX

The Nuer was subjected to considerable criticism from Malinowskians, and an undercurrent of criticism continued throughout the years of its greatest influence. The criticism has two prongs. One is that the fieldwork was inadequate – understandably enough in the circumstances – and that therefore Evans-Pritchard did not really know what was happening on the ground. This led him to develop a highly idealized, abstract analysis, which did not allow for the machinations of calculating man.

This argument is not valid. Evans-Pritchard had done several years' fieldwork in the Sudan, and among the Kenya Luo who are related to the Nuer, before undertaking his Nuer study. He was therefore an experienced observer, as well as an exceptionally able one, working in a familiar country and with personal knowledge of related cultures. Furthermore the very arduous nature of his work may have forced him to grapple with Nuer life at a deeper level than anthropologists have commonly to plumb. As Evans-Pritchard himself said, many years later, 'I was a *ger*, what they call a *rul*, an alien sojourner, among them for only a year, but it was a year's relationship of great intensity, and the quality of a relationship counts for more than its duration.'[39] Moreover, Evans-Pritchard's other books and papers on the Nuer contain such a range of ethnographic detail that it is clear *The Nuer* operated on a high plane of abstraction from choice rather than necessity. The monograph must be understood in the context of a conscious effort to develop structural abstraction in ethnographic analysis.

The other reaction is better founded. The argument is that the abstract model accounts very badly for the observations, especially for the more detailed materials published in 1951 in *Kinship and Marriage among the Nuer*. Specifically, the agnatic, descent principle turned out to be a poor guide to the realities of local grouping, and was obviously in conflict with the strikingly 'bilateral' rules regulating marriage.

In early essays published in *Sudan Notes and Records*, Evans-Pritchard had suggested that the disjunction between the descent system and the system of territorial political groups arose because the Nuer were in a state of transition from a pure lineage system to a territorially based polity. Generations of war and expansion 'broke up clans and lineages to an extent which must have greatly impaired the unifying influence of kinship'. Clans were consequently dispersed 'into small lineages which ... were in frequent feud with their relatives and neighbours. This means that community of living tended to supplant community of blood as the essential principle of social cohesion though in a society based upon ties of kinship the change took place by assimilating symbiotic (i.e., territorial) ties to kinship ties.' He even argued that the clan system now constituted 'the main obstacle to political development'.[40] In short, he offered a traditional evolutionist argument.

The Nuer marked the replacement of this speculative, historical model with a synchronic perspective. In a functionalist model, the principles of descent and territory could not be historically opposed and empirical discrepancies could, therefore, no longer be attributed to an inevitably untidy process of transition. Evans-Pritchard's solution was to claim that his model corresponded not to actual forms of organization but rather to 'a system of values linking tribal segments and providing the idiom in which their relations can be expressed and directed'.[41]

The obvious contrast between Evans-Pritchard's model and what he sometimes termed 'the actualities' was no longer a source of embarrassment. Evans-Pritchard, indeed, increasingly came to glory in the lack of fit between the model and the empirical reports. This was the source of those famous paradoxes, which made him a sort of G. K. Chesterton of African anthropology.

Yet even at the level of 'values' matters were far from certain. In *Sudan Notes and Records*, Evans-Pritchard had asked:

> What exactly is meant by lineage and clan? One thing is fairly certain, namely, that the Nuer do not think in group abstractions called clans. In fact, as far as I am aware, he has no word meaning clan and you cannot ask a man an equivalent of 'What is your clan?'[42]

Some years later, in *The Nuer*, he was a little more confident:

> it is only when one already knows the clans and their lineages and their various ritual symbols, as the Nuer does, that one can easily place a man's clan through his lineage or by his spear-name and honorific salutation, for Nuer speak fluently in terms of lineage. A lineage is *thok mac*, the hearth, or *thok dwiel*, the entrance to the hut, or one may talk of *kar*, a branch.[43]

Apparently the Nuer, like the British anthropologists, had achieved a new certainty by abandoning a 'clan' model for a 'lineage' model. What, then, was their idea of 'lineages', of which they 'speak fluently'?

> A Nuer rarely talks about his lineage as distinct from his community, and in contrast to other lineages which form part of it, outside a ceremonial context. I have watched a Nuer who knew precisely what I wanted, trying on my behalf to discover from a stranger the name of his lineage. He often found great initial difficulty in making the man understand the information required of him, for Nuer think generally in terms of local divisions and of the relationships between them, and an attempt to discover lineage affiliations apart from their community relations, and outside a ceremonial context, generally led to misunderstanding in the opening stages of an inquiry.[44]

The Nuer model, despite its elegance and influence, apparently provides reliable guidance neither to Nuer social behaviour nor to

Nuer values. Even the Nuer are not like *The Nuer*. To what then does the model relate? It relates in the first place to the work of earlier anthropologists, and in particular to the conceptualizations of Morgan, Maine, Durkheim, Robertson Smith and Radcliffe-Brown. Perhaps more specifically, it transmutes something of Evans-Pritchard's experience of the Bedouin, as mediated by his reading of Robertson Smith. Yet for a generation the internal coherence – and philosophical resonance – of the model continued to dazzle.

X

Despite the disruption caused by the war, the 1940s was a remarkable decade for British social anthropology. It began with the publication of *African Political Systems*, which established – together with the Nuer, Anuak and Tallensi monographs – the political perspective on social structure. It ended with the symposium, *African Systems of Kinship and Marriage*, published in 1950, which with *The Web of Kinship among the Tallensi* (1949) and *Kinship and Marriage among the Nuer* (1951), marked a breakthrough in the study of kinship systems. The latter development depended upon the former.

Meyer Fortes was the most important figure in the development of kinship theory in this decade, next to Radcliffe-Brown himself. Fortes has pointed out that Radcliffe-Brown – and his American students – tended to regard the kinship system as being equivalent to the social structure in tribal societies. This was to overemphasize the role of kinship even in societies like those of the Australian Aborigines. Moreover, Radcliffe-Brown – like Malinowski – was too apt to assume that kinship relations derived from the inner core of family relationships. In their work, Fortes wrote, 'the kinship system is envisaged as a bilateral network of recognized dyadic relations radiating outwards from the elementary family.'[45] Both writers also laid too much stress on the interpersonal relationships of kinship.

The missing factor in these writings was the external weight of legal and political arrangements, which shaped the kinship system together with the domestic pressures generated within the family group. Fortes later wrote:

> It is my contention that the major advance in kinship theory since Radcliffe-Brown, but growing directly out of his work, has been the analytical separation of the politico-jural domain from the familial, or domestic domain within the total social universe of what have been clumsily called kinship-based social systems.[46]

Evans-Pritchard's Nuer books and Fortes's books on the Tallensi demonstrated this dual context of kinship groups, domestic and political. The point was given concrete form by dividing the studies of Nuer and Tallensi social structure into two volumes. In each case the first volume dealt with clan and lineage relationships, the second with interpersonal relationships of kinship.

Thus the 1940s began with *The Nuer* and the demonstration of the political significance of lineages. They ended with *The Web of Kinship among the Tallensi*, and the analysis of the interaction between external and internal constraints upon kinship relations. The work of Fortes and Evans-Pritchard recognizably derived from Radcliffe-Brown, but it represented only one of the possible developments of his theories. In fact Radcliffe-Brown never fully accepted its implications. In his long introduction to *African Systems of Kinship and Marriage* (1950), he still treated descent groups and other kinship corporations mainly from the internal point of view. But other contemporaries were mostly converted. A notable instance was Audrey Richards, one of Malinowski's closest associates, who demonstrated in her contribution to *African Systems of Kinship and Marriage* the interaction of familial and politico-jural constraints upon central African matrilineal systems, in what was one of the finest examples of the new approach.

Finally, it is important to note that these authors generally accepted the logic of Bateson, and moved beyond the naïve realism of Radcliffe-Brown. Fortes wrote in 1949:

> When we describe structure we are already dealing with general principles far removed from the complicated skein of behaviour, feelings, beliefs, &c., that constitute the tissue of actual social life. We are, as it were, in the realm of grammar and syntax, not of the spoken word. We discern structure in the 'concrete reality' of social events only by virtue of having first established structure by abstraction from 'concrete reality'.[47]

XI

The movement of British social anthropology in the 1930s and 1940s may be charted along various dimensions. There was the shift from the dominance of Malinowski and the LSE to Radcliffe-Brown, Evans-Pritchard and Fortes at Oxford. Oceania, with its small, bounded, apparently uniform cultures was displaced as the main area for fieldwork by Africa, with its large, sprawling, and often highly differentiated societies. In this period, too, anthropologists first adopted and then abandoned the concrete, institution-based functionalism of Malinowski, experimented with various modes of abstraction, and finally adopted a sociological, structuralist position. There was also a shift in topical interest from the family, magic and making a living, to political and kinship systems – from the interests of not only Malinowski but also Frazer and Westermarck, to the different concerns of Morgan, Maine, Rivers and Radcliffe-Brown. These various movements were connected at one level, as should be clear by now.

The whole period may be followed best through its central monographs. These not only reflected current views and preoccupations but also acted as experiments in understanding and explanation. The most successful became models to imitate. For much of the 1950s British social anthropologists of the post-war generation were content to repeat the experiments that Evans-Pritchard had conducted in *Witchcraft, Oracles and Magic*, and *The Nuer*.

The Malinowskian tradition remained alive, however, and the contradictions in the new structural approach, and also its limitations, soon led the more adventurous to explore other routes through the jungle, following paths along which some even met, to their surprise, with a faithful disciple of Malinowski, still making a living, slashing and burning in the bush.

Taking the broadest view, the really remarkable feature of this period was simply the creative energy shown by a group of only two dozen or so, in less than two decades. The achievement of British social anthropology in the interwar years warrants comparison with the *Année* school in its heyday.

4   Anthropology and colonialism

A painting used to hang in the ante-room of former President Kwame Nkrumah. The painting was enormous, and the main figure was Nkrumah himself, fighting, wrestling with the last chains of colonialism. The chains are yielding, there is thunder and lightning in the air, the earth is shaking. Out of all this, three small figures are fleeing, white men, pallid. One of them is the capitalist, he carries a briefcase. Another is the priest or missionary, he carries the Bible. The third, a lesser figure, carries a book entitled *African Political Systems*: he is the anthropologist . . .

– Johan Galtung[1]

'Sequels to colonialism', it is sometimes said of our investigations. The two are certainly linked, but nothing would be more misleading than to see anthropology as a throwback to the colonial frame of mind, a shameful ideology which would offer colonialism a chance of survival.

What we call the Renaissance was a veritable birth for colonialism and for anthropology. Between the two, confronting each other from the time of their common origin, an equivocal dialogue has been pursued for four centuries. If colonialism had not existed, the elaboration of anthropology would have been less belated; but perhaps also anthropology would not have been led to implicate all mankind in each of its particular case-studies. Our science arrived at maturity the day that Western man began to see that he would never understand himself as long as there was a single race or people on the surface of the earth that he treated as an object. Only then could anthropology declare itself in its true colours: as an enterprise reviewing and atoning for the Renaissance, in order to spread humanism to all humanity.

– Lévi-Strauss[2]

I

From its very early days, British anthropology liked to present itself as a science that could be useful in colonial administration. The reasons are obvious. The colonial governments and interests offered the best prospects of financial support, particularly in the decades before the discipline was granted recognition by the universities. At the same time, in the heyday of imperial enthusiasm the thought of its possible utility must have sustained some of those who pursued this esoteric and marginal study in Britain.

Readiness to shoulder arms in the colonial cause was widespread, though by no means universal. Haddon, for instance, went out to British Columbia in 1909 to pursue researches in Indian culture. While he was there the police moved against dissident Chinese labourers, and Haddon was pressed into service together with other white visitors. He excused himself from taking part in the actual raid, pleading short-sight, but volunteered to guard the sixty-six prisoners who were taken. In a letter home he wrote:

> This is not exactly what I came out for to do ... instead of Indian Ethnology I have had a practical lesson in Sociology. ... But I am having a great time, full of new experiences, some of which will be useful for teaching and others for yarning.[3]

One cannot imagine someone like Frazer participating so actively. Indeed, Frazer represented the contrary position, the ivory tower scholar reluctant even to specify the possible uses of his studies. In his inaugural lecture at Liverpool in 1908 he warned his audience:

> But if you wish to shatter the social fabric, you must not expect your professor of Social Anthropology to aid and abet you. He is no seer to discern, no prophet to foretell a coming heaven on earth, no mountebank with a sovran remedy for every ill, no Red Cross Knight to head a crusade against misery and want, against disease and death, against all the horrid spectres that war on poor humanity. It is for others with higher notes and nobler natures than his to sound the charge and lead it in this Holy War. He is only a student, a student of the past, who may perhaps tell you a little, a very little, of what has been, but who cannot, dare not tell you what ought to be. ...[4]

However, in general, anthropologists were eager to advertise the possible uses of their subject, above all as a means of gaining recognition. The diplomas at Oxford, Cambridge and London were justified in part as providing training for colonial officers. The Royal Anthropological

Institute also stressed the uses of the subject in its repeated attempts to gain funds for research and teaching positions in the discipline, sometimes working in collaboration with the Folklore Society and the British Association. At the simplest level, of course, there was a case. Anyone working in the colonies would be better prepared if he knew something about the peoples with whom he would be dealing. But it was difficult to persuade the British government that the anthropologists had anything very specific to offer.

In 1909 a deputation of colonial administrators, Members of Parliament and scholars called upon Mr Asquith, then the Prime Minister, with a request for a grant of a mere £500 a year to establish a teaching centre in anthropology for the benefit of colonial officials and traders. They pressed the commercial value of anthropological knowledge, and even tried to persuade Asquith that such an institute would mean a saving in the long run:

> The need for this might be illustrated by the case of an official untrained in anthropology, whose action led to a misunderstanding on the part of a border tribe. A military expedition followed, the cost of which was probably ten times as much as the Institute asked for in the next hundred years.

But in their next breath they gave themselves away.

> Professor Ridgeway proceeded to deal with the need of anthropometry, an important branch of the science, whose claims he advocated. Measurements and other details of physical characteristics should be taken in every school.

> *Mr. Asquith*: That would cost a lot of money.

Sir Harry Johnston advanced another argument – 'As a race we were very snobbish and if a grant were made and the institute called "Royal" by permission of the King, anthropology would receive an enormous impetus.'[5] All to no avail. The Anthropological Institute received the title 'Royal' in 1907, but the new teaching institute was never funded, or even established with such a resounding title. Sir Herbert Risley might spend a speech day at Winchester, as he did in 1910, telling the boys that they should study anthropology before going to India, but they were never to be required to do so. The demand for anthropological instruction was never widespread, and it never became established outside the African empire. Nor were the anthropologists to succeed in getting money and recognition for many years.

They kept plugging away, even during the war, this odd alliance of opinionated administrators and relatively obscure scholars. Today their initiatives seem rather funny, when they were not a little sinister. At one of Sir Richard Temple's endless special meetings, this time of a committee under the aegis of the British Association, in 1914, Colonel Sir Matthew Nathan, representing the African Society, contributed this assessment:

> The application of the study differs somewhat in East and West Africa as compared with South Africa. In the case of East and West Africa we want to know all about the native in order to develop his capacity to the fullest extent, and gradually to increase that capacity so that he may, in the future, assist in the administration of the Government and of the business of his own country.
>
> In South Africa we want the study of Anthropology to assist in dealing with the ever present native problem. I have always felt, and I think I have sometimes said, that the more we look upon the native in South Africa as a scientific problem the less we shall feel that he is a social danger. It is with nations as with individuals, *tout savoir, tout pardonner*.[6]

This analysis seems to have impressed Temple, because when in 1921 he launched yet another of his appeals for a school of applied anthropology it was under the title 'Tout Savoir, Tout Pardonner' – and, he added in conclusion, 'Tout Gagner'.[7] But few of the anthropologists were particularly interested in this aspect of things, except as a device for selling their wares. Characteristically, Seligman's comment on one of these lectures by Temple was that the most useful function of a central bureau of imperial anthropology might be in publishing reports, adding, 'I know of at least three pieces of first-class work, two African and one Pacific, held up because no publisher will take them without a substantial subsidy.'[8]

II

If the British government and the public were not easily stirred to a sense of the possible uses of anthropology, the colonial governments were equally unimpressed. In the East the tradition was that administrators would benefit by studying the languages and legal systems of the complex societies they administered, but sociological research was not generally encouraged. In India, for example, 'ethnology' seems never to have meant more than the development of the census to include some social and cultural data, and, to a limited extent, the study of 'tribal' peoples. For the rest anthropology was used mainly in the African empire, although in 1920 the Australian administration in Papua appointed a government anthropologist.

The record in Africa is not very striking, at least until the 1930s. Government anthropologists were appointed in southern Nigeria in 1908, after difficulties with local administration, but their contracts were not renewed. In 1920 the Gold Coast government appointed Rattray, an administrative officer, to the newly created post of government anthropologist. In the following year the Nigerian government decided that the census should contain substantial ethnological information – on the model, it seems, of the Indian census. Accordingly Meek, another administrator with some anthropological training, was appointed Census Commissioner in the Northern Province. In 1927 he and Talbot were sent to southern Nigeria in order to carry out investigations following the breakdown of local administration there. These were mainly *ad hoc* appointments, however; and the role of government anthropologist was not institutionalized on any scale in west Africa.

In east Africa, Seligman had been contracted to carry out anthropological researches on behalf of the Sudan government, a brief he passed on later to Evans-Pritchard. No use was made of their expertise. Evans-Pritchard has recalled:

> Professor Seligman once told me that in all the years he had worked in the Sudan or on Sudanese problems he was never once asked his advice and that the only time he volunteered it, in connection with the rain-makers of the Nuba Hills, it was not taken. During the fifteen years in which I worked on sociological problems in the same region I was never once asked my advice on any question at all.[9]

Elsewhere in east Africa only the Tanganyika government set up a post for a government sociologist.

In southern Africa, Schapera worked for many years in close partnership with the Bechuanaland government, and in the Union the government created an Ethnological section of the Native Affairs Department in 1925. The work of this body – later much expanded – did not go much beyond the routine of making ethnological censuses, advising on the claims of various candidates for chiefships, and, more recently, devising pseudo-traditional forms of tribal administration. The intellectual underpinnings of *apartheid*, such as they were, came from the Afrikaans ethnologists (*volkekundiges*), inspired by German romantic ideas and deeply suspicious of the 'liberal' British anthropology.[10]

Until the mid-1930s, then, there was little in the way of official anthropology in the British Empire and dominions. Taking the empire as a whole, it is not too much to say that by this time the direct anthropological contribution to administration was nugatory.

On the other hand, there was an indirect effect through the training of colonial officers in anthropology. The colonial governments were not averse to their officers having a smattering of the subject. As a governor of the Gold Coast remarked, if anthropology 'is to prove of any practical benefit to the administration [it] must be carried on by officers who are enthusiastic over the study of it, and regard it more in the nature of a pleasurable pursuit than that of a duty'.[11]

Relatively few officers could have got more than a smattering of the subject, even after the watershed in colonial policy which the 1930s represented. The cadet's training was brief, and the emphasis was upon law and practical techniques such as accounting, surveying and so forth. Languages were encouraged, but few mastered them, and anthropology was only one of the options which competed for their attention.

The record of anthropological research by colonial administrators compares unfavourably with that of the missionaries. The journals which some of the colonial governments published contained little anthropology, though more ethnohistory and curious anecdote. They reveal how the more studious of the administrators were drawn rather to the study of the flora and fauna of their territories, an escape, no doubt, from their tiresome contacts with the human inhabitants.

III

British colonial policy in Africa began to change in the 1930s. It was decided to 'develop' the colonies economically and administratively, and the hitherto neglected African colonies were stimulated to engage in more positive administrative planning. The depression, and then the war, delayed the implementation of many plans, but the shift in policy had its effect upon the anthropologists. First of all, the International African Institute at last landed enough money to support fellows in the field, so coincidentally swinging Malinowski's seminar round to focus on 'culture change' in Africa. Secondly, the Rhodes–Livingstone Institute was founded in what was then Northern Rhodesia. It set the pattern for the colonial social research institutes which were to provide such a stimulus to anthropology after the war. Thirdly, Lord Hailey was commissioned to carry out his African survey. He came up

with proposals for spending comparatively huge sums of money
on research, and part of this was to trickle in the direction of the
anthropologists.

The International Institute of African Languages and Cultures – to
give it its full title – was set up in 1926, with the backing of anthropologists, linguists, missionaries and colonial officials from various
European countries. The first council, for example, included Lugard,
the great colonial figure, Edwin Smith, the missionary anthropologist
and the first director, and such scholars as Lévy-Bruhl, Fr Schmidt
and Seligman. The Institute's work was for some years in the field
of pure scholarship, perhaps its most notable achievement being the
proposals on African orthography.

Although its active members were mainly based in Britain, the
international character of the body, and the distinction of its leading
members, made it a good vehicle for the funds which were gradually
being made available. There was nothing dramatic on this front:
the first year's income, from a charitable trust, grants from various
metropolitan and colonial governments, and membership fees
amounted to little over £3,000. A grant from the Carnegie
Corporation helped to raise the third year's income to nearly £7,000,
but the income of the Institute was not stabilized at a reasonable
figure until in the early 1930s the Rockefeller Foundation decided
to support fellowships through the Institute, and raised the income to
£9,000. It was these research fellowships that made the Institute such
a force in anthropology in the 1930s.

There were not many of these fellowships and grants; but then there
were very few anthropologists in the interwar years. The impact of
these grants was out of all proportion to their number. The first three
fellows were Fortes, Nadel and Hofstra. Other anthropologists who
were supported in part or entirely by the Institute in the following
years were Monica Hunter (later Wilson), Schapera, Forde, Read,
Gordon Brown, and Hilda Beemer (Kuper). The small sums of money
disbursed for research yielded an extraordinary return in intellectual
terms. Moreover the Institute was able to subsidize the publication of
the monographs and symposia that followed from this fieldwork,
becoming for a time the most important anthropological publisher in
the world.

When the Institute received the Rockefeller funds, it worked out a
five-year research plan, which was published in 1932. The plan is
of interest as a statement of what 'applied anthropology' meant to
the new generation of functionalists, for it reflected their interests,
and those of the more sophisticated missionaries. The plan's initial

assumption was that the limited resources of the Institute should be directed towards the solution of one major problem, and this was defined as follows:

> The fundamental problem arising from the inter-penetration of African life by the ideas and economic forces of European civilization is that of the cohesion of African society. African society is being subjected to a severe strain, and there is a danger lest the powerful forces that are entering the continent may bring about its complete disintegration, the results of which must be calamitous for the individuals who compose it and at the same time render impossible an orderly evolution of the community. It is proposed, therefore, that the enquiries fostered by the Institute should be directed towards bringing about a better understanding of the factors of social cohesion in original African society, the ways in which these are being affected by the new influences, tendencies towards new groupings and the formation of new social bonds, and forms of co-operation between African societies and Western civilization.[12]

This formulation suggests the functionalist illusion – which, of course, some functionalists escaped – that because their models of society assumed equilibrium between the parts, change meant disintegration. The image of the pathetic remnants of Australian and North American tribes haunted them. Nevertheless, the plan went on to insist that the Institute was neither for nor against 'change'. It aimed to make an objective and scientific study of the processes of change, without commiting itself for or against any particular policy. The administrator would simply be given the information which might help

> in determining the right relations between the institutions of African society and alien systems of government, education, and religion, in preserving what is vital in the former and in eliminating unnecessary conflict between the latter and African tradition, custom, and mentality.[13]

But the Institute's fellows did very little in the way of studying 'change'. They spent most of their time and energy on what they considered more academic and more scientific studies of the bases of social cohesion. Some did participate in small 'applied' projects, on the invitation of their host governments. Thus Fortes gave an account of Tallensi marriage law for use in the courts, and was asked for some general advice on re-ordering the administration of the remote

Northern Territories of the Gold Coast. Margaret Read did a study of the effects of migratory labour on village life in Nyasaland. Nadel advised on the setting up of 'pagan courts' alongside the Islamic courts in the Nupe area of Nigeria. He also provided economic data for use in reassessing the scheme of taxation. There were a few other limited studies of a similar nature, by-products of more fundamental anthropological research on social structure.

The academic publications of the anthropologists were of little interest to the colonial administrators, while the applied projects were few and unambitious. The colonial governor, Sir Philip Mitchell, was speaking for many when he complained that anthropologists,

> asserting that they only were gifted with understanding, busied themselves with enthusiasm about all the minutiae of obscure tribal and personal practices [from which studies] resulted a large number of painstaking and often accurate records ... of such length that no one had time to read them and often, in any case, irrelevant, by the time they became available, to the day to day business of government.

A different kind of development was foreshadowed by the establishment of the Rhodes–Livingstone Institute in 1938. It was founded to direct social research in 'British Central Africa', and it set the pattern for a number of similar centres established in other colonial areas. For the first time social research personnel were employed on the same generous terms as senior government officers, but the research-workers were nevertheless allowed considerable autonomy. This was made easier by the fact that although the Institute was sited in Northern Rhodesia, it was concerned with a group of countries and so could avoid domination by the demands of one colonial government. The beginnings were small, and at first only one or two research officers were employed. As elsewhere, growth had to await the passage of the Colonial Development and Welfare Act in 1940. This act grew in part from Hailey's *An African Survey*.

Hailey was a retired senior official of the Indian Civil Service, who undertook his survey on the suggestion of Smuts and with funds from Carnegie and the Rhodes Trustees. His report was concerned mainly with administration, but he was critical also of the anthropologists. He was not impressed by the claims Malinowski had been making. One achievement of applied anthropology the anthropologists were used to citing was the discovery that the Golden Stool of the Ashanti had a ritual value such that the Ashanti would never accept its abuse by any-one without war. Hailey's comment on this was full of common sense:

The attempt of the Gold Coast Administration in 1899 to take possession of the Golden Stool of Ashanti has often been quoted as an instance of ... misunderstanding, though it was perhaps evidence of flagrant disregard of popular feeling rather than of ignorance of indigenous custom.[14]

The anthropologists were being excessively naïve if they thought that conflicts were the result of misunderstandings as often as they stemmed from fundamental conflicts of interest.

His scepticism went deeper. Although he accepted that administrators should try to have all the available information, he pointed out that the British administration in West Africa had managed to do a great deal before the first significant inquiry into African institutions was launched – the West African Lands Committee, which was appointed in 1912. Moreover, he felt that if the policy of Indirect Rule was abandoned, as he hoped it would be, the already limited utility of anthropology would be further restricted. He wrote:

The problem of the maladjustments in African society created by the extension to it of Western economic or political institutions is no more amenable to treatment by the anthropologist than by anyone else. The most conspicuous field where his studies still have a direct application is in the elucidation of customary rules of law regulating marriage, succession, and land tenure. Here they have a definite use, and their value is not limited to the field in which they can be immediately applied, for it is probably even greater in its illumination of the context of African custom and values within which all administrative action must work.[15]

Hailey's report appeared at a time when colonial policy was being reviewed, in the light of events in India and the Middle East. The war stimulated more radical rethinking of colonial issues, and in 1940 the government published the Colonial Development and Welfare Act. It provided, among much else, for the allocation of up to half a million pounds a year for colonial research. The government explained that this decision was inspired largely by Hailey's report.

The funds provided for research only reached half a million pounds in the late 1940s, but by the early 1950s they had passed the million mark. However, it must be remembered that these funds were for all research, in all the colonies. The largest portions went on research in agriculture, animal health and forestry (35 per cent), and medical research (16 per cent). All social and economic research accounted for only 9 per cent of the total. After the war the Colonial Social

Science Research Council (CSSRC) was set up, with a committee of nine, including Firth and Audrey Richards, to allocate these funds. The anthropologists were the main group of social scientists working in the African field, and so sufficient funds were available to permit a dramatic expansion of the profession after the war. Such was the shortage of trained people to take up these fellowships, that some were given to Americans, a strange reversal of the traditional funding relationship.

The majority of CSSRC fellowships in anthropology were given to people working in the African field. Africa remained virtually an academic monopoly of the anthropologists until the 1950s. It was also the primary focus of their field research after 1930. In 1943 Braunholtz, then President of the Royal Anthropological Institute, complained about 'The natural tendency of British anthropologists to study the inhabitants of British colonies'.[16] He might well have added 'in Africa'.

This concentration on Africa is not easily explained. The Indian sub-continent and the Middle East were increasingly disturbed politically after the First World War, but Africa was by no means uniformly calm – Evans-Pritchard had studied the Nuer shortly after they had been most brutally 'pacified'. Of course, some anthropologists did go else-where. In the 1930s, for example, Firth went to Malaya and Leach to Burma; but until the 1950s few followed them. Nor did many British anthropologists return to Oceania after the mid-1930s – this was left to the Australians. It was not simply a matter of funds. In 1947 the Scarborough Commission, reflecting Foreign Office anxieties on the eve of the Cold War, tried to stimulate research in the strategic areas of the Orient, but the anthropologists in general steered clear. It *is* a puzzle – but we must remember that in the interwar period particularly, we are concerned with the movements of a handful of people, who were very closely involved with one another. In such a milieu the chance influence of a successful example, or the views of a powerful man – or woman – on a particular committee, must have been very important.

IV

When, more or less reluctantly, the anthropologist 'did some applied work', he tended to pick one of a limited range of topics. (I say he, but applied work was often regarded by the more mandarin as less demanding intellectually, and therefore as best suited to women. Malinowski's first student to be despatched to do a study of 'culture change' in Africa was chosen because it was thought she was still too new to anthropology to do a conventional tribal study.) The issues which recur in these studies are land tenure, the codification of traditional law, particularly marriage law, labour migration, the position of chiefs, especially subordinate chiefs, and household budgets. No British anthropologist attempted a study of the way in which a total tribal system might be systematically altered; and only Godfrey Wilson and Lucy Mair concentrated specifically upon 'change'. The Brown and Hutt experiment in Tanganyika is illuminating in this respect.

Gordon Brown was a Canadian, who had been trained by Malinowski. He had served as superintendent of education in Tanganyika, and through a concatenation of accidents he teamed up with a sympathetic district commissioner, Hutt, in an attempt to discover how the anthropologist and the administrator could co-operate. Brown and Hutt agreed to separate the roles of anthropologist and administrator as fully as possible. Brown was not to judge policy; Hutt was not to question the anthropologist's facts, but was simply to ask for information on particular topics and use it as he thought best.

What did he ask? His first three questions referred to the registration of marriage and divorce, the extent of polygyny, and the effect of capital punishment as a deterrent to murder. As the experiment proceeded, in 1932, the questions became rather more wide-ranging, but Hutt specifically resisted Brown's attempts to prepare an analysis of the total social situation in the district. He did not want the study to become too 'academic'. The anthropologist was thus treated as merely a source of reliable information on specific and immediate questions. In other districts, the DC would put similar questions to a trusted local clerk.[17]

Very few anthropologists presented governments with a significant body of commissioned material. Hans Cory, the Tanganyika government anthropologist, was one exception. Another was Schapera, who worked for many years in close alliance with the Bechuanaland government. He recorded Tswana law, for the chiefs and the courts, wrote an account of the various systems of land tenure in the country, and reported on the effects of migrant labour, as well as preparing confidential reports on more specific and delicate matters. More typically, anthropologists prepared piecemeal analyses when they were asked nicely, and perhaps the majority did nothing at all in this line.

Godfrey Wilson reported on a typical example of the sort of bitty work which was occasionally done on behalf of African colonial governments. The Tanganyika government successfully introduced coffee to the Nyakyusa in the early 1930s. After initial successes the scheme ran into difficulties, owing to the Nyakyusa habit of moving their homes with great frequency, and deserting their fields, and also their odd customs with respect to land tenure. Under some government pressure to act, the chiefs passed a law that coffee bushes should be the 'absolute property' of their planters, but this proved unworkable.

Godfrey and Monica Wilson had done fieldwork among the Nyakyusa, and Godfrey Wilson was in the field in 1938 and was asked for advice. He pointed out that nothing could be done about the mobility of the population. The answer must be to produce a more flexible law, perhaps modelled on the Nyakyusa law regarding banana trees. This was that the trees should be given into the care of new settlers, but that the original planter had to be compensated with a proportion of the crop. The officials received this suggestion well, but at the time Wilson was writing – in 1940 – a decision was still being awaited.

Several points should be made about this little story. First of all, Godfrey Wilson was the closest British social anthropology got in this period to producing an expert on 'social change', and he had a keen interest in applied work. He had recently become first director of the Rhodes–Livingstone Institute, and he and his wife published the first attempt by functionalist anthropologists to produce a theory of social change.[18] Yet in this article on applied anthropology, published in 1940 in *Africa*, the journal of the International African Institute, he could not dredge up any more inspiring story to illustrate the possibilities of such work. If this marginal, perhaps neglected piece of advice was worth boasting about, the performance of British social anthropologists in applied anthropology was clearly not very impressive.

Reviewing the work that was actually done, the scepticism of the colonial administrators is very understandable. Of course, intellectuals were appalled by their smugness, their arrogant assumption of omniscience, and their philistine opposition of the 'Practical Man' (as they liked to call themselves) to the scholar. But the anthropologists played into their hands, participating only grudgingly (as a rule) in the little studies dreamt up by the administrators, and accepting the view that they should not speak out on matters of policy, not being 'practical men'. The worst of it was that Malinowski had promised so much. As Audrey Richards confessed, 'the anthropologist often offers his help, but seldom condescends to give it.'[19]

V

The reasons for this state of affairs are not difficult to identify. For one thing, although the anthropologist might often be financed by colonial governments or interests, his or her future lay in academic life. British universities have traditionally rewarded the pure scholar rather than the technician, and the anthropologist's commitment to theoretical studies almost always overrode the desire, such as it may have been, to contribute to policy-making. Moreover, doing applied research was seldom a major condition of fieldwork grants. The grant-giving bodies shared the priorities of the scholars, and took the longer view that it would benefit Britain to have a store of knowledge, and a body of teachers, who could help perhaps one day in refining policy. Even after the war, when there were several institutes of social research in the colonies, with scholars on comparatively long-term contracts, few did primarily applied studies, although fieldworkers were more often asked to collect material, as a sideline, for a survey someone was doing for government on the level of education of sub-chiefs, or something of that sort.

On his side the colonial administrator was often suspicious. In 1956 a former American government anthropologist, H. G. Barnett, reviewing the progress of anthropology in administration throughout the world, concluded, 'No matter how tactfully it is phrased, the truth is that anthropologists and administrators do not, on the whole, get along well together.'[20] The colonial officer in British Africa was no exception. He believed that he knew the relevant facts, and suspected the anthropologist's commitment to his own goal of peace and quiet, or, more idealistically, 'evolutionary development'.

Many District Commissioners believed that they 'knew the native', and that their years of experience made them far more expert than the anthropologist with only one or two years' residence. This may have been in part a defensive reaction, a fear of being shown up, but there was more often something in it of the anthropologist's own jealousy about 'his tribe'. District Commissioners were often suspicious of all outsiders in their territory, and the anthropologist, with his unique opportunities for 'making trouble' – particularly if he was a 'do-gooder' at heart – was a source of anxiety. Joyce Cary, who had been a District Officer in Nigeria, wrote a novel about this, with the foolish American woman anthropologist stirring up forces she cannot control, and eventually being the indirect cause of the death of the decent, understanding, District Commissioner, who had become her lover.[21]

The anthropologist often upset local white opinion by hob-nobbing with the Africans. The more orthodox District Commissioners – particularly in east and central Africa – were easily convinced that they were going native, and letting the side down. Audrey Richards was forced to be rather defensive about this, on behalf of the anthropologists:

> While it is probably sheer romanticism to suppose that he, or she, is ever really accepted as a member of a native tribe, as has sometimes been claimed, anthropologists do participate in native life much more closely than do other categories of Europeans living in the community. They must, for instance, live in a native village and not in the nearest European settlement. They must share in the work and play of the people and attend their ceremonies. It would be difficult for Europeans occupying positions of high authority, or closely identified with a particular Church, to attend beer drinks or magic ceremonies with the same freedom as the anthropologist does. An African district officer might be equally limited by what it was thought fitting for him to do. For this reason it is inevitable that the anthropologist should quickly acquire the reputation of a 'wild man of the woods', and should be constantly accused of 'going native'. There can be few who have not been described at one time or another as 'dancing round a tom-tom in a loin cloth'.[22]

Not only was the anthropologist's life-style disturbing, he or she was also regarded as a romantic reactionary, who wanted to preserve 'his tribe' from any outside contacts, and to keep them as museum exhibits in splendid isolation from trade, government and Christianity. Despite the myth of Indirect Rule, the colonial governments were all committed to the extension of the cash economy, to the support of missions and mission education (with some local exceptions), and to the establishment of new forms of law and government.

This caricature of the anthropologist's politics was in general certainly grossly unfair, but it had some relationship to reality. The liberal position on colonial affairs for much of the 1920s and 1930s was that 'change' was dangerous; that cultures all have a value, which should be respected, and that tribal cultures are peculiarly vulnerable to corruption, even disintegration, on contact with outside forces; and that therefore the forces of decency should be ranged against radical changes of any kind. The liberals warred particularly against the changes which had already caused measurable damage to African interests – white settlement, migrant labour, and so forth. Many anthropologists who rejected this position in part or entirely identified rather with the views of the more progressive administrators. Others became advocates for the sectional interests of 'their' tribes. Some became radical anti-colonialists. But overall, the anthropologists failed to develop a coherent view of the structure of colonial societies, and so, with their functionalist orientation, they were easily cast into the mould of the stereotype.

The tension in these attitudes emerges in a paper that Fortes contributed to a Fabian symposium on colonial affairs immediately after the war. On the one hand he attacked the myth that anthropologists wanted to preserve untouched African societies as museum pieces:

> Those who put it about merely show their ignorance of modern anthropological research work, as well as a shocking lack of understanding of the historical processes of our times. In fact, nostalgia for the 'unspoiled savage' is usually found among those who get their living from breaking up primitive societies and 'corrupting' the savage – government officials, traders, missionaries, etc.

But on the other hand he wrote that forces from the West were having a revolutionary effect on African societies, and commented that

> the centre of gravity of the equilibrium characteristic of a stable and homogeneous primitive society lies in its scheme of cultural values; and that a primitive society undergoing rapid social breakdown is apt to become a rabble of acquisitive or exploited individuals and the prey of irrational mob impulses if they cease to have common cultural values.[23]

The final belief of the liberals, which perhaps more anthropologists shared, was that once the facts were known all persons of goodwill would do the decent thing; and so the tabulation of the causes of (say) Bemba idleness or Tswana indecency was a contribution to tolerance and the eradication of conflict. But as Hailey often pointed out, the problem was seldom one of misunderstanding. The two sides understood each other only too well.

All in all, perhaps the most telling comment on the general colonial and settler attitude to anthropologists in the British commonwealth, as late as the 1940s, was the reaction of the Union government as soon as South Africa entered the war. It immediately closed all African reserves to anthropologists. So much for the dependence of the colonialists upon the anthropologists.

It is ironical that the great period of financial support for anthropological research, the 1950s, coincided with Britain's rapid disengagement from colonial responsibilities. The East African Institute of Social Research, under Audrey Richards and, later, Fallers and Southall, and the Rhodes–Livingstone Institute under Gluckman, Colson and Mitchell specialized in ethnographic studies. They rapidly provided the best regional ethnographic coverage in Africa. Their fellows also paid attention to the emerging social trends, in the towns, the trade unions, and the cash-cropping areas. But their advice was still not often sought. Audrey Richards in Uganda worked in close partnership with that most enlightened governor, Sir Andrew Cohen, but this was exceptional. The economist and the rural development expert were the new gurus. When universities were set up, from Ibadan to Makerere, anthropologists had to squeeze into departments of sociology.

Moreover, as African studies became fashionable – particularly after the independence of Ghana in 1957 – other social scientists crowded in. They found the anthropologists studying every aspect of social life, and made a place for themselves by attacking the anthropologists. It is only now that the political scientists, the historians, and even the economists are recognizing the immense value of the work that the anthropologists have produced, and the scientific advantages of their humble methods, which brought them into prolonged and intimate contact with the rural people and the urban workers.

VI

The inescapable conclusion is that there was never much of a demand for applied anthropology from Whitehall or from the colonial governments. Even in the days of the CSSRC, when committee members talked hopefully about relevant research, the anthropologists in general went their own sweet academic way. Perhaps other colonial powers have been greatly helped by anthropologists, but the reality is that British anthropologists were little used by the colonial authorities, and despite their rhetoric when in pursuit of funds, they were not particularly eager to be used.

Perhaps this is to take too narrow a view of the sort of support anthropology might have given to colonial regimes and imperial policy in general. The Belgian anthropologist Maquet has written:

Although many exceptions could certainly be pointed out, it seems not unfair to say that during the colonial period, most anthropological studies were – unwillingly and unconsciously in many cases – conservative: first, in that Africans were described as so

different from 'civilized' peoples and so 'savage' just at the time that
Europe needed to justify colonial expansion; and second, in that
later on, the value of the traditional cultures was magnified when it
was useful for the colonial powers to ally themselves with the more
traditional forces against the progressive Africans. We do not
believe that these parallels are mere coincidences.[24]

The point is worth making, although the first generation of nationalist
politicians were even more determined to define traditional African
values, and to exalt traditional cultures. Many anthropologists
shared their motive: the desire to remove the philistine stigma from
the cultures of Africa, and to foster an informed African pride in their
heritage.

Another, more difficult, question is more relevant to the theme of
this book. What effect did the colonial environment have on the
development of British social anthropology? The colonial situation
did not simply generate academic anthropology. The other European
colonial regimes failed to produce schools of anthropology of a
similar kind, and the Spanish and Portuguese produced hardly any
anthropology at all, of any kind.

Nor can the policy of Indirect Rule be isolated as the progenitor
of anthropology, functionalist or other. This policy was applied
only to some British territories, and never in the sense of the myth.
It is generally recognized by historians that the contrast between
the 'indirect rule' of the British and the 'direct rule' of the French
diminishes to vanishing point when one considers the situation on
the ground, and individual British territories differed greatly from
each other. In virtually all the colonies local African leaders, recruited
on neo-traditional grounds or not, had to be used to administer local
divisions according to a more or less home-grown system because
the alternative was simply too expensive to contemplate. Moreover,
whatever was said about 'indirect rule', major forces of social change
were deliberately unleashed in all British colonies from a very early
stage – notably the decisions to impose cash taxes, stimulate migrant
labour, and regulate force. From the 1930s all British colonies began
to introduce planned developments in the fields of government
and economy which simply made no sense in terms of any doctrine of
indirect rule.

Yet was functionalism not peculiarly apt as a theory for colonial
anthropology – as Maquet, for example, suggested? This is a question
which one cannot hope to answer definitively, but a few points may
helpfully be made. First of all, the theory which most British colonial

administrators accepted more or less without question was an evolutionist one. They were trained in their public schools in the traditions of the Roman Empire, and they saw themselves as bringing the benefits of civilization, with a minimum of the ills, to backward peoples who might – after centuries of 'evolution' – reach the stage when they could be entrusted with their own fates.

Secondly, diffusionism was also quite a good candidate in the circumstances. Malinowski himself defined the business of the new African anthropology as the study of the diffusion of European culture to Africa, and he gave courses on 'culture contact' as the foundation of the new discipline. This was also the line of approach advocated by Americans like Herskovits. It is significant that Malinowski's functionalism was greatly altered when he developed his ideas on contemporary Africa. His view was not anything like the caricature of the functionalist.

And, most significantly, it was precisely the crude functionalist view that was immediately abhorrent to the administrators, who scoffed at the anthropologist's supposed reluctance to countenance even gradual change, or to accept the presence of the trader, the missionary and the administrator. The functionalist failure to cope with change was *not* something which endeared anthropologists to colonial administrators – quite the contrary. The colonial administrators also recoiled from the implicit relativism of the functionalist position. They mocked the – perhaps mythical – anthropologist in New Guinea who argued that head-hunting was very good for his tribe, and said that it should not be judged by inappropriate western standards of morality. The colonial administrator was firmly committed to an evolutionist theory, which included an evolutionary scale of values up which he felt bound to chivvy his charges.

Yet it has been plausibly argued that functionalism can be seen as an implicit refusal to deal with the total colonial reality in a historical perspective, and this has been attributed to the colonial situation, which may have inhibited, or even blinded, the anthropologist. This line of argument underplays the broader context of functionalist theory in sociology. Functionalist-type studies were not peculiar to interwar British social anthropology in the colonies. Studies of a similar sort were carried out by sociologists in Europe and America, and by the few British social anthropologists working outside the colonies. The functionalist approach was an experiment with synchronic analysis which made sense in terms of the intellectual history of the discipline, and functionalists claimed that it fostered better ethnographies than any previous approach. It was for this reason that Whyte adopted the method in his study of Boston's slums, and Arensberg and Kimball adopted it in their studies of Irish rural society in the 1930s. Equally it should be emphasized that it was quite possible to write historical studies without considering the colonial context, as many American and German ethnologists demonstrated. The refusal to consider Marxist theory – with a few notable exceptions – is also something that was not peculiar to colonial social anthropology. This was an omission which characterized most of the social sciences in the West.

Although a number of the arguments currently fashionable are crude and based upon misinformation, it is nevertheless inescapably true that the colonial situation constrained the development of British social anthropology at the theoretical level, while no doubt facilitating access to funds and to field-sites. The acid test is, what happened to British social anthropology after the loss of the empire? The rapid changes in the discipline after the mid-1950s must be attributed in part to the changes in the political environment.

Two effects stand out. Firstly, the anthropologists did not treat the total colonial situation in a scholarly fashion. Few studied settlers and administrators, for example, and this robbed their work of a vital dimension of reality. This is perhaps why the great studies of the colonial period dealt with kinship, with political constitutions of tribes, and with cosmological systems. It was in these fields that the restrictions of the colonial setting became the anthropologists' strengths.

Secondly, British social anthropologists were inhibited from discarding the racialist and evolutionist adhesions of their pre-functionalist past. The functionalists did not really feel that their subject was concerned with a special type of person, the 'primitive' or 'savage' – or at any rate leading figures like Radcliffe-Brown rejected this idea. But they slipped into accepting that their speciality was the study of the colonial subject, and they allowed him to be identified with the erstwhile 'primitive' or 'savage' of the evolutionists. This was an easy assumption, a convenient blurring of definition, but the consequence has been to identify anthropology with the mass-humiliation of colonialism. The British social anthropologist is so often an object of suspicion in the ex-colonial countries because he was the specialist in the study of colonial peoples; because, by identifying his study in practice as the science of coloured people, he contributed to the devaluation of their humanity.

But there were numerous exceptions to these generalizations, and indeed to the broad picture I have described so sketchily. There was a considerable amount of valuable work which burst the constraints of the paradigm. In South Africa Gluckman and Hilda Kuper examined the racial set-up in dynamic and radical terms, and Hellman pioneered the study of urban African workers. At the Rhodes–Livingstone Institute Gluckman published an account of Lozi land tenure and included for comparative purposes the constitution of a Soviet collective, an action which the settlers considered little short of sedition. As a group – with a few exceptions – the Rhodes–Livingstone fellows were politically on the left. Worsley's analysis of cargo cults in New Guinea became a telling critique of colonial policy and an account of the beginnings of a nationalist movement. Kenyatta, Busia and Z. K. Matthews were trained in anthropology, as were other future nationalist politicians, and they learnt through it new respect and understanding for their cultural heritage. One could go on, but my point is simply that in treating this complex and diffuse problem all generalizations must be qualified.

In conclusion, one characteristic of British functionalist social anthropology should be stressed. After Malinowski, the anthropologists based their methods upon participant-observation, which required intimate and free contact with the peoples they studied. They therefore had to break down the barriers of the colour bar, which existed in most colonies, and they had to challenge the basic, unspoken assumptions of all colonial regimes. Their individual examples of how sophisticated Europeans could happily adopt many tribal habits and live on a basis of friendship with illiterate and poor peoples constituted a constant irritation to settlers and many colonial officers. Their example still has its point.

5 From charisma to routine

Andrew Lang once said to me on a memorable occasion, when I walked back with him, after a dinner-party, to Merton where he was staying: 'If I could have made a living out of it, I might have been a great anthropologist!'

– Marett[1]

I

The hiatus caused in the development of British social anthropology by the Second World War was not complete. Some anthropologists were drafted as colonial administrators, notably Evans-Pritchard and Nadel, and Audrey Richards went into the colonial office. Others served in intelligence units, or on special missions, and Leach had an adventurous war with guerilla units in Burma. But the Royal Anthropological Institute maintained a centre for lectures and meetings and the handful of anthropologists kept in touch with one another. Further, some young men serving in the armed forces had their first experience of Africa or Asia, which decided them to study anthropology when peace came.

With peace, British social anthropology entered a period of relatively spectacular expansion. At last money was plentifully available for research, new departments were established, and new institutes of social research staffed in the colonies. For the first time social anthropology offered a career structure in Britain. The graduate student was no longer taking a crazy gamble, but was entering a profession.

With the establishment of the Colonial Social Science Research Council, the previous dearth of funds was succeeded by a glut. It was a struggle to find enough trained students to take up the new fellowships. Teaching positions also started to open up. African and

Oriental studies began to enjoy public favour. The potency of nationalist movements in India and the Middle East stimulated new thinking
about colonial problems, particularly in the Labour party, which came
to power at this time. All this provided a favourable environment for
the expansion of teaching in anthropology. New chairs were created
at University College London, the School of Oriental and African
Studies (which expanded greatly after the Scarborough Report), the
University of Manchester, and Edinburgh University. Anthropologists also found niches in some other departments, or in universities
which did not have fully-fledged departments of anthropology. In
1953 (when Forde published a survey of the position) there were
38 teachers of social anthropology in British universities. Some sort
of instruction in the subject was available in 12 universities. About
160 students were reading for degrees in social anthropology, roughly
half of them postgraduates, and perhaps 500 students were taking
subsidiary courses in anthropology.

There was therefore a rapid increase in the numbers recruited into
the profession after the war. One good measure is membership of the
professional association, the Association of Social Anthropologists
of Great Britain, founded, significantly, in 1946. It began with 14
members based in the United Kingdom, and 7 based overseas. By
1951 membership in both categories had doubled. In 1953, when
Forde found there were 38 teaching posts in social anthropology
in Britain, there were 60 members of the association, over a third of
whom were based outside the United Kingdom. By the end of the
decade there were over 120 members, and in 1968, when the Social
Science Research Council reviewed the situation of British social
anthropology, there were 240 members. At the same time there were
about 150 British postgraduate students in training, perhaps half of
them proceeding to the doctorate.

Many of the new wave of recruits found employment abroad, in
the USA, the new colonial universities of Africa and Asia, and the
'white commonwealth'. Others found opportunities in the institutes
of social research which were established in the colonies after the
war, particularly the Rhodes–Livingstone Institute, the East African
Institute of Social Research, which was founded in 1950 at Makerere,
in Uganda, and the institute attached to the growing university
at Ibadan, in Nigeria. A few positions in 'applied anthropology' also
opened up in Britain. The base of the profession, however, remained
the teaching departments in Britain itself. There was not to be another
dramatic increase in the number of departments, and most of the
'plateglass universities' of the 1960s preferred to open departments of

sociology. None the less the established departments expanded, and social anthropologists found openings in departments of sociology. Such was the shortage of trained sociologists during the great expansion in the teaching of the subject in the 1960s, that a number of sociology chairs went to social anthropologists.

Research funds became available from a number of sources, and the winding up of the CSSRC did not have much impact. In the period 1961–6 the eighty British-based members of the Association of Social Anthropologists spent nearly a quarter of a million pounds on research. Only 35 per cent of this came from government sources; 35 per cent came from foundations (often based in America), and the balance from universities, international organizations, industry, etc.[2]

Thus in the years following the war the resources of British anthropology, human and financial, expanded greatly. The discipline was entrenched with a reasonably broad university base, and a flow of students was available. One consequence was to make social anthropology a recognized profession in Britain, and this was reflected in organizational developments.

The structure of the profession was influenced by its odd demographic characteristics. It remained small enough to be a cohesive group throughout our period, and recruitment had been concentrated in three distinctly marked phases. The first phase was the late 1920s and the 1930s, when Malinowski's students came into anthropology. There was then a lull until after the war, when there was a relatively large influx. As the Ardeners concluded from a survey of the ASA 1961 register, 'the striking "bulge" in members born between 1915 and 1929 may be taken as real evidence of a great expansion of intake into the discipline which occurred after World War II.' But this group

> included as its core persons of various ages who shared in common the circumstance that they had had opportunity for little or nothing but a war-service career by 1945. Some read for new qualifications in social anthropology in the succeeding years, others completed previous partial qualifications. Since for practical purposes those born between 1915 and 1929 entered social anthropology almost within the same university generation, the age-group pattern alone is not a fair guide to the relative abruptness of the post-war expansion.

And comparing the prewar and postwar groups, they went on:

> The latter move with steady progression from qualification to field-work and then to publication: the group were in the field

within a year or two of qualification, and within five years its publications follow. The pre-war group tended frequently to do its field-work before it gained its first anthropological or sociological qualification (at least in the 'twenties and early 'thirties) and seems to have published, on the whole, more quickly.

Their conclusion was that 'The "professionalization" of the discipline for which the prewar generation worked was overwhelmingly realized in the postwar "bulge" group.'[3] The third group was recruited from about 1963, when the rate of increase in the membership of the ASA suddenly doubled. This group – born after about 1938 – was the product of the great postwar boom in higher education, particularly after the Robbins report.

Until around 1970, these three generations coexisted in the profession. The prewar intake held the professorships and senior appointments; the war-veterans filled the middle-range teaching positions; and the young intake of the 1960s filled the junior positions and held posts in some of the new departments of sociology. This age-grade structure (elders, warriors, youths?) was dramatically evident when the first generation reached retiring age in a group between 1969 and 1972, vacating the senior positions and bowing out in a shower of *Festschriften*, to be replaced by those warriors who had not moved into departments of sociology or been seduced by North American universities.

II

The pioneer generation achieved professorial rank as a group in the years immediately following the war. In 1944 Firth was appointed to the chair vacated by Malinowski at the LSE. In 1945 Daryll Forde was appointed to University College London, where he had to build up a department virtually from scratch, for little had been done since Perry's retirement before the war. In 1946 Evans-Pritchard succeeded Radcliffe-Brown in Oxford. In 1949 Gluckman went as Professor to Manchester, to start a new department. In 1950 Fortes was appointed Professor at Cambridge, and Schapera moved from Cape Town to join Firth at the LSE (where students began to call the department 'We the Tikopia and I. Schapera'). Nadel had gone to Durham as reader and first head of the department of anthropology in 1948; in 1950 he travelled to Canberra to take up the new chair in anthropology and sociology in the Research School of Pacific Studies. In 1951 von Fürer-Haimendorf was appointed Professor of Asian Anthropology at the School of Oriental and African Studies.

These men controlled the profession for two decades, only Nadel dying before the end of the period. Few new chairs were created and where they were established they were usually personal or auxiliary chairs, which did not carry with them departmental headships. The power of this professoriate was impressive. Like most British professors, the leading anthropologists had the decisive voice in the appointment of staff and often in the choice of students, particularly graduate students. The professor could effectively withhold or grant promotions, leaves and other privileges; and his recommendation was crucial in any application for a research grant or for a position elsewhere. He was generally the only effective channel of communication with the university authorities and grant-giving bodies.

This base was reinforced by appointments to the bodies that dispensed patronage. The small group of anthropology professors held key positions on government grant-giving committees, and in the major institutions, such as the anthropology section of the British Academy, the International African Institute, the Association of Social Anthropologists, and the Royal Anthropological Institute (though here power was shared with the physical anthropologists and some archaeologists). This monopoly of influence had its comic side, as the professors solemnly succeeded one another as Presidents of the Royal Anthropological Institute and office-holders in the ASA, and disbursed to one another the various prize lectureships and honours at their disposal. But it was a serious matter, since whatever their personal or academic differences the professors formed an effective cartel, presenting a united front to the grant-giving agencies and to their juniors.

The ASA was set up in 1946, partly in reaction to the plethora of amateurs and non-social anthropologists in the Royal Anthropological Institute. It was explicitly a professional body, and its first committee reflected the power structure in the profession. The president was Radcliffe-Brown, an honorific post reflecting his continued dominance of theory. The chairman and secretary was Evans-Pritchard, and the committee consisted of Firth, Forde and Fortes. The only notable omission was Gluckman, who soon became chairman and secretary in his turn. This was the power map and it remained the same for twenty years.

The outstanding man outside this magic circle was Edmund Leach, who never became head of a department though he did become Provost of King's College, Cambridge. In 1972 Cambridge awarded him a personal chair. Despite the prominence of women in Malinowski's seminars, none became head of a department of anthropology. This is perhaps less surprising when one notes how rare it was until very recently for women to be appointed heads of departments in any subject in universities, but the position outside Britain was different. Monica Wilson and Eileen Krige became professors in South Africa, and Elizabeth Colson and Audrey Richards were directors of institutes of social research in British African colonies.

I have stressed the power that office gave to the new professoriate after the war. This power also had its non-material side, for the men and women who came into the field were in general ready to accept the intellectual leadership of at least some of the professors. For most of their period in office, they dominated the theoretical debate as well.

This is not to say that the professors were in complete agreement on theoretical matters. Far from it, although they did share certain fundamental assumptions about the nature of their study. There were frequent conflicts on theoretical questions, and polemical exchanges were a favourite sport. Each professor had a distinctive set of interests, and specialized in a particular area. In this situation, given the power of the professor, there were what amounted to distinct schools. Most of the professors developed departments in their own image, appointing staff and producing students who shared their orientations. The theoretical map of British anthropology between about 1950 and 1970 was largely, though never entirely, the same as the map of the major departments.

The key points on the map were the three London departments, and Oxford, Cambridge and Manchester. Firth was the most powerful influence at the LSE, where he was joined by Richards, Nadel, Schapera, Mair, Leach and Freedman, at one time or another. The department did not have a firm 'party-line', but it inclined towards the Firthian recension of Malinowskian functionalism. Of all the English departments, it was here that the structuralism of Radcliffe-Brown was least important. The central concerns were with individual manipulation of political systems, the context of economic choices, and the sphere of optation in kinship systems.

Forde came to University College London with an unusual background. He had worked under Kroeber and Lowie in California, and was professionally competent in geography and archaeology as well as in social anthropology. He shared with the Americans a traditional view of anthropology, embracing not only social anthropology but also human biology and archaeology, and he had a strong interest in problems of evolution and ecology. His department specialized in providing an all-round anthropological education. Forde also became director of the International African Institute, and most of his students did fieldwork in West Africa, as he had done.

Von Fürer-Haimendorf could claim to be the only cultural anthropologist in the major British departments, and his department at the School of Oriental and African Studies placed great emphasis upon ethnographic and linguistic competence. For many years it was the only anthropology department in Britain with a strong interest in India, and the recruitment of Adrian Mayer and F. G. Bailey strengthened this commitment. However, there was no particular theoretical emphasis associated with the school.

The three leading departments outside London were all more firmly dominated by the views of their professors. At Oxford Evans-Pritchard abandoned many of Radcliffe-Brown's dogmas and moved increasingly towards a historicist position. The main job of the anthropologist, as he came to see it, was the translation of cultural values into the language of the anthropologist's culture – an essentially humanist rather than a scientific pursuit. He also came to insist upon the necessity for a historical perspective. These orientations came to dominate the Oxford school which he built up, and, while referring always to the classics of the *Année* school, the Oxford anthropologists began to develop an idealist position that marked them off from their colleagues elsewhere in Britain. These tendencies may have been related to the odd fact that several of the members of the department were converts to Roman Catholicism, including Evans-Pritchard himself. In many cases students coming to Oxford were converted first to the vogue theoretical position, and subsequently to Roman Catholicism; the professor acted as godfather at their baptism. The department (or as it was called, almost by accident, the 'institute') at Oxford did not until recently offer an undergraduate degree in anthropology – although Evans-Pritchard once tried to persuade the university authorities to provide one – and so it concentrated upon the training of graduate students, most of whom were recruited from other disciplines.

Meyer Fortes took over a weak, pre-functionalist department in Cambridge in 1950, and he set about its transformation with great energy. For several years he did much of the teaching himself, assisted by visiting professors of social theory – Radcliffe-Brown, Talcott Parsons and George Homans. A number of his early students became professional anthropologists, and he also drew in many of the ablest graduate students in the country. In 1953 Leach came to Cambridge, and Audrey Richards, who held a university readership in Commonwealth studies, was closely associated with the anthropologists. Goody, the student closest to Fortes's theoretical interests, also joined the department.

Unlike most other departments, Cambridge came to have two main theoretical prongs, the neo-Radcliffe-Brown line which Fortes represented, and the shifting but always exciting line of Leach. This divergence was intensified by their different regional interests. Fortes and his students were predominantly concerned with Africa, while Leach and his students worked mainly in South Asia. However, all the members of the department shared a central interest in the study of kinship, and this was the major field in which Cambridge made its mark on modern anthropological theory. When people talked loosely of the Cambridge school in this period they referred to a central focus of interest, in problems of descent theory particularly, rather than to a specific theoretical stance.

Manchester was different again. Max Gluckman had built up a research school at the Rhodes–Livingstone Institute, and he brought a number of its alumni with him to Manchester. They came to write up their theses, returned as visiting Simon Fellows, or joined the department as lecturers. Far more than anywhere else, a single line dominated the department. As they used to joke, 'We are all Maxists here.' The main regional interest continued to be Central Africa, to such an extent that the few people who had not worked there felt at a serious disadvantage. The theoretical issues were also carried over from Gluckman's days at the Rhodes–Livingstone Institute – particularly problems of conflict, process and ritual integration; and the methods were the extended-case study, and later, network analysis. The department had close links with some departments abroad and, later, in the north of England, which became part of the Manchester 'empire'. As soon as a member of the school was appointed to a post elsewhere, he tried to surround himself with his fellows.

The Manchester school was so solidary that in many typical publications only other members of the school were cited. Collections of essays edited by one member of the school normally included essays only by other members. A characteristic example is Epstein's *The Craft of Social Anthropology*, published in 1967. Its list of contributors reads like a roll-call of the Manchester school – Gluckman, Colson, Mitchell, Barnes, Turner, Van Velsen, A. L. and T. S. Epstein, and Marwick. Other prominent members of the school who did not work in Central Africa (and so, perhaps, were judged to be lacking in the essentials of the craft of social anthropology) were

Frankenberg, Peters and Worsley. As might be expected in such a situation, deviants and turncoats were treated with great ferocity internally, but no criticism was tolerated from outsiders.

III

The theoretical position to which British anthropology returned at the end of the war was that of Radcliffe-Brown and his Oxford adherents. The key texts had appeared in 1940: Radcliffe-Brown's lecture 'On social structure', Fortes and Evans-Pritchard's *African Political Systems*, and Evans-Pritchard's *The Nuer*. The movements that developed in the following years had to define themselves with reference to this orthodoxy; none more so than the reactions against it. Fieldwork continued to be done in the Malinowskian manner, but if fieldwork was still functionalist, analysis and theory were dominantly structuralist.

Fortes remained faithful to the orthodoxy, though he developed it in his own way, but most of his professorial colleagues soon reacted against it. The reaction took various forms – one might almost say that the attacks came from the right and from the left. Firstly, Evans-Pritchard repudiated Radcliffe-Brown's scientific pretensions, and adopted an idealist position, with historicist implications. Secondly, Firth and to some extent Nadel and others revived Malinowskian theory, reacting against the formalism of the structuralists, and demanding that greater attention be given to the irrepressibly selfish, manipulative individual. Thirdly, there was the conflict theory of the Manchester school. And finally, in the 1950s, but increasingly in the 1960s, Lévi-Strauss's radical development of the *Année Sociologique* tradition was received into British social anthropology.

This is a first rough sketch of the position, and it must be said right away that a number of the most interesting anthropologists in the period cannot be so neatly pigeon-holed. Nevertheless, let us accept this broad plan for the time being, and explore the contours after getting a first orientation.

In this chapter I shall discuss the positions taken up in the 1950s by Evans-Pritchard, Firth, Fortes and Nadel, and what might be called the mainstream of 'normal science'. In the next chapter I turn to the two key mavericks, Leach and Gluckman. Then, in Chapter 7, I summarize the impact of Lévi-Strauss's structuralism on British social anthropology. This plan involves a departure from the straightforward chronological presentation that was possible earlier. This is unfortunate, but the complexity of the situation in the postwar decades makes it necessary. Yet there is an element of sequence in the presentation. The early 1950s saw the publication of the main orthodox monographs of the postwar generation, and also the statements of position from the leading professors. In the mid-1950s Leach and the Manchester writers became influential, and the Lévi-Straussian movement first made a significant impact in the 1960s.

IV

Evans-Pritchard accepted Radcliffe-Brown's theoretical position at least until the war, but shortly after succeeding him at Oxford in 1946 he issued a manifesto of rebellion. In the following years some of his associates have attempted to represent his career as a unity, without a sharp break, and it is therefore necessary to make something of an issue of what might otherwise be simply taken as read.

I have already cited the Radcliffe-Brownian manifesto which Evans-Pritchard fired off from his field-camp in East Africa, prescribing 'the methods of inductive logic which have been found necessary in the natural sciences' and advocating the use of comparison 'in order to discover general tendencies and functional relationships that are common to human societies as a whole'. He added: 'I am assuming that there are functional interdependencies in culture. If there are not, then Social Anthropology will have a position as an art, like History, in humanistic studies.'[4]

Thirteen years later, in a Marett lecture delivered in 1950, he reversed himself completely. He now argued (almost echoing the phrasing of his earlier manifesto):

> that social anthropology is a kind of historiography, and therefore ultimately of philosophy or art, . . . that it studies societies as moral systems and not as natural systems, that it is interested in design rather than in process, and that it therefore seeks patterns and not scientific laws, and interprets rather than explains.[5]

What happened in between is difficult to establish, not least because the actual date of the change of mind cannot be firmly pinned down. After all, his inaugural lecture delivered at Oxford in 1948 had apparently been an orthodox Radcliffe-Brownian performance. Evans-Pritchard later tried to explain the lecture away in a letter to *Man*, which deserves to be quoted in full.[6]

> Sir,
>   I have sometimes been criticised for having in the course of the years changed my viewpoint in my writings. I do hope this is true,

for consistency is surely the worst of all vices in science. I do however accept – and this is why I write this letter - that my Inaugural
Lecture at Oxford (*Social Anthropology*, 1948) does require a 'for
the record' comment; though I do not think that, on re-reading it
after many years, I would wish to speak very differently; for I was
cautious.

In writing the lecture I first of all took the view that I should
represent the Institute of Social Anthropology, which meant that
I should not publicly dissociate myself from the teaching of
Radcliffe-Brown, for whom I had personal regard, though less
intellectual sympathy or appreciation, or from my colleague Dr
Fortes, whose agreement with Radcliffe-Brown's views was
then, and has been since, manifested. Apart from this what might
be called 'collective' attitude, there was a further complication,
and this is where I was perhaps unwise. Radcliffe-Brown had
given, a few years before mine, his Inaugural Address, and it was
a disaster. He had been used to talking to students in parts of
the world where intellectual standards were not so high as in
Oxford and he misjudged the calibre of his audience. The lecture
was therefore never published – 'significantly' as Professor
Firth wrote in Radcliffe-Brown's obituary notice for the British
Academy. When I came to give my Inaugural Lecture Radcliffe-
Brown, to my embarrassment, brought me the script of his
and asked me to present to the University the same viewpoint, to
emphasise the main points in his address, and then to destroy his
manuscript. There is nothing to Radcliffe-Brown's discredit in
this, only perhaps to mine. How could I have refused his request?
But maybe I should have done so. Such is a tiny piece of anthropological history, but I hope you will think it worth reading.

E. E. Evans-Pritchard

This moving portrayal of loyal self-denial is difficult to reconcile
with the fact that only two years later Evans-Pritchard was to use the
equally official Oxford platform of the Marett Lecture to signal his
repudiation of Radcliffe-Brown's ideas. However, the letter implicitly
concedes that a change of mind had occurred.

Evans-Pritchard may have experienced an intellectual conversion
during the war. I think it likely that his increasingly impassioned postwar crusade against determinist ideas can be linked to his conversion
to Catholicism in 1944. His closest colleague, Godfrey Lienhardt, has
suggested that Evans-Pritchard's shift was in part an accommodation
to the mores of Oxford.

His later insistence, against his earlier ambitions for the subject, that social anthropology was a form of historiography and even of art, was to some measure an attempt to restore its reputation among academics for whom Radcliffe-Brown's 'scientific' principles cut no ice – quite the contrary, in some they produced glaciation.[7]

Evans-Pritchard now increasingly stressed the use of history, arguing that there was little essential difference between history, particularly social history, and social anthropology. This was certainly contrary to the narrowest functionalism, but Monica Hunter (Wilson), Gluckman and Schapera, to name but three, had always used historical materials in the interpretation of African societies. Others (for example Jack Goody and I. M. Lewis) continued to do so after the Marett lecture, without, however, abandoning the preoccupations of the mainstream. Moreover, Evans-Pritchard's historical study of the Sanusi, published in 1949, produced a structural analysis strongly reminiscent of that which emerged from his strikingly non-historical study of the Nuer. The real revolution in African ethnohistory occurred only in the following decade, when Jan Vansina and others showed how oral tradition could be tapped – something Evans-Pritchard never did to any great extent, preferring to draw upon published and documentary sources.

Evans-Pritchard always published his material piecemeal, over many years, before drawing it together into a book, and so it took some time before the implications of his new position became fully apparent; or perhaps he became more anti-sociological as he went on. He came to describe himself as an ethnographer rather than a social anthropologist, and in the 1960s he published mainly ethnographic texts. His final monograph, *The Azande: History and Political Institutions*, published in 1971, was almost perversely ethnohistorical and diffusionist, replete with details on the origins of totems but innocent of any sociological analysis. It was hardly different from monographs published at the turn of the century, and it was ignored by his colleagues. He also published papers on theories of religion and on the French and Scottish masters, which expressed a blanket scepticism about the value of sociological analysis and the possibility of generalization.

V

In 1951 Evans-Pritchard published a series of semi-popular lectures in which he expounded his latter-day views on social anthropology.

In the same year Nadel and Firth presented ambitious attempts to synthesize a theoretical basis for the discipline. Both Firth and Nadel challenged the old Oxford orthodoxy, but on lines different from Evans-Pritchard. They were both in their fashion neo-Malinowskians.

Nadel's dense, rather Germanic book, *The Foundations of Social Anthropology*, reflected his discovery of Weber, and also his earlier training in psychology; nevertheless its central thesis was distinctly Malinowskian, although he was much more concerned with social systems than Malinowski had been in his later period. Beneath the philosophical flourishes the old message emerged – institutions are mutually adjusted to fulfil the basic needs (or in Nadel's terminology, 'innate action potentials') of individuals. He went beyond Malinowski in his concern with the logical interconnections of institutions, and with psychological theory. It may be that he was writing as a Parsonian, although he did not say so, for Talcott Parsons took the same elements of theory and constructed an even denser and more tortuous version of functionalism, with the same bias towards the integration of psychological analysis into sociology.

In 1955 Nadel visited the LSE on leave from Australia, and delivered a series of lectures later published (posthumously) as *The Theory of Social Structure*. This book served even more clearly to define his opinion of the two traditions of modern British anthropology. The bulk of the book is a critique of the utility of the notion of 'social structure'. In conclusion he wrote that

> the 'structuralist' judges his own frame of reference to be not only heuristically useful and promising, but to be more useful and promising, and indeed more important, than the other frame of reference, resting on the concepts of utility, purpose, or 'function' . . . . I cannot accept this judgement, and . . . I feel it is not enough merely to acknowledge the two ways of analysing social existence. As I see it, social existence belongs to a universe of discourse governed by the concepts of purpose and utility; the approach through structure cannot but be subordinated to them.[8]

For the rest, in this book and in the *Foundations*, he developed the tool of role analysis beyond anything previously attempted by anthropologists, and he gave his support to the experiments being made in the development of social psychology (as it would be called now), and network and mathematical models. However, his central argument was simply that the structuralist orthodoxy was inadequate by itself – it had to be wedded to a functionalist perspective which would incorporate psychological theories.

Firth's book, *Elements of Social Organization*, constituted an even more direct attempt to graft something of Malinowski's theory back on to the main growth of British social anthropology, but his emphasis differed from that of Nadel. He preferred to concentrate upon the 'calculating man', the figure Bateson had discerned as the most promising member of Malinowski's conceptual team. Firth may have been ready to use this approach since it fitted in with the pre-Keynesian economics he had learnt, with its obsessional interest in individual choice-making. In any case, such an approach was certainly subversive of the rather idealist structuralism in vogue at the time.

In perhaps the key passage of *Elements of Social Organization*, Firth wrote:

> Social organization has usually been taken as a synonym for social structure. In my view it is time to distinguish between them. The more one thinks of the structure of a society in abstract terms, as of group relations or of ideal patterns, the more necessary it is to think separately of social organization in terms of concrete activity. Generally, the idea of organization is that of people getting things done by planned action. This is a social process, the arrangement of action in sequences in conformity with selected social ends. These ends must have some elements of common significance for the set of persons concerned in the action ... Social organization implies some degree of unification, a putting together of diverse elements into common relation. To do this, advantage may be taken of existing structural principles, or variant procedures may be adopted. This involves the exercise of choice, the making of decisions.[9]

With the major thesis went a (late Malinowskian) concern with social and cultural change, though not with history in Evans-Pritchard's sense.

While his professorial colleagues set out their reservations, or raised banners of revolt, Fortes continued to develop the central tenets of the original Oxford structuralists. In 1953 he published several statements of position, in which he defended the orthodoxy, stressed the role of 'social structure' as a central organizing concept, relegated the study of 'culture' and individual variation to a subsidiary position, and energetically attacked Evans-Pritchard's lapse from the true faith.

VI

Despite these sounds of conflict, the outstanding feature of British social anthropology to outsiders was its cohesiveness; and when faced with a challenge from outside the British drew together. It is worth considering one of the most influential of these challenges, Murdock's critique of 1951, for it dramatized the parameters within which all British social anthropologists operated in the 1950s.

Murdock, a leading figure in American anthropology, published his attack in the *American Anthropologist*. It was sparked off by the symposium, *African Systems of Kinship and Marriage* (1950), and expressed a mixture of admiration and dissatisfaction that was widespread among American anthropologists at the time. He wrote that

> the descriptive and analytical writing of the British social anthro-
> pologists attains an average level of ethnographic competence and
> theoretical suggestiveness probably unequalled by any comparable
> group elsewhere in the world. This explains and justifies the
> respect so widely accorded them. Offsetting these merits, however,
> are a number of special limitations which many professional
> colleagues abroad find difficult to understand and impossible to
> defend.[10]

He listed these limitations as their 'exclusive' concentration 'on kinship and subjects directly related thereto, e.g., marriage, property and government [*sic*]'; and their geographical concentration on British colonial dependencies, and, consequently, their lack of a broad ethno-graphic range. Further, they 'are as indifferent to the theoretical as to the descriptive writings of their colleagues in other lands', and ignored their interests in history, culture change and psychology. Murdock laid the blame unambiguously – 'These various limitations reflect the overwhelming influence of Radcliffe-Brown.' The consequence of all this, Murdock said, was that the British social anthropologists were not anthropologists at all. Ignoring the notion of 'culture', they had become sociologists, of a rather old-fashioned sort.

Stripped of its polemical trimmings, the description was reasonably accurate. Firth and Fortes both accepted it, more or less, but answered that given the limited resources of British social anthropology a limitation of ambition was reasonable. Or, to put it more positively, British social anthropologists had decided to concentrate on a limited set of issues, and their work had all the strength of these self-imposed limitations. Actually the dialogue was in a sense between social anthropologists and cultural anthropologists – between the course British social anthropology had followed under Radcliffe-Brown and that which had been charted by Frazer, or Tylor, or Boas.

The British anthropologists felt no regrets in ignoring the culture and personality work so fashionable at the time in America, or the continued 'salvage' ethnological studies of American Indians, or the rather uncritical statistical cross-cultural studies of Murdock himself. They believed not only that they were bound to concentrate their energies, but, even more, that the results proved that they had chosen rightly in concentrating upon the structure of social relationships. Their postwar students were trained to follow suit, and they did.

VII

The monographs produced in the 1950s by the postwar intake certainly had a great deal in common. Two issues predominated. First there was the study of politics more or less in the terms laid down by *African Political Systems*. The key problem was the political role of lineages in segmentary systems and in states, and virtually every monograph which appeared in this period tackled this question. The fine late Malinowskian studies of African states were admired but did not generate comparable theoretical interest. These were Nadel's *A Black Byzantium* (1942), the Kriges' *The Realm of a Rain-Queen* (1943), and Hilda Kuper's *An African Aristocracy* (1947). All of them were more or less centrally concerned with the organization of the ruling class in African states, and this was a problem – obviously central to any political understanding - which did not particularly interest those who derived their inspiration from the Oxford studies.

The orthodox studies followed on each other's heels throughout the 1950s. In 1954 Barnes published an account of the Ngoni state, showing the way in which it had marched through southern Africa, segmenting and accreting in classical form. In the same year Leach published a radical analysis of Kachin political systems, but despite its great originality the central problem was defined in the same terms – the Kachin political communities embraced segmentary and state systems, and Leach concentrated upon the problem of how the one type was transformed into the other. In 1956 Fallers produced a monograph on the Soga of Uganda, in which he investigated the way in which the bureaucratization of the Soga state affected traditional political roles and the functions of clans and lineages. In the same year Southall published his analysis of another Ugandan society, the Alur, and made a great issue of the fact that they were neither a classical segmentary society, based on lineages, nor a centralized state, but something in between, a combination of the two classical types, which he described as a 'segmentary state'. Mitchell's *The Yao Village*, which also appeared in 1956, investigated the way in which competition for authority in this centralized Malawian tribe occurred simultaneously within the matrilineages and the system of offices, the two arenas of competition being closely interlinked. Also in 1956, M. G. Smith's essay 'On segmentary lineage systems' attempted to raise the issues of the day to a more general level of significance, arguing that segmentation is a feature of all political action, although the fact that segmentation occurred in some systems on a lineage basis had significant consequences. In *Government in Zazzau* (1960), he produced the most complicated of the orthodox studies, but one of his central concerns was still the relationship between centralized administration and lineage-based competition and fission. In 1958 Middleton and Tait edited a new symposium on African political systems, *Tribes Without Rulers*, which was even more restricted than its prototype to problems of lineage organization. Its contributors were all members of the postwar cadre, and the book reflected the dominance that lineage theory exercised in the work they carried out.

There were two important differences between these studies and the monographs published by Evans-Pritchard and Fortes in the 1940s. The first was in the very general use of historical materials, a development that owed something to the influence of Evans-Pritchard. The second was a shift towards a concern with bureaucracy. This interest was suggested partly by the problems of 'states within states' in the late colonial period, but it was fostered also by the discovery of Weber.

The other major concern of the period was with 'magico-religious' systems, to use what was already a rather dated term. This kind of study usually treated one of two main issues, both of which had been stated in monographic form by Evans-Pritchard. First there was the whole problem of witchcraft. The studies in the 1950s took up Evans-Pritchard's observation that witchcraft was a way of identifying a socially relevant cause of misfortune. They examined the way in which accusations of witchcraft and sorcery dramatized social tensions, and transformed them. This analysis often appeared as a subsidiary theme in the monographs of the period – for example in Mitchell's study of the Yao, or Turner's *Schism and Continuity in an African Society*. It was often integrated with a conventional study of a segmentary lineage system, witchcraft accusations being seen as an aspect of the process of lineage fission. Marwick's study of the Cewa was an analysis of the stresses of the lineage system seen through the prism of sorcery accusations. In due course this field of studies generated its own symposium, Middleton and Winter's *Witchcraft and Sorcery in East Africa* (1963).

The other problem was a larger one, the study of religious systems proper, which had been neglected by Malinowski and his students. The key texts here were Radcliffe-Brown's essay on 'Religion and society' (1945), and Evans-Pritchard's essays on Nuer religion, pulled together in a monograph in 1956. Radcliffe-Brown's position was essentially determinist – ancestor-worship, for example, was to be understood as a functional requisite of certain kinds of lineage system. Evans-Pritchard accepted the fact that religions are conditioned by their social environment, but as in his study of Zande witchcraft he was more concerned to explore the logical interrelations of their cosmological notions. Both these positions had their adherents, but the difference between them was really only one of the emphasis. Middleton's *Lubgara Religion* (1960) treated ancestor-worship in a Ugandan tribe in much the same way as some of his contemporaries treated witchcraft - as a function of lineage structure, and, in action, as a reflection of the processes of lineage segmentation. Lienhardt's *Divinity and Experience: The Religion of the Dinka* (1961), was a superb complement to Evans-Pritchard's *Nuer Religion* – the two tribes were neighbours in the Sudan.

Gluckman's analyses of rituals of conflict surrounding the office of kingship in African states were congruent with the studies treating witchcraft and ancestor-worship as modes of conducting and adjusting tense social relationships. Here once again Evans-Pritchard had provided the paradigmatic analysis, in his essay 'The divine kingship of the Shilluk' (1948).

The Malinowskian preoccupation with myth was not much in evidence in this period, except in connection with the evaluation of historical evidence. An exception was Leach's neo-Malinowskian analysis of the political functions of myth in *Political Systems of Highland Burma* (1954), although his analysis was also influenced by the work of the lineage theorists on the manipulation of genealogies. The revolution in the analysis of myth that Lévi-Strauss was to bring about was in no way foreshadowed in the work being done in Britain in this period.

Perhaps unexpectedly, the study of kinship was relatively neglected after the publication in 1950 of *African Systems of Kinship and Marriage*. Contrary to Murdock's view of the position, political organization was the primary interest, and problems of kinship theory were investigated mainly in relation to descent theory. There was, for instance, a flow of studies emerging from Fortes's essay 'Time and social structure' (1949). These were concerned with the developmental cycle of the domestic group, but in terms of the constraints imposed by the politico-jural system. This sort of analysis featured as a minor theme of many monographs, and was the centrepiece of the first volume in a new series of papers in social anthropology which the Cambridge department began to publish in 1958. Another issue which commanded attention was raised by Gluckman in *African Systems of Kinship and Marriage*, where he argued that the divorce rate is a function of the lineage structure. The classical, purely kinship topics were neglected - kinship terminology, marriage rules, incest and exogamy, interpersonal roles of kinship. They came into prominence again only at the end of the decade, when a debate between Leach and Fortes directed attention to the theories of Lévi-Strauss, and when Firth, Freeman and Leach raised the problem of non-unilineal kinship systems, and the question of the role of choice in the formation of kinship groups.

Of course there were other problems being written about and studied in this period. The CSSRC commissioned reports on land tenure, budgets and other economic matters, and some colonial governments requested studies of labour migration. Some of these studies had an impact on contemporaries – perhaps most notably the demonstrations by Schapera and Watson that labour migration was not necessarily disruptive of the social structure. But in general the economic reports were of restricted interest, and there was little development in economic anthropological theory. Firth alone made this a central preoccupation, and a few students influenced by him tried to apply economic theory in exotic circumstances. However, it was not until the 1960s that economics, and ecology, began to re-emerge as issues of primary importance, as Malinowski had seen them to be.

Law was another field that concerned colonial governments, and a number of studies in legal anthropology or 'social control' appeared in this period. Some, like the work of Goody and Bohannan, were really aspects of the study of segmentary lineage systems. Others, particularly the work of Gluckman and Schapera, were more concerned with problems of jurisprudence. Once again, however, law was not a field which attracted great interest in its own right.

If Murdock was broadly correct in picking out the limited range of interests of contemporary British social anthropologists, however wrongly he specified them, he was certainly right to stress the geographical limitations of their work. The 1950s continued this trend. To a certain extent it was a function of departmental special-ization, and of connections set up by 'old boys' with institutes and universities in the colonies. The Oxford anthropologists continued to travel to the Sudan, though some also explored the Middle East and Catholic Europe. Cambridge set up a strong link with the East African Institute of Social Research, under the directorship of Richards and, later, Southall and Stenning, but a number of Fortes's students continued to work in Ghana, while Leach directed his own students to South-East Asia. Manchester continued its close association with the Rhodes–Livingstone Institute, and its students overwhelmingly worked in Central Africa. The London professors also tended to send their students to the areas in which they had themselves done fieldwork - so Forde's students went to Nigeria, and Firth's to Malaya and Oceania. Elsewhere, the Australian departments naturally concentrated on the Aborigines, but in the 1950s they moved into the new ethnographic region of highland New Guinea.

I shall be coming shortly to consider the cross-currents of the 1950s and early 1960s, but it is remarkable how consistent and how sharply focused on a small range of issues modern British social anthropology was in the 1950s. This was a function of the small size of the profession and the overwhelming power of the professoriate. The rapid expan-sion of the early postwar years gave a new impetus to the discipline, but it did not displace the theoretical dominance of the point of view that had been established at Oxford in the years immediately before the war.

6 Leach and Gluckman

Law and order arise out of the very processes which they govern.
But they are not rigid, nor due to any inertia or permanent mould.
They obtain on the contrary as the result of a constant struggle not
merely of human passions against the law, but of legal principles
with one another.

– Malinowski[1]

I

The last chapter was concerned primarily with the mainstream, the
developments within the orthodoxies established by Radcliffe-Brown
and Malinowski. Throughout the 1950s and 1960s there were eddies
and currents that moved against the main flow, and in this chapter
I shall discuss the two leading mavericks, E. R. Leach and Max
Gluckman. Although both published their first important essays in
1940, they came into their own in the 1950s.

There may be some resistance to considering Leach and Gluckman
in one breath. Leach once described Gluckman as 'my most vigorous
opponent in matters theoretical',[2] and represented him as amongst
the least repentant adherents of the kind of organic equilibrium
theory that Leach himself rejected. Furthermore, despite his later
apostasy, Leach was often thought of primarily as the English
prophet of Lévi-Strauss, as Radcliffe-Brown was of Durkheim, while
Gluckman never showed any interest in the preoccupations of the
neo-structuralists. Yet it is probably more accurate to see Leach's
Lévi-Straussian period as a secondary development, which never
really jelled with his major work. As he once wrote:

I myself was once a pupil of Malinowski and I am, at heart, still
a 'functionalist' even though I recognise the limitations of

Malinowski's own brand of theory. Although I have occasionally used the 'structuralist' methods of Lévi-Strauss to illuminate particular features of particular cultural systems the gap between my general position and that of Lévi-Strauss is very wide.[3]

In the next chapter I shall deal with the impact of Lévi-Strauss's work on British anthropologists; and Leach will figure prominently there. Here my concern is with the broadly political topics which were the subjects of Leach's monographs. It is in this field that the convergences, and divergences, with Gluckman are of interest.

Leach and Gluckman only just belonged to the senior age-grade of British anthropologists. Leach was born in 1910, Gluckman in 1911. Both came into anthropology in Britain in the mid-1930s, after the majority of the first generation had completed their doctoral training, and at a time when Malinowski's influence was giving way to that of Radcliffe-Brown. Both men attended Malinowski's seminars in this period, but Gluckman was commuting from Oxford, where he was formally under the supervision of Marett, while Leach was a student at the LSE. Gluckman later came under the influence of the new structuralism in Oxford, being particularly impressed by the early work of Evans-Pritchard. Leach was never greatly influenced by either Radcliffe-Brown or Evans-Pritchard, and after Malinowski's departure he was closest to Firth at the LSE.

They were the brilliant new recruits of the two main schools. Both set out to develop the insights of their masters in novel ways. But although Leach remained recognizably a Malinowskian in much of his writing, and Gluckman was always an Oxford structuralist at bottom, there was a real convergence of interest. Both were drawn to problems of conflict of norms and the manipulation of rules, and both used a historical perspective and the extended-case method to investigate these problems. (By a sad coincidence, they also both lost the field-notes of their most important studies during the war!) Their students took up similar problems, if one excepts those of Leach's students who pursued the interests of Lévi-Strauss. Barth, Barnes and Bailey – three of the liveliest anthropologists of the 1950s and 1960s – demonstrated in their work the ultimate convergence of Leach and Gluckman.

A fuller and more nuanced comparison might well wait until the work of these two scholars has been reviewed in detail. At this stage it is sufficient to note that Leach and Gluckman, the figures intermediate between the pioneer generation and the postwar generation, were primarily concerned with advancing the range and sharpening the bite of the theories that had been established in the 1930s. Following their work new options were realized, and, at last, their contributions can be seen to have supported each other. If one had to sum up in a sentence the message both propagated it was this – that the central dynamic of social systems is provided by political activity, by men competing with each other to enhance their means and status, within the framework set by often conflicting or ambiguous rules.

The reader should also know that both were 'charismatic' figures, large men, emphatic, committed, outspoken. Both attracted strong personal loyalties, but, intolerant and at times overbearing, they inevitably alienated some colleagues.

II

Gluckman was born in Johannesburg, of Russian-Jewish parents. He first studied social anthropology at the University of the Witwatersrand under Mrs A.W. Hoernlé. She was a successful teacher. A number of her pupils went on to become professional anthropologists, and Gluckman's contemporaries included Ellen Hellman, Hilda Beemer (Kuper) and Eileen Jensen (Krige). Gluckman has suggested that Winifred Hoernlé developed his interest in conflict theory, but there is nothing in her work, or in that of her other students, to suggest this. Trained in Cambridge, she was a follower of Radcliffe-Brown, and Gluckman's generous tributes to her may be read as in part an attempt to individuate his genealogy with reference to a maternal ancestress. However, Mrs Hoernlé did instil in her students the values of scholarship, which were not strongly represented in South African universities. As a group these students also saw their commitment to anthropology partly in political terms. At a time when their British-based contemporaries tended to avert their eyes from the realities of power and deprivation in the colonial societies, they found it difficult to ignore the context of the systems which they investigated.

In 1934 Gluckman went to Oxford as a Rhodes scholar, taking his D.Phil. in 1936. He did fieldwork in Zululand between 1936 and 1938. In 1940 his first major essays appeared: a chapter on the Zulu in *African Political Systems*, and the first part of the brief monograph, *Analysis of a Social Situation in Modern Zululand*. In these papers he dealt with the kind of segmentary opposition that was the great focus of Oxford theory, but he introduced also a concern with other forms of opposition and conflict, which were to preoccupy him more in the years to follow.

In his contribution to *African Political Systems* Gluckman described two stages of pre-colonial Zulu society, and argued:

The essence of both the systems described is the opposition of like groups and the potentially conflicting loyalties of the people to different authorities. The nation was a stable organisation, for this opposition was principally between the tribes which were united in the king's position and his regiments . . . In actual administration, the loyalties of the people and the competition of officers did not often conflict, since the administrative machinery worked through the heads of groups of different type: the main opposition was between similar groups, co-operating as parts of a larger group.

This segmentary opposition produced coherence and equilibrium. The conflicts that occurred were even positively functional - like the Nuer feud. However, Gluckman went on to contrast these stable systems with the situation he found in the field:

Today the system is not stable, for not only is Zulu life being constantly affected and changed by many factors, but also the different authorities stand for entirely different, even contradictory, values. . . . The modern political organization of Zululand is the opposition between the two colour-groups represented by certain authorities. . . . The opposition between the two groups is not well-balanced, for ultimately it is dominated by the superior force of Government. . . . The threat of this force is necessary to make the system work, because Zulu values and interests are so opposed to those of the Europeans that the Zulu do not recognize a strong moral relationship between themselves and Government, such as existed, and exists, between themselves and their king and chiefs. They usually regard Government as being out to exploit them, regardless of their interests.[4]

This was the only analysis to deal with the context of racial domination in the whole of *African Political Systems*.

The *Analysis of a Social Situation in Modern Zululand*[5] went further in showing how the plural political society formed by colonial or settler domination must provide the framework for the understanding of local 'tribal' systems. Using a novel form of presentation, Gluckman described in great detail the scene at the opening of a new bridge in Zululand – the comings and goings, the speeches and comments, the taking of tea – always drawing attention to the social allegiances of the actors, from the white magistrate and his entourage, to the chief and his followers, even to the anthropologist himself. Gluckman's point was that although the members of the different colour groups were symbolically and actually divided and opposed at every point, yet they were forced to interact in spheres of common interest.

This did not mean that the situation was stable; on the contrary, despite the cross-cutting ties that existed, contemporary Zululand represented the type of social system in which conflicts could not be properly resolved without radical structural changes. This type of system was contrasted with pre-colonial Zulu society where, despite changes, often radical enough, there were long periods of comparative stability when the conflicts generated by the system could be absorbed by it. Gluckman argued that the social anthropologist should study these periods of comparative stability, when the social system approached a state of equilibrium.

The essence of Gluckman's position, as it developed, was that social equilibrium is not a simple affair, resulting from the neat integration of groups or norms. On the contrary, it emerges through the balancing of oppositions in a dialectical process. As he and Colson once wrote, social groups have 'an inherent tendency to segment and then to become bound together by cross-cutting alliances ... conflicts in one set of relationships are absorbed and redressed in the countervailing relations'.[6] Equally, the norms governing social life are often critically ambiguous, or even conflicting. For example, the rules of succession to a chieftaincy are often so phrased that there will inevitably be several 'rightful' claimants who will compete for office. But since it is in the interests of all the claimants to unite in boosting the central value of the office, the very competition generated by the rules will strengthen the consensus about the value of the office. In ritual, too, Gluckman saw conflict and not merely some sort of transcendent unity being expressed; but in the expression of its conflicts the society was temporarily purged. He came to see ritual, that is,

> not simply as expressing cohesion and impressing the value of society and its social sentiments on people, as in Durkheim's and Radcliffe-Brown's theories, but as exaggerating real conflicts of social rules and affirming that there was unity despite these conflicts.[7]

This sort of analysis, focusing on the achievement of consensus and social equilibrium through the contained expression of conflict, is familiar to sociologists in the work of the German scholar Simmel (1858–1917), but Gluckman developed his views in ignorance of Simmel's work. Even Weber was virtually unknown to British anthropologists until after the Second World War. One may also detect in some of Gluckman's work the influence of Freud's notion of ambivalence, and he was certainly familiar with Freudian thought, and sympathetic to it. There is an even more direct appeal to

Bateson's analysis of schismogenesis. Nevertheless the immediate inspiration was closer at hand, in the work of the Oxford structuralists.

Radcliffe-Brown had expressed his 'principle of opposition', and Evans-Pritchard had developed the idea in his analysis of segmentation and feuding among the Nuer. Evans-Pritchard went even further in his analysis of Anuak politics, and in his outstanding essay, 'The divine kingship of the Shilluk', published in 1948. There he wrote, in terms Gluckman was to use also,

> Shilluk rebellions have not been made against the kingship. On the contrary, they were made to preserve the values embodied in the kingship which were being weakened, or it was believed so, by the individual who held office. They were not revolutions but rebellions against the king in the name of the kingship.[8]

In their attempts to rewrite history, and to detach him from his British sources, some of Evans-Pritchard's followers have also tried to disown much of the work which derived from his major analyses, and particularly Gluckman's work. Pocock, for example, has argued that Radcliffe-Brown and Gluckman confused two meanings of the notion of 'opposition' – antagonism, and structural juxtaposition. In discussing Evans-Pritchard, Pocock (and Dumont) tried to bring him into line with the modern French structuralists, for whom 'opposition' is a process that occurs at the level of the classification of groups rather than at the level of the confrontation of two bodies of people. Thus Pocock argued that Gluckman vulgarized Evans-Pritchard's model, and imposed upon it a distorting functionalist emphasis.[9]

I do not believe it is fruitful to discuss whether Gluckman's development of Evans-Pritchard's ideas was legitimate or not. It is clear enough that the line of development he followed differed from that followed by the majority of Evans-Pritchard's postwar students, but then after the war Evans-Pritchard's own views altered fairly drastically. My point is simply that Gluckman's theories were one possible development of the ideas he had learnt at Oxford from Radcliffe-Brown and Evans-Pritchard.

The most vulnerable feature of Gluckman's theory, as it evolved, was the concentration upon what he had identified as repetitive as opposed to changing social systems. This sometimes led him to ludicrous extremes, and he later modified his position. Discussing the views he advanced in the 1940s and 1950s he wrote, in 1963, 'I was still thinking in crude functional terms of institutions – even civil war, which after all can be an institution – contributing to the maintenance of a rather rigidly conceived social structure.'[10] This emphasis, he explained, grew out of his study of white-ruled Zululand, 'which, despite its many unresolved and irresoluble conflicts, "worked"', obliging him to consider 'how social systems could contain the deep conflicts which are present in all of them'.[11]

III

Gluckman's essays on the Zulu set out the sociological ideas that he carried over to Central Africa when he joined Godfrey Wilson at the Rhodes–Livingstone Institute, in 1939. He became acting Director in 1941 and served as Director from 1942 to 1947. This was a period of intense activity at the Institute, and Gluckman's ideas were taken up by the fellows who now came to do fieldwork. Although Gluckman's views represented a shift of emphasis rather than a total divergence from the position of the prewar Oxford structuralists, their adoption had significant consequences. The fieldworkers who were influenced by Gluckman came to conceive of social reality in a way that differed markedly from the more conventional views of the students of Evans-Pritchard and Fortes, and consequently the work of the Rhodes–Livingstone fellows in Central Africa is distinctive, and stands in sharp contrast to much of the work of the Oxford and Cambridge anthropologists in East and West Africa.

Outlining the research plans of the Institute in 1945, Gluckman stressed his interest in the total social system of the region, including whites and Indians. He wrote:

> I must emphasize that I do not view the social processes at work as entirely disintegrative . . . My whole formulation of the problem depends on recognizing that there is a Central African Society of heterogeneous culture-groups of Europeans and Africans, with a defined social structure and norms of behaviour, though it has many conflicts and maladjustments.[12]

Following from this, it was necessary to study urban as well as rural areas, and to see African workers in the towns not simply as displaced peasants but as workers, operating within an industrial, urban social system. This ambitious programme contrasted sharply with the research plan that the International African Institute had published a decade earlier. While the promised studies of white and Asian communities unfortunately never materialized, the settlers and administrators are present in the Rhodes–Livingstone studies in a way distinctly unusual in the anthropological reports of the period.

One of the problems that this orientation raised concerned the role of the village headmen, the NCOs of district administration, caught between the demands of the alien authorities and those of their own people. This was a situation in which the inherent conflicts of colonial administration were exposed, and it was one Gluckman had explored in his Zulu studies. Most of the Rhodes–Livingstone fellows tackled it at one time or another.

Gluckman's detailed analysis of a single 'social situation' in Zululand had indicated a dissatisfaction with conventional modes of presenting illustrative ethnographic material. It represented a reaction against the selectivity of the Malinowskian technique of 'apt illustration'. Mitchell used the 'social situation' approach in *The Kalela Dance*, but other fellows searched for alternatives. Their experiments came to fruition in Turner's use of 'social dramas', later termed 'extended-case studies', a technique particularly well suited to the study of processes of conflict and conflict resolution. The members of the Institute also used statistical methods more successfully and conscientiously than did most of their contemporaries, and Barnes and Mitchell made advances in the refinement of statistical methods to meet the exigencies of anthropological research. Finally, Gluckman's example of the use of historical data to identify stages of comparative stability and equilibrium that could be analysed and compared to the contemporary situation also inspired imitation and development, particularly in the hands of Barnes.

Thus Gluckman brought to the study of Central African societies not only his theories of the role of conflict in the social process, but also an insistence that the total political situation should be taken into account, and an openness to methodological innovation. He passed on his ideas at the Institute through close and constant interchanges at seminars, and visits in the field, and also in his review articles and contributions to the Institute's journal.

His own major research in this period, however, was at a tangent to the work he inspired. This was his study of Lozi law. He had some legal training, and his main interest was in the principles of jurisprudence used by the Barotse, and in their convergence with the principles of European law. This work was influential in the development of legal anthropological theory, but except in some of Epstein's work in the Copperbelt it did not have much effect on the studies of the Rhodes–Livingstone fellows.

IV

In 1947 Gluckman left the Rhodes–Livingstone Institute to take up a teaching appointment at Oxford, and after a couple of years he moved again, to open a department of anthropology at Manchester University. But throughout he maintained close connections with the Institute, now under the control of his associates, first Elizabeth Colson, and later Mitchell. A number of the fellows of the Institute were later associated with the Manchester department, some closely and for many years, and even those who were not remained committed for a considerable period to the tenets of the 'Manchester school'. Perhaps the best known of these fellows were Barnes, Cunnison, Epstein, Marwick, Turner, Van Velsen and Watson. Others who worked in Central Africa were drawn into the circle – the administrator C. M. N. White and the agronomist Allan were two of the more sympathetic.

The studies they published exhibit a remarkable degree of uniformity. With the occasional exception of Cunnison, their work is almost always readily identifiable as 'Manchester' in theme and inspiration. Perhaps this is because they represent a special case in the formation of anthropological schools. Most develop in a university, through the intellectual domination of the professor. This emerged in the field, and in conditions of greater camaraderie and equality, while all the members were engaged in similar, demanding enquiries. Certainly the cohesion that developed was unusual – though not, of course, without an undercurrent of conflict.

Virtually all the monographs on Central African rural societies which members of the school produced concentrated upon village structure, and analysed the processes of conflict and conflict-resolution inherent in the structure of the community. They also examined the position of the headman as an 'inter-calary' figure in the local admin-istration; studied witchcraft and ritual as channels for the expression, and resolution, of social conflicts; and experimented with statistical and extended-case material. Each of the monographs had its particular focus – village fission for Turner, vertical political integration for Mitchell on the Yao, labour migration for Watson, sorcery accusations for Marwick, and so forth. Yet each can be read as a particular projection of the fundamental model they all shared, and which they took from Gluckman.

Less work was done in the tense urban areas, but Epstein and Mitchell produced studies of the Copperbelt and Watson contributed his analysis of labour migration seen from the rural end. Here too the characteristic preoccupations of the school were evident. The analyses brought out the situationally defined structural oppositions, over-ridden at times by shared interests, which had been analysed in the rural communities.

Turner's study of the Ndembu, *Schism and Continuity in an African Society* (1957), was the most satisfying of these studies. Turner began with a problem that Malinowski had raised and which Richards had analysed some years earlier for the matrilineal societies of Central Africa. This was, how do matrilineal societies reconcile the conflicting interests of men as members of a matrilineage, brothers, husbands and brothers-in-law? The Ndembu village is built around a core of male matrilineal kin. They normally bring their wives to live at their homes, and their sisters move away to live with their husbands. But every man is succeeded by a sister's son, who must therefore be brought in at some stage to the core community of matrilineally related men. The ambitious men try to build up their communities, and to this end they try to keep their own children at home as well as recovering their sisters' children. The resulting conflict between the pulls of family and matrilineage was a basic problem for the Ndembu – 'Thus both marriages and villages are inherently unstable and in-laws struggle continually for control over women and their children.'[13] In this situation the only solidary unit was the matricentric family, the group formed by children of one mother. It was this unit which was pulled between the competing father and mother's brother.

There were other structurally generated conflicts as well, between men and women, with their different economic roles and different functions within the matrilineages; and between the men of the core matrilineal community itself, competing for authority and property within the village. Turner analysed the resulting pattern of relation-ships both in broad terms, by a statistical survey of the composition of a number of villages, and in depth, by analysing the conflicts within one village.

Turner used what he called 'social dramas' to present his analysis of the way in which these conflicts worked themselves out in the village. He argued that overt conflicts brought out the underlying strains of the social system; they therefore dramatized the inherent stresses within the structure. By dealing with a series of confrontations involving the same actors one could look at the way conflicts developed and were resolved, and also test the fundamental analysis. The result was a new kind of monograph, with a long story of quarrels, tensions and resolutions running through it. Barnes has compared this sort of study to a Russian novel, in its diversity of actors and complexity of motives – not to mention its proliferation of impossible names.

The theoretical analysis was cast in Gluckman's mould; for example:

> People live together because they are matrilineally related, but just because they are matrilineally related they come into conflict over office and over the inheritance of property. Since the dogma of kinship asserts that matrilineal kin participate in one another's existence, and since the norms of kinship state that matrilineal kin must at all times help one another, open physical violence between them seldom takes place. Their struggles are phrased in the idiom of sorcery/witchcraft and animistic beliefs. . . . Conflict is endemic in the social structure but a set of mechanisms exist whereby conflict itself is pressed into the service of affirming group unity.[14]

Turner himself freely acknowledged his debt to Gluckman, and like many of the works of the school, the book carried an approving introduction by Gluckman. Turner's analysis also referred back directly to the work of the Oxford structuralists, and particularly to Fortes's Tallensi study, in his analysis of lineage fission and the operation of ties of kinship outside the lineage.

Although it is fair to say that Turner's analysis was not theoretically innovative (as his studies of Ndembu ritual were to be), the quality of the case material and the care with which it was presented and analysed put the monograph in a class of its own. The reader was given a fresh, complex understanding of the cut and thrust of inter-personal relationships in an exotic social context, came to know the protagonists, saw them acting out their roles and appreciated the conflicts which faced them. Turner's account of Ndembu village life carried a conviction that was never so fully achieved by the disorderly books of Malinowski, or the excessively orderly books of the structuralists. Because the focus was upon the individuals – in their prescribed roles – the path from this sort of study was to lead to network analysis, game theory, and other modes of conceptualizing the strategies of everyday life. The Rhodes–Livingstone fellows were beginning to move away from the structuralists and towards what has been called 'methodological individualism'; but this was not yet fully apparent in the 1950s.

V

In the urban studies of Epstein and Mitchell the central structural opposition was, of course, between whites and blacks, as it had been in Zululand. The Copperbelt towns were organized around the mines. They were divided into white municipality and African township, and the Africans were separately administered by government officials. The Africans were drawn from several countries and over seventy tribes, and they were in turn divided in two ways – by tribal origin, and by occupation, or urban prestige.

The whites, drawing upon their experience of rural administration, reinforced by their stereotype of the African, believed that Africans should be governed on a 'tribal' basis, even in the towns. Urban administration should operate through 'tribal elders' of some kind. But although Africans were fairly willing, in general, to consult these 'elders' on some matters, they did not accept their leadership in the industrial context. The 'elders' were accused of selling out to the whites, and when the workers rioted on the Copperbelt in 1935, the 'tribal elders' who had been elected had to seek refuge with the whites, in the same way as the hated black policemen.

The fact was that in some contexts occupational ties overrode tribal loyalties. But the structure of employment generated its own tensions. The whites occupied the highest positions of power and prestige, and they set the standards for individual aspiration. The educated, westernized Africans held the highest-paid white-collar jobs below the colour line. This group naturally provided much of the African leadership, but their style of life separated them from their fellows, and their position of comparative privilege put them in a dilemma when the lower-grade workers went on strike. Therefore although they built up the trade unions which provided leadership after the 'elders' had been ditched, they were in turn displaced from the leadership in favour of more militant if less educated underground workers.

This situation was further complicated by other factors. Firstly, there was considerable overlap between tribal origin and 'class' position. Some 'tribes' were disproportionately represented in certain occupations, since they were favoured by educational advantages in their home areas. This served to confuse the lines of division in some situations, in others to reinforce them. Secondly, the meaning of 'tribal' identification was very different in the town and in the rural areas. In the towns it did not connote acceptance of a whole series of ascribed positions of authority, but rather served as a primary mode of grouping people into possible friends and probable foes. Finally, Epstein and Mitchell demonstrated that different identities were asserted in different situations in urban life. Sometimes a man might side with Bemba against non-Bemba; at other times with clerks against underground workers; and then again line up with fellow Africans against the white mine authority or the government.

Many of the subsidiary themes developed by Epstein and Mitchell were transformations of the themes they and their colleagues had investigated in the rural areas of Central Africa. But the conflicting norms and competing interests of the rural society became alternative types of action and utterly opposed racial blocks in the towns. This led them to concentrate particularly upon the situational selection of allegiances and hence of modes of behaviour, choices generated by the organization of 'class' and 'tribe', and, ultimately, by the over-arching structure imposed by the dominant white group.

One cannot readily separate the development of Gluckman's ideas and the work he inspired at the Rhodes–Livingstone Institute. They fused in the productions of the 'Manchester school', which in the 1950s became a distinct mutation of British structuralism. At the same period Leach was working alone, from a different starting-point, but my argument is that his development converged with 'Manchester' to a degree that can be appreciated only now, in retrospect.

VI

Leach was one of the few British anthropologists of the prewar vintage with a 'conventional' upper-middle-class background. At Cambridge he read for a degree in engineering. He then spent some years in the East, in China, before abandoning his first career and entering the LSE in the mid-1930s, as a student of Malinowski. In 1938 he spent a few weeks doing fieldwork among the Kurds, but although he had envisaged a return the war found him engaged in a more ambitious field study of the Kachin in Burma. The war was spent in irregular military units, often with Kachin. He lost his field-notes, but eventually, after the war, prepared a thesis based largely upon published materials. He became a reader at the LSE under Firth, where he was for some time regarded as an expert on material culture. In 1953 he went to Cambridge as lecturer, and a few years later did a further field study, in Ceylon. Although his old college, Clare, refused him a fellowship on the grounds of his militant atheism, he was elected to a fellowship at King's, and later became Provost. In 1972 he was belatedly awarded a professorship by personal title.

Leach's first monograph, *Social and Economic Organisation of the Rowanduz Kurds*, appeared in 1940. This was a tentative piece of work, based on only five weeks in the field, and it was rather neglected at the time. After all, the same year saw the appearance of Evans-Pritchard's political studies of the Nuer and the Anuak, and of *African Political Systems* (which contained, with much else, Gluckman's first essay on the Zulu). Yet it was a suggestive little book, and set out some of the ideas Leach went on to develop in later years. The book also provides a solid link between the neo-Malinowskian position that Firth was setting out and the explorations with which Leach was later to dazzle his colleagues.

Leach's central observation was that the Kurds were passing through a period of rapid change, as a consequence of external administrative interference. He pointed to 'powerful and perhaps irresistible forces at work tending not so much to the modification as to the total destruction and disintegration of existing forms of tribal organization'.[15] This was a state of affairs that presented a problem to the functionalist, whose basic premise was that the system he was studying was well-integrated and in equilibrium. Gluckman had recognized the dynamism of social systems, but had posited the existence of periods of comparative calm and equilibrium of forces which could be studied in more or less conventional terms. Leach rejected this. All societies maintain only a precarious balance at any time, and are really in 'a constant state of flux and potential change'. The norms that exist are neither stable nor inflexible. 'There can never be absolute conformity to the cultural norm, indeed the norm itself exists only as a stress of conflicting interests and divergent attitudes.' This is where one may identify the source of the dynamism. 'The mechanism of culture change is to be found in the reaction of individuals to their differential economic and political interests.'[16]

This being the case, Leach argued,

> in order to make the description intelligible at all, some degree of idealisation seems essential. In the main therefore I shall seek to describe Kurdish society as if it were a functioning whole and then show up existing circumstances as variations from this idealised norm.[17]

Analysis must therefore operate at two levels. First the anthropologist builds up a model of how the society might be expected to work *if* it were in equilibrium, if it were well-integrated. But this is an idealization of limited value. To get back to the historical reality one must look at the interplay of personal interests, which can only temporarily form a balance, and which must in due course alter the system.

The emphasis on change, and on the creative force of individual demands, and the view of 'norms' as unstable ideals based upon temporary configurations of interests, all went back to the Malinowskian position. What Leach added was his use of a model, an ideal type, abstracted for limited heuristic purposes. Gluckman had seized upon the part played by competing interests and conflicting norms which were present, but secondary in Radcliffe-Brownian structuralism. Leach brought a highly sophisticated structural approach to the aid of Malinowskian analysis, which was too much obsessed with the vagaries of 'calculating man'.

After the war Leach wrote his doctoral thesis on Kachin society, and in 1954 published perhaps his outstanding book, *Political Systems of Highland Burma*. This grew out of the thesis, and the comparatively crude arguments of 1940 re-emerged in a more mature and elaborate form. The communities of highland Burma, roughly classified as Kachin and Shan, form a bewildering variety of linguistic, cultural and political units. Leach argued that the notion of a bounded 'tribe' was of no use in understanding the situation. The whole set of interacting communities had to be seen as comprising in some sense a single social system. But it was not a system in equilibrium. As he had argued in 1940, so now he insisted that equilibrium could be assumed only for purposes of analysis at a certain level. One had to remain aware of the fictional nature of this assumption, and recognize that 'the reality situation is in most cases full of inconsistencies; and it is precisely these inconsistencies which can provide us with an understanding of the processes of social change.'[18]

If the anthropologist needed an ideal pattern to provide an orientation, so did the people themselves. In their case this was set out in ritual, which from time to time expressed symbolically 'the system of socially approved "proper" relations between individuals and groups'; rituals 'momentarily make explicit what is otherwise a fiction'.[19] Ritual expression - broadly understood as an aspect of all behaviour – and the cultural symbols through which it worked did not correspond, however, to normative rules of behaviour. They were too ambiguous, and evoked too spasmodically. Indeed the ambiguity of ritual and symbol, the levels of uncertainty inherent in ritual and cultural communication, were necessary. They permitted the actors a range of legitimate choices.

The structural analysis of the anthropologists and the rituals of the people are therefore both idealized abstractions, attempts to impose an *as if* fictional but comprehensible order upon the flux of social life. Beneath these attempts at formalization lies the reality of individuals in pursuit of power. In this continual competition the actors make a series of choices that may cumulatively alter the structure of their society.

There were three basic types of political system in the Kachin Hills area - the egalitarian, almost anarchic system of the *gumlao* Kachin; the unstable, intermediate *gumsa* form, a sort of mini-state; and the Shan state. These were ideal types, but useful to the people and the anthropologist in classifying real communities. Communities swung from one type to another, and the *gumsa* communities were particularly unstable. Leach examined in depth the categories used by the people to describe these systems, and showed that they were represented in terms of the same set of symbols, in different combinations. When a community swung from one type to another, as a result of political activity, the people might then weight the value of the various symbols differently, while still in a sense speaking the same ritual language.

The difference between these systems is reminiscent of the classical anthropological opposition between kin-based societies and states. This was the basis of Fortes and Evans-Pritchard's opposition between states and stateless societies organized by a segmentary lineage system. Leach's conception was related to theirs, as he said, but his analysis was particularly concerned with the mechanisms by which one 'type' of system was transformed into another.

The Kachin lineages differ from the African stereotype in that they are ranked relative to each other. Rank is fixed by a system of marriage alliances. One cannot give a wife to a lineage from whom one takes a wife, and vice versa. This rule permits an ideal ranking of lineages, with wife-givers superior to wife-takers who are their vassals. The combination of lineage and rank is at the root of the instability of the *gumsa* system. As Leach summarized the position:

> The *gumsa* ideal order consists of a network of related lineages, but it is also a network of ranked lineages. As the process of lineage fission proceeds there comes a point at which choice has to be made between the primacy of the principle of rank or the principle of kinship. Rank implies an asymmetrical relationship. . . . Kinship implies a symmetrical relationship. . . . The weakness of the *gumsa* system is that the successful chief is tempted to repudiate links of kinship with his followers and to treat them as if they were bond slaves. It is this situation which, from a *gumlao* point of view, is held to justify revolt.[20]

There is an equivalent structural defect at the heart of the *gumlao* system. Leach wrote that a *gumlao* community, unless it happens to be centred around a fixed territorial centre such as a patch of irrigated rice terraces, usually lacks the means to hold its component lineages together in a status of equality. It will then either disintegrate altogether through fission, or else status differences between lineage groups will bring the system back into the *gumsa* pattern.[21]

In both cases, the dynamic for change is provided by individuals competing for power. The dissatisfied man with some inherited status might decide to seek office in a hierarchical system or to repudiate hierarchy; to be a rebel against the incumbent chief, or a revolutionary against the *gumsa* system. The influential figure in a *gumlao* system may choose to repudiate democracy and swing his community towards a *gumsa* structure. Each system carries within itself the seeds of its contrary, and communities swing between the *gumlao* and *gumsa* extremes.

When Leach came to demonstrate his thesis that the Kachin Hills communities exemplified something like Pareto's succession of lions and foxes, he was faced with serious difficulties. He used two methods. First he presented a detailed analysis of one small and unstable *gumsa* community as it was in 1940, concluding that

> Hpalang in 1940, in my view, was probably in process of changing from a *gumsa* to a *gumlao* type of organisation. It was restrained from completing the change over only by the arbitrary dictates of the paramount power whose officers objected to the *gumlao* system as a matter of principle.[22]

This was by no means conclusive. His second test was historical, but the historical sources were unsatisfactory. They provided a clue to the forces making for instability and change – in myths the *gumlao* leader is presented as 'a minor aristocrat of ambition and ability who might himself have been a chief if the accident of birth order had not dictated otherwise. The myth is a description of the real man.'[23] But so far as his thesis as a whole was concerned, Leach could show only 'that there is nothing in the history of the area which conflicts with my interpretation'.[24]

Yet it is difficult to see how this thesis could have been disproved by historical materials. In a preface to the 1964 reprint of the monograph Leach remarked that 'my own attempt to find systemic ordering in historical events depends upon the changing evaluation of verbal categories and is, in the final analysis, illusory.'[25] For what changes when a community swings from *gumlao* to *gumsa*? Discussing his community of Hpalang, he had remarked that while the kinship composition of the community had remained more or less unaltered over the past 40 years, there had been radical changes in the internal authority structure. The leaders of the community still used *gumsa* categories to describe the respective status of groups and persons; they attached importance to the notion of aristocracy, the title of chief, and to the rights of chiefs ... But all this was largely pretence. Had the community been organised on *gumlao* principles with no aristocrats, no chiefs and no tributary dues, the de facto situation would have been almost the same. This is an illustration of the fact that the contrast between *gumsa* and *gumlao* is a difference of ideal order rather than empirical fact.[26]

This suggests a central problem which the book raises. If there is such a difference between 'ideal order' and 'empirical fact' – presumably, a difference comparable to that between ideology and action – with which level is Leach concerned? Or is he engaged in an attempt to analyse the complex and dynamic interaction of these two levels? Presumably the latter, and the book can be read in this way. But the uncertainty is there, and it is significant. Leach's subsequent writings swung between the extremes of an idealist view of social structure and a perception of structure as a map of power relations. He generally maintained that political relationships were in some way primary, but the distance between his later neo-structuralist essays and, say, *Pul Eliya*, is at first blush very striking.

If there is a higher unity in his work it lies in the Malinowskian premise that the people's model is a sort of screen behind which the actual competitive relations of community life are worked out. The people's model is expressed in inexact and symbolic terms, so they can manipulate alternatives with an easy conscience, and resolve apparent contradictions at the ideological level. The anthropologist's model is also, necessarily, at several removes from the empirical facts. It is an equilibrium *as if* model, differing from the sort of model used by the people themselves mainly in the precision of its categories. But this necessary precision freezes the model, and it cannot accommodate change. To understand the actual flux of social relations the anthropologist must consider the anomalies and contradictions in the folk models, and discover the ways in which ambitious individuals are manipulating political resources.

Political Systems of Highland Burma was, then, a difficult monograph but daring and experimental, particularly in its model of cyclical change. None the less it lacked the aggressively revolutionary tone of Leach's next book, *Pul Eliya*, which appeared in 1961. This was an explicit frontal attack on those he called 'Oxford structuralists', represented (in Leach's summary) by Radcliffe-Brown, Fortes and Evans-Pritchard.

Leach opened with a definition of social anthropology as the study of the way in which 'custom' constrained individual behaviour. He identified three approaches to this issue, all deriving ultimately from Durkheim. First there was the Oxford model, which analysed society as an assemblage of roles, the occupants of the roles being under moral and jural constraints to fulfil them. The second approach, deriving from the Durkheim of *Suicide*, took the statistical norm as the basic datum. This was the Malinowskian position - 'Custom is what men do, normal men, average men.'[27] Both these approaches were deficient, but in different ways. The first did not begin to cope with individual variation, while the second evaded the problem of how the norm established itself and was institutionalized.

Leach derived the third approach rather more shakily from Durkheim's notion of collective representations:

> Here the thesis is that 'the sacred' and the 'profane' are distinct categories of verbal and non-verbal behaviour and that the former is, as it were, a 'model' for the latter. In some developments of this argument, ritual is looked upon as providing an 'outline plan' in terms of which individuals orientate their day-to-day behaviour. The divergencies of individual behaviour from any standard norm are not then the result of moral error or of unenlightened self-interest, but arise simply because different individuals, quite legitimately, fill in the details of the ideal schema in different ways.[28]

This was basically the line Leach had taken in *Political Systems of Highland Burma*, while stressing that 'ritual' was an aspect of everyday behaviour, not something restricted to 'sacred' contexts. In *Pul Eliya* the set of symbols which the people use to orientate their lives are based on kinship. But now he tried to identify an objective reality behind the ideological orientation. In the Kachin study, action was shaped by power relations; in the Singhalese village of Pul Eliya the basic constraints were even more down-to-earth. The layout of the village fields and the irrigation arrangements, which could not easily be changed, presented a set of objective constraints to which the villagers had to adapt their behaviour. For purposes of analysis, 'custom' is still the statistical norm, while the ideal norm becomes the gloss upon it, but the ecology determines interests and choices.

The thesis was sharpened by taking 'kinship' as the central issue. Kinship theory was dominated by Fortes at this time, and Fortes operated in terms of an equilibrium model of the kinship system, which was perceived in jural terms - as a system of rules, rights and duties pertaining to particular kinship roles. The continuity of the social system might be maintained by the perpetuation of corporate lineage groups, that is, enduring assemblages of rights and duties focused on a particular 'estate'.

To this Leach opposed the view that at least this one village in the dry zone of Ceylon was ordered above all by material factors. It was 'locality rather than descent which forms the basis of corporate groupings'.[29] Indeed,

> The group itself need have no rules; it may be simply a collection of individuals who derive their livelihood from a piece of territory laid out in a particular way. The continuing entity is *not* Pul Eliya *society* but Pul Eliya itself - the village tank, the *gangoda* area, the Old Field . . . [30]

Kinship was an epiphenomenon of property relations, an elastic and fairly ambiguous idiom in which people talked about property relations. The 'kinship system' did not constrain behaviour: it was a mode of describing choices that were constrained rather by material factors.

The argument was demonstrated by way of the extended-case method which had been developed by the Manchester school (though Leach seemed to imply that this was all his own invention). The detailed land-tenure records of the village, which had been preserved for decades, allowed him to examine specific manipulations and their consequences over time. His conclusion was always that the kinship rules were bent or reinterpreted to permit the villagers to make the adaptive, economic choices. For example, discussing the *variga* ('sub-caste'), he wrote:

> Ideally the cardinal rule is that land should never be allowed to pass outside the *variga*. Sales and gifts of land should only be between members of the same *variga*. If these rules were always maintained *variga* heirs would necessarily be within the *variga*. . . . in the past, the operations of the *variga* court were such as to ensure that all tolerated spouses of *variga* members were themselves treated as *variga* members whatever their actual origin. Thus by a legal fiction the rule of *variga* endogamy was maintained and inherited land necessarily stayed within the *variga*.[31]

It is instructive to compare the argument with that of the Burma monograph. There the actors made choices in terms of a power model of the community, and tried to maximize power. The cultural symbols defined gross alternatives, and permitted the actors to make a traditional sort of sense out of whatever real structure emerged. In *Pul Eliya* the actors' choices were constrained by the actual layout of the agricultural resources, and they attempted to maximize wealth. (In both societies, one might argue, the ultimate goal was the improvement of social status. Power and wealth may be converted into each other.) The cultural symbols in Pul Eliya, and specifically 'kinship', provided the idiom within which choices could be talked about and, ultimately, legitimized.

In *Pul Eliya* the 'ritual' dimension was granted less autonomy than in the Kachin study. This was in keeping with the polemical tone of Leach's attack on Oxford 'idealism', but it served to weaken the interpretation. As Fortes was able to show in his counter-attack, Leach's own data indicated the ways in which the kinship categories and rules in themselves served to constrain choices.[32] The argument was nevertheless consistent, both internally and with regard to Leach's own earlier works, and it represented a development of Malinowski's position. The 'reality' of the social situation is the statistical pattern created by individuals maximizing satisfactions. The 'ideal' norms are no more than a rough and ready mode of conceptualizing or orientating action, and their utility depends upon their ambiguity.

I have so far concerned myself with only one aspect of Leach's writing. Particularly in his essays, he was often more concerned with the 'ritual' dimension itself. This concern led to his prolonged flirtation with Lévi-Strauss's structuralist methods, at first sight so foreign to his basic approach. Leach had defined the issue as early as 1945, in his essay 'Jinghpaw kinship terminology', and the terms he used then were echoed in *Pul Eliya*, sixteen years later. He wrote:

In my own field work, I have found the determination of socio-logical norms extremely difficult. . . . The field worker has three distinct 'levels' of behaviour pattern to consider. The first is the actual behaviour of individuals. The average of all such individual behaviour patterns constitutes the second, which may fairly be described as 'the norm'. But there is a third pattern, the native's own description of himself and his society, which constitutes 'the ideal'. Because the field worker's time is short and he must rely upon a limited number of informants, he is always tempted to identify the second of these patterns with the third. Clearly the norm is strongly influenced by the ideal, but I question whether the two are ever precisely coincident. In the study of kinship this is an important distinction, because any structural analysis of a kinship system is necessarily a discussion of ideal behaviour, not of normal behaviour.

But while the ideal statements did not simply reflect the statistical norms, they could usefully be treated as an internally consistent system. Therefore one could, for example, show that Jinghpaw kinship terminology,

> which is superficially extremely complex, would appear simple and consistent to a man living in an ideal society, organized according to certain very simple rules. These rules constitute the ideal pattern of Jinghpaw society, to which the actual society is now, and probably always has been, a somewhat remote approximation.[33]

In his essay on Jinghpaw kinship terminology Leach made up his own methods for the analysis of the system. When he later adopted Lévi-Strauss's methods this was because he saw them as a superior means of analysing ideal systems. With very few lapses he remained what he called a functionalist, since, in contrast to Lévi-Strauss, he never believed that the structure of the ideal system was congruent with the statistical pattern that emerged as the sum of individual choices in a dynamic social and ecological context.

But this is still only part of the story. Leach has also consistently been a hammer of orthodoxy, ready to challenge any received ideas. He urged his colleagues to rethink their basic category assumptions, to dare to reconsider familiar facts, and to experiment with alternative procedures. In 1959, delivering the first Malinowski memorial lecture, which he provocatively entitled 'Rethinking anthropology', Leach challenged his audience to think mathematically about society. They should abandon their obsession with typologies – this was just an anthropological version of butterfly-collecting. They should drop comparison in favour of generalization. This could be achieved '*By thinking of the organizational ideas that are present in any society as constituting a mathematical pattern*'.[34] In the course of his lecture he characteristically singled out three living anthropologists as exemplars of folly. They were Fortes, Goody and Richards, his three senior Cambridge colleagues! For at least a decade he brandished Lévi-Strauss's reputation as a weapon in these polemics, arguing that his colleagues were being parochial, smug and backward in ignoring the significance of the French scholar's work.

One might suggest a sociological correlate of Leach's iconoclasm. He was, like Gluckman, a figure intermediate between the generation of Malinowski's first students and the postwar generation. He was also the most prominent senior anthropologist in Britain never to become a professorial head of department (no doubt from choice). He has himself pointed out that his eminently gentle social background was rather unusual among the social anthropologists of his time. He was, then, structurally something of an outsider, though an outsider who could very smoothly become Provost of King's College, Cambridge. He clearly relished this position, and his self-confidence permeates his polemics and allows, perhaps, his bold departures from the conventional route.

VII

Have I exaggerated the parallels between the work of Leach and the Manchester school? To some extent the similarities, such as they are, must have been the product of working at the same time in the same professional environment; and the dissimilarities are certainly striking enough. Yet at the heart of all their work there was a shared concern with the ways in which social systems somehow recognizably persist despite their inherent contradictions, and despite the fact that individuals are always pursuing their self-interest. Leach tended, like Malinowski, to stress the individual's manipulation of the rules, while Gluckman, like the Oxford structuralists, placed greater emphasis upon the coercive force of rules and values, yet each edged away from the position he inherited and perhaps unwittingly moved closer to the other. It is certainly interesting that where Leach studied 'ritual' aspects of social relations, Gluckman preferred to emphasize 'legal' aspects, but the convergence was there. Perhaps it was simply that this area of tension between individual interests and the values propagated by the 'society' was obviously the area to investigate after the dichotomous statements of Radcliffe-Brown and Malinowski had been assimilated.

Turner was perhaps the most creative of the Central Africa/ Manchester group that formed around Gluckman. In the 1960s he developed his analysis of Ndembu ritual, which he saw in the way Leach saw ritual, as a language for communicating statements about structural relationships, but a language infinitely suggestive and ambiguous; a language fitted to the transformation of social conflict. Barth, one of Leach's most original associates, developed another theme, directing attention to individual strategies and the manipulation of values, and elaborating 'transactional' models of social relationships. Gluckman's student Bailey – another intermediate figure, since he worked in India, a terrain of Leach and the neo-structuralists – developed a different thread of Manchester theory until it converged with Barth. These and other convergences between some of the students of Gluckman and Leach suggest that the parallels I have drawn between their work are not merely surface coincidences.

Leach, Gluckman and their students were leading figures in British social anthropology in the late 1950s and the 1960s. Together (though not in partnership) they formulated the basis of a new synthesis from the thesis of Malinowski and the antithesis of Radcliffe-Brown. But another, very different challenge to the British orthodoxy was being developed at the same time, on the other side of the Channel, and the British anthropologist who was to engage most passionately and creatively with the new theory was Edmund Leach.

7   Lévi-Strauss and British neo-structuralism

In anthropology as in linguistics . . . , it is not comparison that supports generalization, but the other way around. If, as we believe to be the case, the unconscious activity of the mind consists in imposing forms upon content, and if these forms are fundamentally the same for all minds – ancient and modern, primitive and civilized (as the study of the symbolic function, expressed in language, so strikingly indicates) – it is necessary and sufficient to grasp the unconscious structure underlying each institution and each custom, in order to obtain a principle of interpretation valid for other institutions and other customs, provided of course that the analysis is carried far enough.

– Lévi-Strauss[1]

I

The three levels of social reality that Malinowski identified demand different strategies of social enquiry. People are observed to pursue their interests competitively and in alliances; they tell one another what to do, and they explain to the ethnographer how things should be done; and they think – as Lévi-Strauss says – socio-logically, in terms of the categories and images presented by their cultures.

The Malinowskian obsession with 'what really happens' survived the Oxford structuralist movement and continued as a central thread in British social anthropology. The Oxford school of the 1940s was primarily concerned with the rules of the game, the explicit code of social behaviour. But the interest in how people think, in what used to be called psychological problems, in the logic of belief and myth, so central in the work of the British pre-functionalists, had been virtually absent from British social anthropology for a generation. As

Murdock had noted, this was the price of the sociological orientation which had been chosen, and the consequent neglect of the tradition of Tylor and the culture concept. The most recent monograph of importance which could be directly related to that tradition was Evans-Pritchard's classic, *Witchcraft, Oracles and Magic among the Azande* (1937). Lévi-Strauss reintroduced this range of concerns to British social anthropology. He revived an appropriate analytical tradition, stemming from the later Durkheim and from Mauss; and he drew also on the work of the American cultural anthropologists, with whom he had worked in New York during the Second World War, and on linguistic theory.

British social anthropology had always drawn its facts from the empire, but its theories traditionally came from France. Radcliffe-Brown had transplanted the theories of Durkheim, although it can be argued that Durkheim's ideas had suffered a certain impoverishment in their journey across the Channel. Radcliffe-Brown created a rather British Durkheim, a no-nonsense, down-to-earth sort of chap with a sound theory about how social groups in 'primitive societies' cohered through the dramatic recreation of appropriate sentiments and the enforcement of norms. Religion and perhaps all aspects of cosmology were ultimately epiphenomena of group structure.

Lévi-Strauss's Durkheim (of whom he was, he confessed, 'an inconstant disciple') and even more his Mauss were very different figures, though there was, of course, a certain family resemblance to the British Durkheim. Perhaps this made the intrusion of the disturbing new Gallic figure a little easier.

The tradition of the *Année* school that Lévi-Strauss developed was concerned with 'primitive classification' and 'primitive logic'. It was this, with Mauss's theory of exchange, which provided Lévi-Strauss's initial impetus. (The connection between these two theories may emerge later.) He married these strains with others which he picked up during his American exile in the 1940s – the structural linguistics of Jakobson and the Prague school, and the Boasian tradition of cultural anthropology.

My purpose here is to examine Lévi-Strauss's impact upon British social anthropology, not to present a rounded picture of his total contribution. His influence in Britain became evident around 1960, though it had begun to grow in the 1950s, some time between the partition of India and the independence of Ghana. The moment was ripe. Not only was there a certain boredom with conventional theory, but the empire was falling apart – and with it, some felt, the traditional laboratory of the discipline. Many were ready to shift their interest from norms and action to symbolic systems; and they were prepared to make the necessary shift in theoretical orientation.

The leaders of the new British 'structuralism', as it emerged, were Leach, Needham and Mary Douglas. Their success in converting some of the brightest students of the period was facilitated by the almost religious enthusiasm of some of the proponents of Lévi-Strauss's ideas. 'Structuralism' came to have something of the momentum of a millennial movement, and certain of its adherents felt that they formed a secret society of the seeing in a world of the blind. Conversion was not just a matter of accepting a new paradigm. It was, almost, a question of salvation.

I remember attending Lévi-Strauss's Huxley Memorial Lecture in London in 1965. The general public in Britain was then becoming aware of structuralism, the post-Sartre influence from Paris, and the hall was packed. Lévi-Strauss delivered a brilliant but highly esoteric lecture on the future of kinship studies to a rapt audience. Leach was called upon to give the vote of thanks, and he prefaced it by remarking that he had no idea why so many people had attended the lecture, since only he himself and a handful of others could possibly have understood it. In the same vein, he introduced a collection of papers by British social anthropologists, dealing with Lévi-Strauss's theories of totemism and myth, with the comment that some of the contributors did not appear even to have read Lévi-Strauss, and that their criticism depended 'either on English arrogance or straight misinformation'.[2]

Lévi-Strauss's first major work, *The Elementary Structures of Kinship*, appeared in French in 1949. Its reverberations continued to be felt in British social anthropology until, ironically, the English translation appeared in 1969. In the early 1960s Lévi-Strauss published his two volumes dealing broadly with what he termed *la pensée sauvage* (untamed thought – wild pansies?). Finally, in the mid-1960s he published the first of his series of volumes on South American myths, the fourth and final volume, *L'Homme nu*, appearing in 1971. The absorption and development of Lévi-Strauss's stimulating and contentious theories of kinship engaged the attention of a number of talented anthropologists in Britain, as elsewhere, throughout the 1950s and early 1960s. His analyses of structures of thought also inspired a number of new studies. In the field of mythology, however, Lévi-Strauss's work has had little perceptible influence in Britain. Leach was the only British anthropologist who made a serious effort to develop Lévi-Strauss's mytho-logic.

II

Durkheim provided Lévi-Strauss with a model of society built up of like or unlike segments, which are integrated by the force of either mechanical or organic solidarity. From Mauss he learned that this solidarity may be best achieved by setting up a structure of reciprocity: a system of exchanges binding the segments in alliances. Exchanges may involve one of three media: goods and services, language and symbols, and the super-gift, women. Underlying any system of exchange is the rule of reciprocity, the rule that every gift demands a return. The return may be direct, in which case one has a system of restricted exchange; or it may be indirect, in which case one has a system of generalized exchange.

Lévi-Strauss argued that the principle of reciprocity was the key to understanding kinship systems, for a kinship system was a mode of organizing the exchange of women in marriage. The precondition of such a system was a rule banning incest. Once men are forbidden to enjoy their own women but must exchange them for others, they are obliged to set up a system of exchanges that provides the basis for the organization of society. The incest taboo is also the beginning of culture for it is the first rule to check natural impulses.

The bulk of *The Elementary Structures of Kinship* was concerned with what Lévi-Strauss saw as the obverse of the incest taboo, that is, the rules specifying which women a man *should* marry. In some societies a man may marry any women not barred by the incest taboo, but in others the category of possible wives is precisely specified. A man *must* marry a woman who falls into a particular kinship category – for example, a 'mother's brother's daughter' – or he must take a woman from a group which traditionally supplies wives to men of his group. Societies with such a 'positive marriage rule' (to use Dumont's phrase) have what Lévi-Strauss called *simple* kinship systems. Societies which have only prohibitions but no positive marriage rule have *complex* kinship systems. Some very simple societies, like the Bushmen, have complex kinship systems in this sense, and Lévi-Strauss insisted that he was not making a crude evolutionary antithesis. (Nevertheless, in its implicit reference to Durkheim's *Elementary Forms of the Religious Life*, in the use of the Australian Aborigines as the crucial case study, and in other ways too, Lévi-Strauss's sophisticated structuralist machine moved easily enough in the old evolutionist tracks.)

If a positive marriage rule exists, it can take one of two main forms, corresponding to the distinction between generalized and restricted forms of exchange. In a system of generalized exchange, *A* gives his sister to *B* as a wife, *B* gives his sister to *C*, and so on until at some stage (to be rather formal and simplistic) someone along the chain gives a woman to *A*, so closing the circle. This is a supple, highly efficient form of integration through exchange, since any number of groups may be included in the circle, and new groups can always be slotted in without disturbing the arrangement. Now, this form of marriage exchange may be conceived of as being equivalent to a system in which men marry their mothers' brothers' daughters. If every man were to do so, a system of generalized exchange would result; and societies that have such a positive rule of marriage tend to gloss it in terms of marriage with a mother's brother's daughter. In formal terms, however, the only rule that is necessary for such a system to develop is that no man can give a woman to a group from which men of his group take wives, and vice versa.

Restricted exchange, by contrast, is a transaction involving two groups only, and it is symmetrical. *A* gives a woman to *B*, *B* gives a woman to *A*. Such a system of 'sister-exchange' is typical of societies divided into exogamous moieties, but it can occur without them, and it may be conceived of as marriage with the 'double cross-cousin', that is, marriage with a woman who is both one's mother's brother's daughter and one's father's sister's daughter.

Poised uneasily between these two major forms of exchange, Lévi-Strauss identified a bastard form, involving delayed reciprocity. *A* gives a wife to *B*, and in the next generation *B* returns a wife to *A* or to his son. This may be represented as a form of father's sister's daughter marriage. Later commentators sometimes argued that such a form of marriage rule could not work, unless there was another rule sharply dividing the generations into separate classes. Otherwise this type of system would collapse into a system of direct, symmetrical exchange.

Lévi-Strauss identified different problems. The trouble with delayed reciprocal exchange was that it bound together only two groups, and thus was less efficient in establishing relationships of solidarity throughout a social system. But generalized exchange had its dangers too: it was essentially speculative, since *A* gives a woman to *B* on the assumption that he will get a wife in return from *C*, or *D*, or *E*. However, he might try to claim wives from two or even more parties. In consequence, some groups might become rich in wives to the exclusion of others, and in his analysis of the Kachin – Leach's own tribe – Lévi-Strauss suggested that this was the sad pass to which they had come. The egalitarian assumptions of generalized exchange had been eroded by its aristocratic consequences. If *Political Systems of Highland Burma* had appeared, he might have suggested that this was responsible for the swing from a *gumlao* to a *gumsa* structure (and it is clear that Leach took some hints from this analysis). Another, related, problem with a system of generalized exchange was that those who felt their return in doubt might abandon this method in favour of the less integrative but more secure direct exchange.

There are thus three types of marriage exchange, and each may be represented in genealogical terms as a mode of cross-cousin marriage. Even in the stark and simplified terms in which I have described the model, some questions might suggest themselves. Is this the way in which the actors conceptualize the system, or formulate the rules? Or is it the observer's model? Do the people follow the rules? And what are the units which are making these exchanges of women? Many of the publications which Lévi-Strauss's monograph stimulated are engaged with such questions as these, and with examining what he really meant. In the later editions of *The Elementary Structures*, and in his Huxley lecture, Lévi-Strauss returned to some of these questions, and, incidentally, repudiated the interpretations of Leach and Needham.

I shall not attempt to unravel the extremely complex and technical debates on these issues, but shall rather concentrate upon the larger question – what was the aim of Lévi-Strauss's long, brilliant and often baffling exploration of Australia, the Far East and India in pursuit of simple marriage systems? In particular, to return to the Malinowskian question, was he concerned with what people say, with what they do, or with what they think?

Despite the assertions of some of his commentators, Lévi-Strauss did not believe that he was dealing only with sets of linguistic categories and their interrelations in his theory of kinship. He was convinced that this theory applied both to the marriage prohibitions and prescriptions, and to the actual marriage choices. This was not because the actual pattern of choices was directly constrained by the rules. Rather, both the rules and the statistical pattern were more or less independent refractions of the single underlying, unconscious grammar of opposition and reciprocity. Given this assumption, one could get at the basic grammar either through an analysis of the people's model, or through an analysis of the statistical distribution of marriage choices. But he conceded that the actual marriage choices are also influenced by extraneous political, economic and demo-graphic factors, which have to be abstracted out before the underlying pattern becomes clear. Therefore the model of the people is the best point of entry to the system.

However, if the models and the choices are independent expressions of the basic grammar, then it is possible that a pattern of choices might be discovered in the absence of explicit rules. This permits Lévi-Strauss to suggest how his analysis of simple kinship systems may be used to illuminate complex kinship systems, in which there are no marriage prescriptions. One must assume that as any marriage system is based on reciprocity it will reflect one of the formulae of exchange; and since we would be concerned here with a complex and diffuse pattern of exchanges it would be a system of generalized exchange. One might find, for example, that in a large sample of French marriages the tendency to marry distant kin on the mother's side is greater than would be expected if the pattern were random. If so, the objective rate of certain marriage choices

> of which members of the society may remain unaware, expresses certain structural properties of the system which I assume to be isomorphic with those which are directly known to us in societies showing the same 'preference' more systematically, that is, in prescriptive form.

This would be 'sufficient to place the society in question in the same group as a theoretical society in which everyone would marry according to rule, and of which the former can best be understood as an approximation'.[3]

Although Lévi-Strauss feels he can identify the major structural features in statistical patterns of actual marriage choices, he is more concerned to get 'behind' the flux of real behaviour to the unconscious generating structure. This is the level he believes one must penetrate if one is to understand how misleading the surface appearances are, but it is also just one stage of the enterprise. Beyond the unconscious models lies the human mind, and the final goal is to uncover the universal principles of human mentality. Kinship systems were above all a way to approach this goal, as languages were to be for Chomsky.

Lévi-Strauss later came to believe that the study of kinship might not be the royal road to the understanding of human mental universals. But before going into that problem, let us consider the impact of his theory of kinship on British social anthropologists.

III

Needham developed what he considered to be an orthodox interpretation of the 'alliance' theory of kinship, as Lévi-Strauss's theory came to be known. His persistent search for simple systems, and his mastery of the literature resulted in a series of ingenious interpretations of various systems of 'prescriptive alliance'. However, Needham insisted upon a dichotomy of 'prescriptive' and 'preferential' systems, on the basis that the theory applied only to systems in which there was a prescriptive marriage rule, and not to those in which there was merely a statistical tendency for marriages to occur more frequently between particular categories of kin. This was to limit the range of application of the theory, for the properly prescriptive systems admittedly embraced only a tiny proportion of all known systems. Indeed, as Needham's analyses proceeded, this proportion showed a marked tendency to shrink. Needham also showed a rather literal faith in the ideal model, and assumed that it corresponded to the practices of actual societies in a direct fashion. When the ethnography was at variance with his assumptions, he either turfed the society in question out of the sacred range of prescriptive systems, or questioned the validity of the observations. As David Schneider, one of his most persistent critics, pointed out, not without justice:

> Needham expects to find, free in nature, a concrete system which precisely replicates his type. If the type has characteristics X, Y and Z in that order, then Needham expects to find that the Purum or the Lamet have characteristics X, Y and Z in that order. Needham works with this type as if it were a kind of 'missing link', a real entity which a really good ethnographer who is a good hunter will be able to find – on Sumba perhaps, or among the Old Kuki. Once it is found we will *see* '. . . how the system really works' (Needham).[4]

After a decade of polemical publications from Needham, Lévi-Strauss repudiated his interpretation, on grounds similar to those which Schneider had adumbrated. Lévi-Strauss insisted that the 'model' was in the minds of the native and the anthropologist. Empirical realities would always diverge from it. The dichotomy between so-called prescriptive and preferential systems was unnecessary. All systems were prescriptive at the level of the rules and preferential at the level of actual choices. Therefore the model had wider relevance than Needham allowed it, for it should apply even to societies that did not have positive marriage rules.

The other major development of the theory was quite happily heterodox. This was the work of Leach and some of his students, particularly Yalman. They took over Lévi-Strauss's view of society as a system of 'communication'. Women were 'exchanged' as a sort of message between groups, and these exchanges were linked up with other forms of communication, particularly the communication of goods and symbols of status.

Leach departed from Lévi-Strauss in arguing that the forms of exchange in society, particularly the system of marriage choices, were adapted to political and economic circumstances. If wife-givers were systematically of higher status than wife-takers (or vice versa), this would correlate with differences in the political and economic status of the groups concerned. This emphasis reflected Leach's primary interest, which was not in psychological universals, but in particular social systems. Where Lévi-Strauss was interested in Man and Society, Leach preferred to investigate actors in specific societies. The model of marriage exchanges must therefore be used to illuminate a total social situation, not purged of non-kinship elements in order to provide clues to human mental universals. Leach also anchored the model more firmly to the ground. What were the units, so vaguely specified by Lévi-Strauss, which exchanged women? In a curious implicit reference to Radcliffe-Brown's Australian studies, Leach suggested that they were universally local groups of adult males recruited by descent.

IV

It was in this form that 'alliance theory' clashed directly with the orthodox British 'descent theory'. Particularly in the hands of Fortes, this had become a highly refined system, but like alliance theory it derived ultimately from a widespread actors' model, and like alliance theory again, it was processed in a Durkheimian mould. The people's models (according to these authors) posit the existence of perpetual corporations, recruited and internally organized on the basis of unilineal descent. These groups are political and legal units. How do they cohere in societies? Mauss's solution, in terms of exchange and reciprocity, was neglected in favour of Durkheim's notion of mechanical solidarity. Integration emerged from the opposition of like segments, balancing each other, at every level of structure. This was the point of view that had dominated *The Nuer*. Fortes stressed that another mechanism was also at work, but at the level of domestic, interpersonal relationships. This was the web of kinship relationships that cross-cut descent groupings. Even in societies which made a great deal of use of the principle of unilineal descent, kinship is reckoned bilaterally. The integrative principle is thus 'complementary filiation' – the use of relationships traced through the mother in a patrilineal system or through the father in a matrilineal system.

To this the alliance theorists opposed the idea of kinship systems providing solidarity through a series of exchanges of women. What was the crucial factor - the exchange of sisters for wives, alliance and affinity, or the transmission between generations of rights in persons and in things, and so descent? This question preoccupied Leach and Fortes in a series of widely read polemical exchanges in *Man* in the late 1950s. Leach argued that Fortes, 'while recognizing that ties of affinity have comparable importance to ties of descent, disguises the former under his expression "complementary filiation".'[5] Fortes countered:

> Leach thinks that it is the relationship of marriage and its concomitant relationships of affinity that form the 'crucial' link between corporate descent groups in the Kachin-type systems. I would put it the other way round and say that marriage and affinity are *the media through which* structurally prior politico-jural alliances and associations are expressed and affirmed, and I would contend that they are effective as such media because they give rise to matrilateral kinship bonds. This is an argument from first principles, not from the data presented by Leach.[6]

Some critics suggested that the differences between Fortes and Leach arose from their concern with different ethnographic regions. Descent theory might be helpful in much of Africa; alliance theory seemed to fit in many South-East Asian societies. Leach, however, insisted that a general theoretical issue was in question, and he pursued the controversy with characteristic vigour: but his attitude to alliance theory was essentially pragmatic. It helped to explain various kinship systems, and in particular it illuminated his Kachin material.

In retrospect one of the most curious features of the debate was the general agreement that the units of kinship systems were generally exogamous lineages, an old but increasingly doubtful assumption.

V

Lévi-Strauss never abandoned the theory of kinship he had published in 1949, though he implicitly accepted criticisms of some particular formulations and analyses. But in the 1960s he moved towards a more direct concern with systems of thought. As he later remarked, in the 'Overture' to *Le Cru et le Cuit* (1964),

In *The Elementary Structures* we had disentangled a small number of simple principles from the apparently superficial contingency and incoherent diversity of the rules of marriage. Because of those principles a very complex ensemble of usages and customs was drawn together into a meaningful system, though at first they seemed absurd and had generally been so judged. There was nothing meanwhile to guarantee that these constraints were of internal origin. It was quite possible that they only reflected, within the minds of men, certain demands of social life which had been objectivized in institutions. Their reverberations on the psychic level would then have been the effect of mechanisms whose mode of operation alone remained to be discovered.

So kinship was perhaps too embedded in social action to provide a sure guide to mental processes. The next step had to be to look for a purer expression of social thought. This was mythology, where 'the mind, freed for conversation with itself and rescued from the obligation of dealing with objects, finds itself reduced in some way to imitating itself as an object'.[7]

But in between the two major projects, on kinship systems and on myths, Lévi-Strauss paused, as he has said, to consider for a moment what had been achieved and what remained to be attempted. In this brief period of assessment he published his two comparatively short volumes on systems of classification – *Totemism*, and *La Pensée Sauvage*, both of which appeared in 1962. In these he examined the way in which the social and natural environment is ordered by verbal categories. We make our own 'logic of the concrete' out of the homely elements of everyday life. These were the most Durkheimian of his books, and provided the most straightforward entry to his world for those British social anthropologists who had absorbed the theories of the *Année* school. The structuralist method was exhibited in operation but free of unfamiliar assumptions about marriage or mythologies.

In these two monographs Lévi-Strauss argued that the most general mode of human thought is analogical rather than logical. This was true of all non-scientific or mathematical thought, and not only of 'primitive mentality'. We impose a pattern on our world by classifying the objects in the natural and social environment. The boundaries of these categories are arbitrary. We may, for example, group living creatures into flying things *v.* earth-bound things, or mammals *v.* non-mammals, or meat-eating *v.* vegetarian species, etc. The categories may be formed on the basis of any set of superficial resemblances or oppositions. But if the terms are arbitrary, the relationships between them have a more universal character. The terms of the systems are grouped as pairs of oppositions, and these pairs are then related to each other to form a system of oppositions. For example, in an imaginary society people may oppose men and women, the sky and the earth, flying things and earth-bound things, right hand and left hand . . . and then relate these sets, so that male things, 'up' rather than 'down', and right hands, are all connected and opposed as a set to female things, 'down', and left hands. In this way the oppositions provide the elements of a system which can be used to 'think about' other kinds of relationships, such as the relationships between social groups.

In this imaginary society, let us say, the people are grouped into 'clans'. Each 'clan' may then have a particular natural species as a totem, so that the relationships which the culture has asserted between the species it has defined become a way of thinking about the relationships between the social groups.

The basic notion is that human beings think by making a series of basic oppositions, each with a concrete reference, and then relating these oppositions. This approach, Lévi-Strauss always says, came to him through the work of Jakobson and the Prague school of structural linguistics. It is also related to approaches used in cybernetics. However, it is a method familiar enough in the social sciences and philosophy. Radcliffe-Brown used a similar approach in his second major paper on totemism. Commenting on that paper, Lévi-Strauss wrote:

> The ideas of opposition and correlation, and that of a pair of opposites, have a long history; but it is structural linguistics and subsequently structural anthropology which rehabilitated them in the vocabulary of the human sciences. It is striking to meet them, with all their implications, in the writings of Radcliffe-Brown, who, as we have seen, was led by them to abandon his earlier positions, which were still stamped with the mark of naturalism and empiricism.

The naturalist error was one from which he felt Radcliffe-Brown never completely freed himself, however, for Radcliffe-Brown always tended to assume that the associations and oppositions which people seized upon were somehow presented to them by their environment. Lévi-Strauss insisted that on the contrary, 'it is this logic of oppositions and correlations, exclusions and inclusions, compatibilities and incompatibilities, which explains the laws of association, not the reverse.'[8] Nevertheless, the basic method was one that the British structuralists could accept fairly easily. And using this method Lévi-Strauss was able to elaborate the most daring hypotheses.

An illustration is appropriate, and I shall summarize the argument of a lecture he delivered in England in 1962, in which he covered some of the same ground as in *Totemism* and *La Pensée Sauvage*. The theme of 'The bear and the barber' is that totemic, equivalent, exogamous clans, of the Australian type, and specialized, ranked, endogamous castes, of the Indian variety, are not completely unrelated forms of social organization. They are rather to be understood as different transformations of the same basic structure.

In a totemic system one finds clans, equal and equivalent, each of which may be identified with a particular natural species, its totem. Thus the relationships which have been posited between natural species provide a way of talking about the relationships between social groups. In some systems, members of a clan should abstain from eating the totemic species so that it becomes more freely available to members of other clans. In other societies, members of a clan are held to be responsible for the fertility of the totemic species. In such ways, totemic prohibitions and rituals may become part of the reciprocal exchanges which bind the clans into a society. However, the exchange of services between clans is restricted. The main exchange is of women in marriage.

In the caste system women are kept within the group, but the groups each provide specialized services for the others. So in a system of totemic groups, there are exchanges of natural objects – women. In a caste system, cultural artifacts are exchanged. 'In other words,' Lévi-Strauss wrote, launching into one of his extravagant philosophical arias,

> both the caste system and the so-called totemic systems postulate isomorphism between natural and cultural differences. The validation of this postulate involves in each case a symmetrical and inverted relationship. Castes are defined after a cultural model and must define their matrimonial exchange after a natural model. Totemic groups pattern matrimonial exchange after a cultural model, and they themselves must be defined after a natural model. Women, homogeneous as regards nature, are claimed to be heterogeneous as regards culture, and conversely, natural species, although heterogeneous as regards nature, are claimed to be homogeneous as regards culture, since from the standpoint of culture, they share common properties in so far as man is believed to possess the power to control and multiply them.[9]

The basic opposition on which the whole conceptual system rests is that between nature and culture, an assumption which runs through much of Lévi-Strauss's work, notwithstanding his recent admission that 'the appearance of certain phenomena has made this line of demarcation, if not less real, then certainly more tenuous and tortuous than was imagined twenty years ago.'[10] In his theory of kinship it was the introduction of the incest taboo, forcing men to exchange their women, that marked the movement from nature to culture. In his writings on systems of classification, and on myth, the various modes of exchange are represented as being implicit in the acts of classification, opposition and association, the most fundamental being the opposition between nature and culture. The total social system rests upon a single structural framework, and the social anthropologist cannot detach the cosmology from the social structure.

Lévi-Strauss's creative impact on his British colleagues has been particularly apparent in the revival of the study of systems of thought. He taught them to see cultural sub-systems as 'codes', media of communication susceptible to the same sort of treatment as language. Behind the manifest content of the sentence lies the grammatical form, the structure which generates the whole variety of possible sentences, and constitutes the essential reality. This grammar of symbolic communication is based upon a series of binary oppositions, of the kind eaglehawk/crow, priest/barber. These are in turn related to each other to form a total system.

He took the argument further in his volumes on myth. The *story* of the myth is only superficially what the myth is about. One must decode it, treating it as a single statement rather than a linear series of statements. The real message is contained in the system of relationships with which the myth concerns itself, and these must be broken up into their opposed, paired elements: nature/culture, raw/cooked, honey/tobacco, silence/noise, etc. Using these terms, myths attempt to provide logical models capable of resolving, at this level at least, some of the insupportable contradictions and problems of the world – such as the problem of mortality, or the more specific contradictions of matrilineal forms of social organization. To all particular problems we apply the same mode of thought:

> the kind of logic in mythical thought is as rigorous as that of modern science, and ... the difference lies, not in the quality of the intellectual process, but in the nature of things to which it is applied ... man has always been thinking equally well; the improvement lies, not in an alleged progress of man's mind, but in the discovery of new areas to which it may apply its unchanged and unchanging powers.[11]

Lévi-Strauss was not so much interested in what people think in any particular social context, but rather in how human beings think in general.

VI

Leach was the most enthusiastic and original of the British social anthropologists who experimented with structuralism. His particular contribution was to extend the range of applications, and to rationalize the method in some ways. There are not only binary oppositions – one needs a third term to define a binary set, a term which is neither *A* nor *B*. Because of its anomalous nature it will become hedged around with taboos. For example, one may classify people as relatives, friends, neighbours, strangers. Animals may be classed as pets, farmyard animals, wild animals, and so forth. There may be a homology between such sets of categories. Moreover, just as one cannot marry a woman who is too closely related, and should not marry one who is too foreign, so one does not eat pets, and in general one eats game only in special, heightened situations. But Leach is particularly interested in the anomaly, the creature which does not fit neatly into any of these categories. For example, the rabbit. It is not quite a pet, not quite a farm animal, not quite a wild animal. It does not quite fit, and so it is the source of ambivalence, and is likely to be tabooed in some contexts. And in fact the various idiomatic terms for rabbits quickly become 'indecent' – cunny, bunny, etc.; and the rabbit (under one name or another) becomes the symbol of various kinds of improper or ludicrous sexual behaviour.

Mary Douglas was also intrigued by the anomalies, which became sources of impurity and danger. Her interest in these problems antedated Lévi-Strauss, deriving partly from her teacher at Oxford, Franz Steiner, whose lectures on taboo were edited and published after his premature death. Nevertheless her works on the sociology of perception show the impact of Lévi-Strauss's structural method, which she used to great effect, for example, demonstrating the way in which the food prohibitions set out in Leviticus can be understood in terms of the Hebrew system of classifying animals, the misfits being taboo. Leach was influenced by this analysis.

Arguments of this kind became familiar in anthropology seminars in the 1960s in Britain, to the fury of some of the old guard. The journals were full of controversies about such matters as what the Nuer meant when they said twins were birds, problems of a kind which most British social anthropologists had neglected for thirty years. The new structuralism particularly influenced the monographs and papers of the younger generation.

Yet there was a distinctive tone to the work of even the most convinced of the new British structuralists, and also a definite continuity with some of the concerns of, say, an Evans-Pritchard, or even with the work of Radcliffe-Brown. Radcliffe-Brown's structural analysis of totemism had been preceded by his analysis of Andaman ritual, in which symbols were treated as 'words' which had to be defined by examining the contexts in which they were used. Victor Turner used this technique in his analyses of Ndembu ritual and symbolism. He did not address the contemporary work of Lévi-Strauss, but he was also using an ultimately paralinguistic technique to analyse a symbolic system, if his concern was with 'semantics' rather than 'phonetics'. One can trace a direct line of descent from Radcliffe-Brown on ritual to Turner. It runs through Monica Wilson, who influenced Turner at a critical stage in his development. Turner was interested in both the emotional resonance of symbols, and their social content. His theoretical approach combined elements from Freud, Radcliffe-Brown and Gluckman. But the distinctive feature of his writing on ritual, which has been so influential, is his analysis of the function of ritual for the development, severance and repair of ongoing social relationships.

Mary Douglas had criticized Lévi-Strauss at an early stage for his intellectualist bias, his failure to take into account the emotive force of symbolic action. Now, citing Turner's example, she developed a more radical critique of Lévi-Strauss's paradigm. Her reaction constituted an interesting insight into the different priorities of Lévi-Strauss and the British neo-structuralists. Turner had emphasized the psychic content of symbols, while Lévi-Strauss assumed that the content of the symbol was arbitrary. Further, Turner's painstaking ethnography, his deep personal insight into Ndembu life, was contrasted favourably with Lévi-Strauss's less humane understanding. And finally, and most significant, Turner had provided 'a convincing demonstration of how the cultural categories sustain a given social structure'. Douglas went on, 'It should never again be permissible to provide an analysis of an interlocking system of categories of thought which has no demonstrable relation to the social life of the people who think in these terms.'[12]

Leach has specified the ultimate contrast between the concerns of the British neo-structuralists and Lévi-Strauss himself:

> Most of those who at present call themselves social anthro-
> pologists either in Britain or the United States claim to be

'functionalists'; broadly speaking they are anthropologists in the style and tradition of Malinowski. In contrast, Claude Lévi-Strauss is a social anthropologist in the tradition though not in the style of Frazer. His ultimate concern is to establish facts which are true about 'the human mind', rather than about the organisation of any particular society or class of societies. The difference is fundamental.[13]

But even though there was an indigenous British tradition of cultural analysis that could assimilate the methods of Lévi-Strauss, and despite the very general reaction against Lévi-Strauss's intellectualist perspective, and his often rather cavalier treatment of the mesh of particular social systems, the impact of his ideas was very great. The work which showed his influence most clearly was quite distinct from the general run of British or American studies, so much so that Ardener felt able to catalogue the assumptions of this 'school', contrast them to the functionalist assumptions, and dub the product 'the new anthropology'.[14] The adoption of a new paradigm involves an almost physical sense of changing one's view of the world; and on this test Lévi-Strauss provided a new paradigm for several senior British anthropologists, and many of those who entered the profession in the 1960s. Lévi-Strauss insists that structuralism is a method rather than a philosophy or even a theory, but it is more than a method, for Lévi-Strauss also directed (or redirected) attention to a particular range of problems. This resulted in a fresh interest among some British social anthropologists in the ways in which people use verbal categories to order their worlds, and the ways in which systems of exchange order social relationships.

8   An end and a beginning

Looking back, it is apparent that as a distinctive intellectual movement, British social anthropology lasted for just fifty years, from the early 1920s to the early 1970s. The ethnographies of the neo-Malinowskians then began to be taught as classics, not as exemplars, and the theoretical preoccupations of the functionalists came to seem increasingly remote. The tradition did not suddenly come to an end but it petered out, and by the 1980s it no longer defined the projects of the new generation.

A variety of internal and external factors undermined the tradition, but one was obviously the end of the empire. To begin with, de-colonization made some anthropologists wonder whether they were not in danger of losing their laboratories. In the newly independent countries, local intellectuals began to formulate their own priorities for social and cultural research. Some were suspicious of anthro-pologists, who were accused of collaboration with colonialism. Moreover, other social scientists were now competing for funds to do research in Africa, India and other former colonial areas. They claimed that they had more effective methods and more powerful theories, certainly better adapted to the real problems that the new states faced.

The social anthropologists now had to rethink the very nature of their scientific object. The colonial subject had been loosely identified with 'the primitive' in the public mind, and even in some ethnographies in the postwar period. Of course, by the 1970s no British anthro-pologist any longer used the old idiom of 'primitives' or 'savages'. In theory, they had abandoned the notion that there was a category of primitive societies and primitive religions, which required a special social theory. Yet anthropologists may not have campaigned strongly enough, or often enough, against the lingering Victorian beliefs. The association of anthropologists with the colonial world may even have helped to sustain the intellectually indefensible, and politically unsavoury, idea that the inhabitants of the colonies were uncivilized, backward, and therefore very different from the peoples of the metropolitan countries.

This acquiescence in popular misconceptions had shielded anthropologists from awkward questions about why they spent so much time in the colonies. Now a more considered defence of their research priorities would be required. What justification was there for the traditional focus on the rural peoples of Africa, Oceania and India? If they were not representatives of a different, 'primitive' world, why were they the privileged subjects for ethnographic research? And if social anthropology did not have its special field of research – a particular type of society and culture – then what could it contribute to the broader discourse of the social sciences?

Three possible answers to these questions were proposed, but none was entirely persuasive. The first suggestion was that the scope of ethnography should be extended. Ethnographic studies should be made of western populations and institutions. This had already become a popular option. After World War II, British social anthropologists had written rich ethnographic reports of Welsh, Greek, Spanish and Italian communities. Sociologists had experimented with what they called 'ethnographies' of urban communities, factories, even scientific laboratories. But however desirable such a development might be, it could hardly represent a new programme for the discipline as a whole, unless social anthropology were to merge with sociology, bringing as a dowry only its questionable copyright on a particular method of collecting data.

The second – and contradictory – answer was that social anthropologists had evolved special skills for the study of exotic societies. The discipline had its specially honed methods for doing research in other cultures, its store of accumulated wisdom to draw on for interpreting exotic practices. In short, social anthropology was a specialized discipline with its own proper subject-matter. This subject was not, indeed, 'the primitive', but the peoples who now began to be called, collectively, the Other: the non-western.

And yet, although this claim was a venerable one, it was no longer generally accepted. One complaint was that it was patronizing, even degrading, to the people being studied to treat them as exotics. There were also two intrinsic difficulties. One was that more ethnographers were now working in their own societies. And not only were

European scholars doing field studies in Europe: there were growing schools of social anthropology in countries such as India, Indonesia, Brazil and Mexico, where local scholars were also making ethnographic studies 'at home'.[1] Clearly, social anthropology could no longer be defined as a specialized science of the Other.

The other was that anthropologists no longer enjoyed a monopoly on the study of faraway peoples. Regional studies were flourishing in many parts of the world. Wherever ethnographers went, they had to share their subject-matter with historians, political scientists and other experts, including local scholars. Debates on non-western societies and cultural traditions were increasingly interdisciplinary. Where, once, a British ethnographer might have been the sole authority on 'the Tswana' or 'Fijians', now there were international communities of experts, drawn from different disciplines, who were building up a body of specialist knowledge on Botswana, Fiji and so forth, often supported by new local universities.

The third answer was that social anthropology represented the comparative branch of the social sciences. Its role was to test social science theory by applying it to a range of situations. 'Sociological theory,' Radcliffe-Brown had pronounced, 'must be based on, and continually tested by, systematic comparison.'[2] And who but the anthropologists would provide these tests? Perhaps they might even contribute their own measure of theory. After all, anthropologists had ideas about kinship, totemism, witchcraft; and structuralism, or network analysis, or culture theory could be identified as anthropological inspirations.

Unfortunately, however, anthropologists were at loggerheads with each other on every theoretical question. Even more unsettling was the fact that some influential anthropologists had abandoned hope in the possibility of establishing a viable comparative project. The most ambitious research programmes had fallen into disrepute. Radcliffe-Brown's confident inductivism had been comprehensively anathematized by Leach. In an insult worn by repetition in innumerable undergraduate essays, he remarked that 'the followers of Radcliffe-Brown are anthropological butterfly collectors'. And even if social structures were as real as butterflies, 'arranging butterflies according to their types and sub-types is tautology. It merely reasserts something you know already in a slightly different form.'[3] But British anthropologists were equally suspicious of the deductive gymnastics that Lévi-Strauss's approach required. The structuralist promise was that ultimately general features of the human mind would be revealed, immanent in cultural products, if only at a deep, unconscious level. Even Edmund Leach, the British anthropologist most sympathetic to structuralism, was sceptical of this grand ambition. He said that he remained a Malinowskian at bottom, interested above all in how particular societies operated. Jack Goody experimented with the sample of societies based on the Human Relations Area File, which G.P. Murdock had built up at Yale to allow statistical tests of comparative hypotheses. But Murdock's methods attracted widespread criticism, and few were prepared to follow Goody's example. Some leading social anthropologists virtually abandoned comparison and generalization, and in some moods both Evans-Pritchard and Schapera, for example, had preferred to define themselves as ethnographers, turning their backs on the more ambitious programmes of social anthropology. Yet they were haunted by Radcliffe-Brown's warning, in his Huxley lecture of 1951, that 'Without systematic comparative studies anthropology will become only historiography and ethnography.'[4]

II

The 1960s also saw a new phase in the history of the British universities, the mundane workplace of most British anthropologists. The British university sector expanded rapidly, and a number of new universities were opened, many of which accorded a privileged place to the social sciences. Economics would make Britain richer. Sociology would make society better. (Once a stepchild of the academy, sociology became a very popular undergraduate subject.) Social anthropology, however, now seemed to lack relevance – the key word of the day – and there was little expansion in the teaching of the discipline.

And just at this sensitive moment, confidence low, prospects doubtful, the profession began a traumatic demographic transition. Malinowski's seminar had flourished in the 1920s and 1930s. Its leading members were appointed to the old and new chairs in the discipline between 1945 and 1950, and they ran British social anthropology for twenty years. Between 1968 and 1972 they reached retirement age. Their passage was celebrated in a potlatch of *Festchriften*. Some masters were honoured with three or even four volumes, assembled by competitive cliques of former colleagues and students. In-jokes were made about East African *rites de passage*, but this was no ritual changing of the guard. The retiring elders were extravagantly honoured, but they left a diminished heritage to their successors, the new men (and, eventually, one woman, Jean La Fontaine), who were appointed to their chairs.

After the first burst of expansion, the university sector stopped growing. The outlook grew increasingly sombre in the 1970s. The Royal Anthropological Institute had to abandon its clubby head-quarters in Bedford Square, and gave its library into the care of the Museum of Mankind. Research funds and students grants became scarcer. The social anthropology committee of the Social Science Research Council was suppressed. Some of the leading figures in the field opted for posts abroad in the 1960s and 1970s, as did promising younger scholars. Among those who packed and left were Victor Turner, Mary Douglas, Phillip Gulliver, F. G. Bailey, Stanley Tambiah, John Middleton, Robin Fox and Talal Asad. The impact of these defections was magnified, for social anthropology was a small field, with fewer than two hundred professionals in Britain. Nor could they be made good. In the 1980s there were freezes on appointments, and university administrations encouraged early retirements. The renewal of the discipline, even its reproduction, seemed to be in doubt.

Denied opportunities for patronage, the new professoriate never took effective command. Perhaps, too, there was a certain modesty, or an absence of ambition. The retired elders continued to dominate the intellectual debate in the 1970s, and within the UK only Jack Goody at Cambridge and Rodney Needham at Oxford found a new following. Given the end of empire, the institutional transition, the decline of opportunities, it was hardly surprising that theoretical debate stagnated and that there was a crisis of intellectual identity.

III

To add to the woes of the new professoriate, the very legitimacy of the discipline suddenly came under attack. Powerful critiques of colonial social science were formulated by Frantz Fanon and later by Edward Said, and they were taken up by many Third World intellectuals. 'Orientalism' was identified as the characteristic science of colonialism, dedicated to the treatment of colonial peoples as objects, and to the construction of false and mystifying differences. Anthropologists were among its practitioners. The Vietnam War gave a great impetus to this critique, and stimulated a shift to Marxist theories of social change. Dependency theory was developed by Latin American writers, who argued that social and cultural processes in what was now called the Third World were ultimately shaped by world capitalism.

Another, more enduring critical current came from feminist theory.

At the crudest level, social anthropologists were now accused of having ignored half the populations they studied, or of having taken the word of the men for what women were up to. Feminist writers had drawn attention to the varieties and modalities of women's roles in a range of human cultures, and within American anthropology feminists began systematically to investigate the determinants of gender-based statuses. In Britain, Edwin Ardener argued that among the powerless, muted voices neglected by ethnographers, were the voices of women. Among British anthropologists, Shirley Ardener, Marilyn Strathern and Henrietta Moore developed a fresh interest in the comparative study of gender, and in the social and cultural perspectives of women. Feminist anthropology established a distinct field of discourse that crossed the Atlantic divide, and, even more strikingly, overrode the yet more daunting disciplinary barriers. Within social anthropology, however, it helped to shape the view that the discipline had connived in domination and exploitation.[5]

IV

Above all, social anthropology required a fresh theoretical project. The most serious challenge was a crisis of theory. The neo-Durkheimian social theory that had guided British social anthropology now appeared to be increasingly threadbare. Exercises in typology inspired by Radcliffe-Brown had not delivered robust cross-cultural categories of societies or social institutions. The structuralist theory of kinship had been heavily criticized, and while some followed Lévi-Strauss in his explorations of myth and systems of thought, the British did not believe that structural methods would reveal – as Lévi-Strauss believed – the basic structures of the human mind.

The very assumptions that had sustained the old theories could no longer be sustained. Functionalist and structuralist models had directed attention to the internal workings of a society. They could not easily accommodate broader social forces, such as national political currents, labour migration and religious movements that swept across cultural boundaries. Perhaps for this reason, functional ethnographies had too often ignored the realities of the colonial situation. Yet while the ethnographer might be working in a village, the villagers were usually well aware that they lived in a larger world.

No doubt this line of criticism was pushed too far. Gluckman and the Manchester writers had struggled to set the communities they studied in the broader colonial context. Structural methodologies had encouraged ethnographers to look beyond the borders of notionally bounded societies. Leach's *Political Systems of Highland Burma* (1954) had compared a variety of cultural and political regimes in a large region, which he represented as forming a single multi-centred and dynamic system. Louis Dumont's *Homo Hierarchicus* (1970) had taken all India for its subject. Lévi-Strauss's *Mythologiques* had tracked transformations of myth through South America and even into North America.

Yet there was an element of truth in the charge. The functionalist and structuralist models tended to assume that societies and cultures coincided, and that their boundaries were real. Moreover, these models were notoriously clumsy when it came to the interpretation of social change. Again, the charge that classical social anthropology was antihistorical could be pressed too hard. Evans-Pritchard had advocated a move to historical ethnography. Jan Vansina (trained in social anthropology at University College London by Daryll Forde) had pioneered a new historical African anthropology, which combined ethnographic research and oral history, and drew on archival sources. As more ethnographers embraced a historical perspective, they began to read the social and cultural historians of the Annales school, themselves neo-Durkheimians with a strong and informed interest in social anthropology. Nevertheless, these historical studies sat uneasily with the classical approaches of the discipline.

The compromised role of colonial anthropology, and the failure to treat change, and to take into account broader social and economic processes, became a special target of Marxist critiques in the 1960s. A school of Marxist anthropology emerged in Paris, under the leadership of Maurice Godelier, Claude Meillassoux and Emanuel Terray, and made an impact in British social anthropology. Talal Asad edited a set of studies of colonial anthropology (*Anthropology and the Colonial Encounter*, 1973) that tried to establish connections between particular ethnographies and the demands of colonial policy. Eric Wolf's *Europe and the Peoples Without History* (1982) showed how ethnographies could be situated within a general argument about imperialism.

Typologies were proposed that classified social formations (the new word for societies) by their modes of production: exercises that yielded stages eerily reminiscent of those postulated by the speculative world historians associated with the Scottish Enlightenment. The venerable arguments of Engels were dusted off. Marx's ethnological notebooks were translated and published. The Asiatic Mode of Production was now routinely expounded to first-year undergraduate students, and at a more advanced level obscure Soviet commentaries on Marx were consulted. Lineage systems were reanalysed as incipient class structures, in which the elders exploited women and young men. There were fierce debates as to whether kinship systems were part of the infrastructure, the structure, or the superstructure of social formations.[6]

Some British scholars were converted to these new ideas. In University College London, a Marxist cargo cult swept students and caught up some of the staff, and an innovative journal, *Critique of Anthropology*, was launched. But little came of all this excitement. Marxist approaches lost their appeal very quickly in France and Britain, and were generally abandoned by the late 1970s. A number of anthropologists remained interested in the connections between 'relations of meaning and relations of force, symbols and ideology, domination and determination'.[7] (These concerns inform the work of Maurice Bloch, who became the most creative and interesting of the British Marxist anthropologists.) But the main effect of the Marxist episode was to hasten the decay of the old orthodoxies. The classical functionalist enterprise was now wounded beyond hope of recovery.

Other options began to be canvassed. Beginning in the 1950s and becoming very general in the 1960s, a number of movements across the whole spectrum of the social sciences, and in historiography, had brought into question objectivizing, external, 'behaviourist' explanatory schemes, modelled on the natural sciences. They advocated instead more phenomenological, interpretive, humanist approaches. This reorientation was sometimes spoken of in shorthand as a shift from function to meaning. Peter Winch, a Wittgensteinian Oxford philosopher, had published an influential book, *The Idea of a Social Science* (1958), that gave philosophical grounds for rejecting the conventional projects of social science in favour of hermeneutical enquiries. Evans-Pritchard had turned against Radcliffe-Brown's positivist sociology in the 1950s, and had advocated the interpretive study of what he termed moral systems. The French scholar Louis Dumont, who taught for some years at Oxford, and influenced a generation of Indianists, had given priority to values in social analysis. Lévi-Strauss had already turned the attention of social anthropologists to what he sometimes called – in deference to the Marxists – a science of the superstructure. It was, however, in the US, that an interpretive anthropology was most powerfully established, and a number of younger British scholars began to cast their eyes across the Atlantic.

V

American cultural anthropology had increasingly diverged from British social anthropology since the 1920s. British social anthropology was a tradition in the social sciences, and its intellectual inspiration had been drawn in large part from the school of Durkheim. Its distinctive concept was social structure. The founding father of American cultural anthropology was Franz Boas, who had moved from Berlin to the United States, where he was appointed to a chair at Columbia University in New York in 1899. He brought with him the anti-evolutionist, historical and geographical ethnology that had developed in Germany. He and his students were not in general particularly interested in the sociological issues that preoccupied the British school. Their distinctive concept was, rather, culture.

For the Boasians, 'culture' was initially taken to be equivalent to 'tradition': the values, customs and institutions characteristic of a particular people. It was an accidental growth, made up of borrowings, independent inventions, scraps taken from here and there. As a consequence of these accidental historical accretions, each population had its own culture. But culture was not simply the product of historical contacts and chance innovations: it also operated as a distinct historical agency. Cultures differentiated neighbours from each other, and each culture fostered characteristic strategies of innovation, accommodation and interaction.

Some of Boas's outstanding students – notably Alfred Kroeber, the great linguist Edward Sapir, and Boas's assistant at Columbia, Ruth Benedict – were inclined to argue that however varied its sources might be, a culture was also patterned, internally ordered. Each culture developed a characteristic configuration of values, which the ethnographer had to grasp intuitively, guided by art and mythology. Moreover, this culture imposed distinct modes of experiencing the world. One set of Boas's students argued that cultures and personalities were organized in similar ways, and that each culture also fostered appropriate personality types. Kluckhohn, Kroeber and Sapir began to experiment with psychoanalytic theory, and to focus on the relationships between culture patterns and the individual.

British social anthropologists were typically critical of the concept of culture. Malinowski, it is true, had developed a theory of what he called culture, but he meant, in practice, that in every society there were institutions that met the same basic needs of human beings. He was uninterested in the sorts of things that were traditionally treated under the rubric of culture: religion, mythology, folk cosmologies. He had little to say about cultural variation. For his part, Radcliffe-Brown had objected that culture was not empirically real. One could observe human behaviour in its setting, and 'direct observation does reveal to us that these human beings are connected by a complex network of social relations', which he termed 'social structure'. Culture, in contrast, was not directly observable – 'since that word denotes, not any concrete reality, but an abstraction, and as it is commonly used a vague abstraction'.[8] Religion was for him – as it had been for Durkheim – a reflection of the social structure. Rituals sustained social solidarity. Symbols referred to social roles and institutions.

Evans-Pritchard suggested that American anthropologists preferred to talk of culture – in the sense of tradition – rather than about social processes because they were studying 'fractionised and dis-integrated [American] Indian societies', and also because 'the absence of a tradition of intensive field work through the native languages and for long periods of time, such as we have in England, also tends towards studies of custom or culture rather than of social relations . . . '.[9]

In short, for most British anthropologists, 'culture' meant a rather abstract, formal tradition, which might be far removed from the real business of social life; or it was equated with the symbols and dogmas of an ideology that merely reflected social relations (as in Durkheim's analysis of collective representations). According to Leach, for example, 'Culture provides the form, the "dress" of the social situation. As far as I am concerned, the cultural situation is a given factor, it is a product and an accident of history . . . But the structure of the situation is largely independent of its cultural form. The same kind of structural relationship may exist in many different cultures and be symbolised in correspondingly different ways.'[10]

To some extent, the competitive relationship between British social anthropologists and American cultural anthropologists height-ened this contrast between aspirant sciences of culture and of social structure. Radcliffe-Brown had certainly sharpened the opposition during his years at Chicago in the 1930s. But in mid-century the differences were further exacerbated as American cultural anthro-pologists began to make more insistent claims for the theoretical importance of culture.

In the 1950s, leading American anthropologists were drawn into an interdisciplary project in the social sciences, led by Talcott Parsons at the Social Relations department at Harvard University. Parsons opposed the dominant behaviourism of American social sciences, and introduced the more phenomenological social theory of Max Weber. He also developed a synthetic approach to the study of human behaviour, in which different ontological levels (as he conceived them) were differentiated. Biological, psychological, cultural and social levels had to be distinguished. Each was allocated to a particular discipline: culture was assigned to the anthropologists. (Parsons himself would eventually provide a grand synthesis.)

The Parsonian project had enormous influence in its day, particularly in the United States, and it fostered the development of a specialized anthropology that took culture as its subject and that ignored social structure (the domain of sociologists). Moreover, it stimulated the elaboration of more specialized and narrow definitions of culture. Alfred Kroeber and Clyde Kluckhohn, an anthropologist closely associated with Parsons, published in 1952 a lengthy review in which they listed 164 definitions of culture, before settling on a definition that emphasized a view of culture as a set of 'patterns, explicit and implicit, of and for behaviour acquired and transmitted by symbols'. This was a strikingly mentalist view: 'the essential core of culture consists of traditional ... ideas and especially their attached values'.[11] Clifford Geertz, a graduate of the Parsons–Kluckhohn school, was to develop the most influential formulation of this idealist view of culture 'as a system of symbols by which man confers significance on his own experience'.[12]

As it crystallized in the 1960s and the 1970s, therefore, the idea of culture in American cultural anthropology was essentially cognitive in nature: it had to do with ideas and values, expressed in symbols. Culture and personality studies were displaced in favour of studies dealing with the cultural construction of the individual, the self and the body, which were treated as texts. (All these words became terms of art.) The actor of social theory became a person, a symbolic representation constructed by an anonymous culture, a spiritual being without a mind or a body to call its own.

Linguistic models inspired formal approaches to the study of cultural symbols and categories of thought, although in practice the experiments of the 'new ethnography' were restricted to the fields of kinship terms and ethnoscience.[13] Clifford Geertz argued against the use of formal models, and his programme of 'thick description', of informal, interpretive ethnography, attracted more support, influencing not only cultural anthropologists but also historians, philosophers, and students of art and literature. Cultural anthropology was an exercise in hermeneutics, Geertz insisted. Cultural behaviour should be conceived of on the model of a text. 'Doing ethnography is like trying to read (in the sense of "construct a reading of") a manuscript ... written not in conventionalized graphs of sound but in transient examples of shared behaviour.'[14] The ethnographer constructed, read and interpreted this text, but the crucial act was the construction of a reading, the business of interpretation. 'Believing, with Max Weber, that man is an animal suspended in webs of significance he himself has spun, I take culture to be these webs, and the analysis of it to be therefore not an experimental science in search of law, but an interpretive one in search of meaning. It is explication I am after.'[15]

The Boasian tradition of cultural anthropology was a changing, protean movement, but it was always relativist, insistent that other people saw the world differently from ourselves, diffident about judging the values of others in western terms. It was also notably idealist in tone. The proper subject-matter of anthropology was beliefs, values, conceptual systems, discourses. These had to be understood in their own terms, and should not be reduced to functions or expressions of some supposedly more fundamental reality, such as social structure. And the goal was a humanist one: appreciation, understanding, rather than the positivist ambition of scientific explanation. Anthropology should not pretend to be a comparative sociology.

These arguments were followed from a distance in Europe, but European social anthropology only really came to terms with them in the 1980s, at a time when influences from literary theory began to penetrate the discourse of cultural anthropology, introducing a whole new jargon, and a new pantheon of theorists. What came to be called a 'postmodernist' vogue developed. The postmodernist movement in American anthropology is essentially a radical development of the Boasian programme, and more particularly of Geertz's project. Geertz had argued that the anthropologist both reads and writes a text, he '"inscribes" social discourse; he writes it down ... "What does the ethnographer do?" – he writes.'[16] The contributors to the extremely influential postmodernist symposium *Writing Culture* (1986) argued[17] – strongly influenced by Geertz, and reacting directly to him – that this writing down does not constitute an authoritative interpretation, different in kind from the cultural text it pretends to inscribe. Rather, it constitutes another cultural text. Its author, like the native subject, is trapped in a web of significance that he or she has constructed but cannot escape. The postmodernists accordingly turned the spotlight on the disconcerted ethnographers themselves. No longer could ethnographers view the Other in peace, innocently aspiring to objectivity. They were also cultural actors, caught up in a culturally specific web of meanings, and they shaped their ethnographies for a culturally defined readership.

There could be no single, true, objective account of a cultural event or a social process. The postmodernists preferred the image of a cacophony of voices, commenting upon each other and as they say, somewhat mysteriously, ironicizing. The ethnographic object is multifaceted, it can only be partially and fleetingly glimpsed from any one perspective, and it cannot be analysed. The assertion of objectivity in traditional ethnography had been in reality a display, promoting a claim to authority, political as well as intellectual. The rhetorical performance of the ethnographer was a trick, an exercise in persuasion. The postmodernist ethnographer should be reflexive, critically aware of what he or she was doing, conscious of the problematic nature of ethnographic writing. Experiments in ethnographic representation were encouraged. Films, photographs and museum displays competed with books and articles, and autobiographies, diaries, dialogues were preferred to orderly reviews of cultural practices.

Some postmodernist anthropologists also drew on the critiques of western anthropology that followed the publication of Edward Said's *Orientalism* (1978). Establishment anthropology had been the servant of imperialism. A relativizing, post-colonial anthropology had to unmask the pretensions of colonial scholarship, and should take care not to claim a specious authority to speak for the Other. Postmodernist ethnographers should allow the views of the people to be heard; and if they had to pick and choose, they should give priority to the muted voices of the oppressed.[18]

The arguments became more and more abstract, formulated often in romantically vague terms, but all this high theory was ultimately directed against the very possibility of social theory. Grand theory, ambitious historical narratives, were modernist dinosaurs, surviving from an epoch in which scientists had promised that they would understand the world and change it for the better. Theories were just ideologies in disguise, and their day had passed. At the time of the Hitler–Stalin pact, the British Foreign Office spokesman declared that all the *isms* had become *wasms*. This was perhaps premature, but it was certainly prophetic. A new era had now come to pass in which there were only local, culturally specific, temporary, partial truths.

There was also a view that the world itself had changed, though there was much debate as to precisely when and how this transformation had occurred, and what had actually happened. We no longer lived in the modernist world of bounded societies and cultures, in which an imperial metropolis planned the futures of closed local communities. The world was now multi-centred, but equally all cultures were now plural, interpenetrating. In this postmodern epoch, African villagers watched the World Cup on a communal television set; London and Paris were cities of immigrants, many from the former colonial world, who sent home remittances to support rural relatives; and Vietnamese peasants, who had fled the war to California a generation ago, now sent their children to Berkeley and holidayed in Hawaii, where they were entertained by troops of native dancers. There was no global culture – yet – but nor were there isolated, traditional communities whose main feature of interest was their difference.[19]

Some British social anthropologists were intrigued by these new movements. (Marilyn Strathern was perhaps the most fully engaged in the contemporary American debates.[20]) However, this culturalist, idealist discourse seemed to exclude too much that seemed central to the British: politics became simply rhetoric; ethnic identity was merely an ideological construction; a religion was a system of beliefs and rituals, but apparently lacked churches, hierarchies, congregations; economics was about conceptions of nature, production and reproduction, but excluded such mundane factors as land law, labour, budgets or calculations of profit and loss. The British social anthropologists were, on the whole, reluctant to abandon the study of social institutions, social processes, social history, even, perhaps, social structures.

The context was also very different. American debates about multiculturalism did not find ready echoes in Britain, or elsewhere in Europe. In America, identity politics flourished, and culture became the ground for the assertion of identity. Internal ethnic differences were celebrated. But in Europe identity politics had a bad record, and still seemed potentially dangerous. The movement towards European integration, and the disintegration of the Soviet empire, put a very different complexion on these matters.

VI

American cultural anthropology was not, however, monolithic. Another tradition had persisted from Victorian anthropology. This was evolutionism, which aspired to document and explain the history of the human species within a framework of Darwinian theory. In the early twentieth century, anthropology departments had brought together social or cultural anthropologists with physical anthropologists and archaeologists, and, in the United States, even linguists, in the service of this great project. In Britain, this alliance survived through the twentieth century in only three anthropology departments, in Cambridge, Durham and University College London, and in the Royal Anthropological Institute, which still provided an umbrella for the various anthropologies. But by mid-century the cohabitation was purely formal, even in these institutions. Social anthropologists had abandoned the study of human evolution. They had more in common with sociologists and historians than with their immediate colleagues in anthropology. Although *Man* published articles on archaeology and physical anthropology alongside articles on social anthropology, the social anthropologists skipped the contributions of their colleagues. The Association of Social Anthropologists, established immediately after World War II, admitted only social anthropologists.

In the United States, as well, there was a growing disjunction between the branches of anthropology, but although many cultural anthropologists distanced themselves from their colleagues, others remained committed to an evolutionary anthropology. Leslie White and Julian Steward renewed evolutionary theory in mid-century, abandoning the old, unilinear models of progress and introducing a fresh and vital concern with ecological factors. In the 1960s, young scholars sympathetic to Marxist theory took up this programme, notably Eric Wolf and Marshall Sahlins. Marvin Harris was a successful popularizer of these interests, and, like Leslie White before him, he engaged in polemics against the cultural relativists in the Boasian tradition, and against social anthropology.[21] In the 1970s, sociobiology introduced a neo-Darwinian theory of selection to explain cultural evolution, inspiring another line of attack against the cultural relativists (and provoking spirited counter-attacks).[22]

In Britain, some leading scholars developed an interest in social evolution or in the history of whole epochs. Jack Goody wrote wide-ranging studies of the development of kinship systems in Europe, Asia and Africa.[23] Ernest Gellner – who was appointed to the chair in social anthropology at Cambridge, in succession to Goody – published an ambitious model of general social and intellectual evolution.[24] In the next generation, Tim Ingold was more systematically engaged with the full range of evolutionary debates.[25] But social evolutionism still remained a minority interest.

Another development in the 1970s and 1980s, piecemeal and pragmatic, saw the establishment of programmes in what were called the human sciences, in Oxford, Durham, University College London and Brunel. Here social anthropology students were taught anthropology

together with human biology and psychology. But while these undergraduate programmes are popular and successful, they have not
yet generated new research projects. Few social anthropologists
collaborate with biologists. A tiny group began to examine the possible
applications of the new cognitive psychology – once again, an
interdisciplinary field that was developing rapidly in the United
States. The French scholar Dan Sperber argued that models drawn
from cognitive psychology suggested fresh perspectives on cultural
processes, a challenge taken up in Britain by Maurice Bloch and
Christina Toren.

The field in which British anthropologists are most routinely
engaged with biological and psychological theories and problems
is medical anthropology. Medical anthropology is a new, interdisciplinary, applied field. Its central questions concern the ways in
which illness is understood, experienced and treated in a variety
of social and cultural settings, questions that are of considerable
intellectual interest, and also of practical importance in public health.
It is proving to be one of the most fecund areas of anthropological
debate, partly because it is open to a variety of disciplinary
perspectives.

VII

British social anthropologists were reading American cultural anthropology with fresh interest, if some confusion, in the 1980s, but by
the end of the decade their attention was caught by developments
closer to home. Social anthropology had been a somewhat insular,
British field until Lévi-Strauss and Dumont had forced the British to
pay attention once more to developments in Paris. But while social
anthropology in the United Kingdom was undergoing a sometimes
traumatic reorientation, the discipline had begun to spread in
Western Europe.

In the Scandinavian countries, social anthropology had become
established in the 1950s and 1960s. Under the inspiring leadership of
Fredrik Barth, new centres of sociological anthropology developed,
with close links to British scholars. Idealistic young Scandinavians
had been drawn to problems of the Third World, and social anthropologists played a role in the massive overseas development programmes undertaken by Sweden, Norway and Denmark.

In the German-speaking countries, and in Holland, sociology had
been the most popular undergraduate subject in the social sciences in
the radical sixties, but in the 1970s there was increasing interest in

the non-western world, fed by a romantic rejection of modernity. Anthropology departments suddenly found themselves besieged by students. As one German ethnologist put it, anthropology became the Green Party of the social sciences.

The Dutch had a strong indigenous tradition of social anthropology, and Leiden University was a centre of structuralist theory. The established German and Austrian traditions of ethnology had stagnated, however, and some of its leaders had been fatally compromised by collaboration with Nazi racial science. For a generation after the war, the German anthropologists avoided theoretical controversy. Nevertheless, the tradition of ethnographic field research revived, and in the 1970s a new generation of scholars began to take an interest in the theoretical models of French and British social anthropology.

Elsewhere, in Southern Europe particularly, new departments of social anthropology were established in the 1970s and 1980s, often by scholars who had been trained in Paris, Britain and the United States. And then, in 1989, the Soviet empire collapsed, and the departments of ethnology in former Eastern bloc countries turned to Western Europe for models of anthropology. Moscow had been a centre of international ethnographic research, but theoretical debate had been confined to the bounds of Marxist orthodoxy. In Eastern European countries the main focus of research was the home country. Scholars tended to share a traditional, nationalist preoccupation with peasant traditions, and their work had little theoretical content or comparative range. As the walls fell, the Eastern ethnologists began to read western anthropology with impressive, indeed inspiring enthusiasm.

In 1989, a new European Association of Social Anthropologists (EASA) was formed, which, for the first time, established a European society of scholars in the discipline. The very first conference of the EASA, held in Coimbra, in Portugal, in the summer of 1990, was a catalyst. It brought together what was recognizably a European community of social anthropologists. Conferences were held; a monograph series launched; a new journal, *Social Anthropology*, began to appear; a major programme of exchanges of students and staff was organized with support from Brussels.[26] Suddenly social anthropology had an institutional base on a scale never contemplated before.

The new community of European social anthropologists is becoming more significant than the national traditions that it encompasses, and it is shaping the rising generation of scholars. They share the classic commitment to Malinowskian fieldwork, but draw on a range of sociological and historical discourses. They are also engaged with characteristically European concerns about immigrant communities, ethnicity, and the relationships between European, national and local interests. Eastern Europe is the major new field for ethnographic research, but young European scholars are also reviving European traditions of fieldwork in societies beyond Europe. Their work is informed by a very high standard of linguistic competence and historical knowledge. Wherever they travel, they find themselves drawn into sophisticated local debates and arguments between experts from various disciplines who are concerned with the same ethnographic region. (Scholarship may make advances even as theoretical debates seem to drift. Indeed, theoretical cargo cults often distract attention from scholarly research.) The theoretical interests of the new generation are eclectic and interdisciplinary. There is no orthodoxy. They read the American anthropology journals, but they are particularly receptive to modern European social theorists such as Bourdieu, Foucault, Giddens and Habermas, and to the examples of cultural and social historians.

The 1990s have also seen a spurt of institutional growth in British universities. For the first time in a generation, brilliant young scholars are being brought into the field. British social anthropology is finding itself anew in this European environment. The challenge is now to establish a truly cosmopolitan social anthropology, multi-centred, engaged in a range of current intellectual debates. Its practitioners will draw on new models from the social sciences, and confront them with the experiences and the models of their subjects.

Appendix
Some contributions to the history of British social anthropology

Victorian anthropology

In 1966, J. W. Burrow published a book entitled *Evolution and Society: A Study in Victorian Social Theory* (Cambridge: Cambridge University Press). It was the first modern account of the rise of British social anthropology in the second half of the nineteenth century, and set the ideas of the pioneer anthropologists in the context of Victorian social theory. George W. Stocking's *Victorian Anthropology* (New York: Free Press, 1987) covers the same period, taking issue with Burrow on the question of how far Darwin inspired the new science and connecting the ideas of the anthropologists with more general cultural developments of the day. My own book, *The Invention of Primitive Society: Transformations of an Illusion* (London: Routledge, 1988) traces the idea of a primitive society from the 1860s to the present.

Early twentieth century

Ian Langham's *The Building of British Social Anthropology: W. H. R. Rivers and his Cambridge Disciples in the Development of Kinship Studies, 1898–1931* (Dordrecht, Holland: Reidel, 1981) is an account of the 'Cambridge school' established by Rivers and Haddon. J. Urry, *Before Social Anthropology: Essays on the History of British Anthropology* (Chur, Switzerland: Harwood Academic Publishers, 1992) is concerned more broadly with the first generation of professional scholars, who institutionalized the discipline in the early twentieth century. Another useful source on Edwardian social anthropology is *W. H. R. Rivers* by Richard Slobodin (New York: Columbia University Press, 1978).

Modern British social anthropology

A number of publications have appeared since the first edition of this book, which deal with aspects of the history of modern British social anthropology. George Stocking has written an important essay on the development of the fieldwork tradition, 'The ethnographer's magic: fieldwork in British anthropology from Tylor to Malinowski' (in Stocking (ed.), *Observers Observed: Essays on Ethnographic Fieldwork, History of Anthropology* vol. 1, Madison, Wis.: University of Wisconsin Press, 1983, pp. 70–120). See also volume 3 in the same series (also edited by Stocking), *Malinowski, Rivers, Benedict and Others*. There is now something of an industry in Malinowski studies, and a major biography is being prepared. In the meantime we have, *inter alia*, Roy Ellen *et al.* (eds), *Malinowski Between Two Worlds* (Cambridge: Cambridge University Press, 1988) and Robert J. Thornton and Peter Skalnik (eds), *The Early Writings of Bronislaw Malinowski* (Cambridge: Cambridge University Press, 1993), which has a long and informative introduction.

Talal Asad edited a collection of radical essays, *Anthropology and the Colonial Encounter* (London: Ithaca Press, 1973), which provoked some of the older generation to publish rather defensive memoirs in a special issue of *Anthropological Forum* (1977, vol. 4, no. 2) entitled *Anthropological Research in British Colonies: Some Personal Accounts*. Henrika Kuklick, *The Savage Within: The Social History of British Anthropology, 1885–1945* (Cambridge: Cambridge University Press, 1992) is helpful on aspects of the social history, particularly the colonial context. Jack Goody, *The Expensive Moment: The Rise of Social Anthropology in Britain and Africa, 1918–1970* (Cambridge, Cambridge University Press, 1995) is an account of ideological debate and institutionalisation in the form of a memoir and biographical sketches. Joan Vincent's *Anthropology and Politics* (Tucson, Ariz.: University of Arizona Press, 1990) is a general history of political anthropology, but it covers the modern British contribution in generous detail. Richard Werbner has written a valuable essay, 'The Manchester School in south-central Africa', *Annual Review of Anthropology*, 1984, vol. 13, pp. 157–85. On relations between social anthropology and psychology see my essay, 'Psychology and anthropology: the British experience', *History of the History Sciences*, vol. 3, pp. 397–413. *Functionalism Historicized: Essays on British Social Anthropology* (edited by George W. Stocking, *History of Anthropology*, vol. 2, Madison, Wis.: University of Wisconsin Press, 1984) includes several important papers, notably Stocking's own essays on Radcliffe-Brown.

Published in the same volume of *History of Anthropology* is Hilda Kuper's memoir of British social anthropology. Several other valuable memoirs appeared in the *Annual Review of Anthropology*: by Raymond Firth (1975, vol. 4, pp. 1–25), Meyer Fortes (1978, vol. 7, pp. 1–30) and E. R. Leach (1984, vol. 13, pp. 1–23). See also M. N. Srivinas, 'Itineraries of an Indian social anthropologist', *International Social Science Journal*, 1973, vol. 25, pp. 129–48. Interviews were also published in *Current Anthropology* with Edmund Leach (1986, vol. 27, pp. 375–82), Raymond Firth (1988, vol. 29, pp. 327–41) and Ernest Gellner (1991, vol. 32, pp. 63–72) and with Isaac Schapera in the *American Ethnologist* (1988, vol. 15, pp. 554–65).

Notes

Chapter 1 Malinowski

1 B. Malinowski, *The Sexual Life of Savages*, 3rd edn, London, 1932, p. xxix.
2 E. R. Leach, 'The epistemological background to Malinowski's empiricism', in R. Firth (ed.), *Man and Culture*, London, 1957, p. 120.
3 Ibid., p. 124.
4 A. R. Radcliffe-Brown, 'Historical note on British social anthropology', *American Anthropologist*, vol. 54, 1952, p. 276.
5 Report in *Man*, 1906, p. 57.
6 B. Malinowski, *Argonauts of the Western Pacific*, London, 1922, pp. 515–16.
7 A. R. Radcliffe-Brown, 'A further note on Ambrym', *Man*, 1929, p. 53.
8 W. H. Rivers, 'Report on anthropological research outside America', *The Present Condition and Future Needs of the Science of Anthropology*, presented by W. H. Rivers, A. E. Jenks and S. G. Morley, Washington, 1913, p. 6.
9 R. R. Marett, *The Diffusion of Culture*, the Frazer lecture in social anthropology, Cambridge, 1927, p. 4.
10 Henri A. Junod, *The Life of a South African Tribe*, Neuchatel, Switzerland, 1912, pp. 5–6.
11 E. Sidney Hartland, 'Notes on some South African tribes', *Man*, 1907, pp. 49–50.
12 A. M. Hocart, review in *Man*, 1915, p. 89.
13 W. H. Rivers, 'Report', p. 7.
14 Ibid., p. 11.
15 R. R. Marett, *The Diffusion of Culture*, p. 33.
16 In trying to understand Malinowski's background I am indebted to the three papers on Malinowski by Konstantin Symmons-Symonolewicz in the *Polish Review*, 1958, 1959 and 1960, and to A. Paluch, 'The Polish background to Malinowski's work', *Man*, 1981, pp. 276–85. See also Karol Estreicher, 'Zakopane – leur amour', *Polish Perspectives*, Warsaw, June 1971. I am also grateful for guidance from Peter Skalnik.
17 Cf. E. R. Leach, 'The epistemological background'; A. Paluch, 'The Polish background'.
18 This and the following quotations are drawn from Wundt's introduction

to *Elements of Folk Psychology*, the English translation of which appeared in London in 1916.

19 J. A. Barnes, preface to American paperback edn of Malinowski's *The Family among the Australian Aborigines*, 1963.

20 Review in *Man*, 1914, p. 32.

21 R. R. Marett, *Professor Bronislaw Malinowski: An account of the memorial meeting held in London on July 13, 1942*, London, 1943, p. 7.

22 B. Malinowski, *A Diary in the Strict Sense of the Term*, London, 1967, pp. 158–9.

23 Ibid., p. 167.

24 B. Malinowski, *Argonauts of the Western Pacific*, p. 13. The references in the following paragraph are to the same introductory chapter, pp. 17, 24 and 25.

25 From a memorandum by R. R. Marett, quoted by Wilson D. Wallis in 'Anthropology in England early in the present century', *American Anthropologist*, 1957, p. 790.

26 Michael Young (ed.), *The Ethnography of Malinowski*, London, 1979.

27 M. F. Ashley Montagu, 'Bronislaw Malinowski', *Isis*, Harvard, 1942, pp. 146–7.

28 Quoted by Raymond Firth, 'Malinowski as scientist and as man', in R. Firth (ed.), *Man and Culture*, London, 1957, p. 9.

29 E. R. Leach, 'The epistemological background', p. 124.

30 M. Fortes, 'Malinowski and the study of kinship', *Man and Culture*, R. Firth (ed.), London, 1957, p. 157.

31 B. Malinowski, *Argonauts of the Western Pacific*, p. 10.

32 Personal communication from Professor Lucy Mair.

33 *The Autobiography of Bertrand Russell*, vol. 2, London, 1968, pp. 195–6.

34 In an obituary of Malinowski, *Journal of American Folklore*, 1943, p. 208.

35 R. Lowie, *The History of Ethnological Theory*, London, 1937, p. 241.

36 Quoted in R. Firth, 'Malinowski as scientist and as man', p. 10.

37 B. Malinowski, *Crime and Custom in Savage Society*, London, 1926, p. 30.

38 A. Lang, introduction to *Anthropological Essays Presented to Edward Burnett Tylor*, Oxford, 1907, p. 13.

39 B. Malinowski, *Magic, Science and Religion and other essays*, Chicago, 1948, p. 15. The following quotation is from p. 70.

40 B. Malinowski, *Myth in Primitive Psychology*, London, 1926, p. 97.

41 B. Malinowski, 'The impasse on kinship', *Man*, 1930, pp. 19–29.

42 See Chapter 3.

43 M. Fortes, 'Malinowski and the study of kinship'.

44 Special preface to the 3rd edn of Malinowski's *The Sexual Life of Savages*, p. xx.

45 A. R. Radcliffe-Brown, review in *Man*, 1914, p. 32.

46 B. Malinowski, *Magic, Science and Religion*, p. 202.

47 Special preface to 3rd edn of Malinowski's *Sexual Life of Savages*, p. xxxv.

48 B. Malinowski, *Methods of Study of Culture Contact in Africa*, International African Institute, Memorandum XV, London, 1938, p. viii.

49 Ibid., p. xxii.

50 A. R. Radcliffe-Brown, *Structure and Function in Primitive Society*, London, 1952, p. 202.

An end and a beginning

be conceived of on the model of a text. 'Doing et... trying to read (in the sense of "construct a reading of"... written not in conventionalized graphs of sound but... examples of shared behaviour.'[14] The ethnographer constructs... and interpreted this text, but the crucial act was the construct... a reading, the business of interpretation. 'Believing, with Max Weber... that man is an animal suspended in webs of significance he himself has spun, I take culture to be these webs, and the analysis of it to be therefore not an experimental science in search of law, but an interpretive one in search of meaning. It is explication I am after.'[15]

The Boasian tradition of cultural anthropology was a changing, protean movement, but it was always relativist, insistent that other people saw the world differently from ourselves, diffident about judging the values of others in western terms. It was also notably idealist in tone. The proper subject-matter of anthropology was beliefs, values, conceptual systems, discourses. These had to be under-stood in their own terms, and should not be reduced to functions or expressions of some supposedly more fundamental reality, such as social structure. And the goal was a humanist one: appreciation, understanding, rather than the positivist ambition of scientific explanation. Anthropology should not pretend to be a comparative sociology.

These arguments were followed from a distance in Europe, but European social anthropology only really came to terms with them in the 1980s, at a time when influences from literary theory began to penetrate the discourse of cultural anthropology, introducing a whole new jargon, and a new pantheon of theorists. What came to be called a 'postmodernist' vogue developed. The postmodernist movement in American anthropology is essentially a radical development of the Boasian programme, and more particularly of Geertz's project. Geertz had argued that the anthropologist both reads and writes a text, he "inscribes" social discourse; he writes it down.'[16] The contributors to the *Writing Culture* (1986) argued[17] – strongly influenced by Geertz, and reacting directly to him – that this writing down does not constitute an authoritative interpretation, different in kind from the cultural text it pretends to inscribe. Rather, it constitutes another cultural text. Its author, like the native subject, is trapped in a web of significance that he or she has constructed but cannot escape. The postmodernists accordingly turned the spotlight on the disconcerted ethnographers themselves. No longer could ethnographers view the Other in peace, innocently

...ski, *Methods of Study of Culture Contact in Africa*, p. xii.
...ki, *Coral Gardens and their Magic*, London, 1935,
... *Diffusion of Culture*, Cambridge, 1927, p. 4.
...*se and Meaning in the Social Sciences*, London, 1973,
...56.
...' to 2nd edn of Malinowski's *Coral Gardens*
...56.
..., p. 91.
...*Culture*.
...*t Sense of the Term*, p. 119.
...*tion in Primitive Society*,
...ave drawn heavily on
...demy, 1956.
..., 1967, p. 74.
...on's *Sherston's*
...bution to
..., 1955.
...*graphy of a Con-*
...ons from pp. 84–5.
...*ers*, Cambridge, 1922,

...*at Purpose*, p. 109.
...*Oceania*, 1956, p. 247.
...*st on the Murngin*, Royal Anthropological Institute
..., London, 1967, p. 24.
...ffe-Brown, 'Some problems of Bantu sociology', *Bantu*
...22, p. 38.
..., *Proceedings*, p. 302.
... Radcliffe-Brown, *A Natural Science of Society*, Chicago, 1957, p. 83.
... Lévi-Strauss, 'La Sociologie française', *La Sociologie au XXe siècle*,
vol. II, G. Gurvitch and W. Moore (eds), Paris, 1947, p. 531.
23 A. R. Radcliffe-Brown, *A Natural Science of Society*, pp. 45, 55.
24 Sol Tax *et al.* (eds), *An Appraisal of Anthropology Today*, Chicago, 1953, p. 109.

25 A. R. Radcliffe-Brown, *A Natural Science of Society*, p. 58.
26 Ibid., p. 71.
27 Ibid., p. 106.
28 Ibid., p. 102.
29 A. R. Radcliffe-Brown, *Structure and Function in Primitive Society*, pp. 43–4.
30 Ibid., p. 124.
31 Ibid., p. 131.
32 A. R. Radcliffe-Brown, 'The comparative method in social anthropology', 1952, reprinted posthumously in M. N. Srinivas (ed.), *Method in Social Anthropology*, Chicago, 1958, pp. 117–18.
33 C. Lévi-Strauss, *Totemism*, London, 1962, particularly pp. 83–92.
34 A. R. Radcliffe-Brown, 'The study of kinship systems', *Journal of the Royal Anthropological Institute*, 1941, pp. 63–4 (reprinted in *Structure and Function in Primitive Society*).
35 Henri A. Junod, *The Life of a South African Tribe*, Neuchatel, Switzerland, 1912, pp. 227–8.
36 E. E. Evans-Pritchard, 'The study of kinship in primitive societies', *Man*, 1929.
37 A. R. Radcliffe-Brown, *Structure and Function in Primitive Society*, p. 92.
38 Ibid., p. 95.
39 A. R. Radcliffe-Brown, 'A note on functional anthropology', *Man*, 1946, p. 38.
40 Ibid., pp. 39–40.
41 A. R. Radcliffe-Brown, 'Functionalism: a protest', *American Anthropologist*, 1949, p. 321.
42 The quotation from Boas and the comment are in Fred Eggan's essay, 'One hundred years of ethnology and social anthropology', in J. O. Brew (ed.), *One Hundred Years of Anthropology*, Cambridge, Mass., 1968, pp. 136–7.

Chapter 3　The 1930s and 1940s – from function to structure

1 Hortense Powdermaker, *Stranger and Friend*, London, 1966, pp. 42–3.
2 Ibid., p. 36.
3 M. Fortes's memoir of Nadel, in S. F. Nadel, *The Theory of Social Structure*, London, 1957.
4 Hortense Powdermaker, 'Further reflections on Lesu and Malinowski's diary', *Oceania*, 1970, p. 347.
5 R. Firth, 'History of modern social anthropology', preliminary draft, presented at a conference on the history of anthropology held in New York, 1962, cyclostyled, p. 11. I am grateful to Professor Firth for permission to quote from this paper.
6 G. Bateson, *Naven*, Cambridge, 1936; 2nd edn, Stanford, 1958, p. ix.
7 Ibid., 1958, p. 27.
8 Ibid., p. 1.
9 Ibid., p. 281.
10 Ibid., pp. 262 and 281.
11 Ibid., pp. 278–9.

12 E. E. Evans-Pritchard, *Witchcraft, Oracles and Magic among the Azande*, Oxford, 1937, p. 4.
13 R. F. Fortune, *Sorcerers of Dobu*, London, 1932, p. 150.
14 Ibid., p. 135.
15 E. E. Evans-Pritchard, *Social Anthropology*, London, 1951, pp. 99–100.
16 E. E. Evans-Pritchard, *Witchcraft, Oracles and Magic*, p. 106.
17 Ibid., p. 73.
18 Ibid., p. 114.
19 Ibid., p. 270.
20 Ibid., p. 387.
21 Ibid., p. 405.
22 Ibid., p. 544.
23 Ibid., p. 337.
24 Ibid., pp. 540–1.
25 Ibid., pp. 2–3.
26 Ibid., p. 439.
27 E. E. Evans-Pritchard, *Social Anthropology*, p. 96.
28 E. E. Evans-Pritchard, 'Anthropology and the social sciences', in J. E. Dugdale (ed.), *Further Papers on the Social Sciences*, London, 1937, pp. 72–3.
29 E. E. Evans-Pritchard, Preface to John Middleton and David Tait (eds), *Tribes without Rulers*, London, 1958, pp. x–xi.
30 E. E. Evans-Pritchard, *The Nuer*, Oxford, 1940, p. 85.
31 Ibid., p. 110.
32 Ibid., p. 136.
33 Ibid., p. 148.
34 Ibid., p. 159.
35 Ibid., p. 212.
36 Ibid., p. 236.
37 Ibid., p. 248.
38 Ibid., p. 241.
39 E. E. Evans-Pritchard, *Nuer Religion*, Oxford, 1956, p. ix.
40 E. E. Evan-Pritchard, 'The Nuer: tribe and clan', part 3, *Sudan Notes and Records*, 1935, pp. 86–7.
41 E. E. Evans-Pritchard, *The Nuer*, p. 212.
42 E. E. Evans-Pritchard, 'The Nuer: tribe and clan', part 1, *Sudan Notes and Records*, 1933, p. 28.
43 E. E. Evans-Pritchard, *The Nuer*, p. 195.
44 Ibid., p. 203.
45 M. Fortes, *Kinship and the Social Order*, London, 1969, p. 49.
46 Ibid., p. 72.
47 M. Fortes, 'Time and social structure: an Ashanti case study', in M. Fortes (ed.), *Social Structure*, Oxford, 1949, p. 56.

Chapter 4 Anthropology and colonialism

1 Johan Galtung, 'Scientific colonialism', *Transition*, vol. 30, 1967.
2 C. Lévi-Strauss, *The Scope of Anthropology*, 1967, pp. 51–2 (first published in French, 1960).

3 A. Hingston Quiggin, *Haddon: The Head Hunter*, London, 1942, p. 136.
4 Frazer's inaugural lecture is reprinted in *Psyche's Task*, London, 1913, quotation p. 161.
5 *Man*, 1909, pp. 85–7.
6 *Man*, 1914, p. 67.
7 *Man*, 1921, p. 93.
8 *Man*, 1921, p. 173.
9 E. E. Evans-Pritchard, 'Applied anthropology', *Africa*, 1946, p. 97.
10 See John Sharp, 'The roots and development of *Volkekunde* in South Africa', *Journal of Southern African Studies*, 1981, pp. 16–36.
11 H. G. Barnett, *Anthropology in Administration*, Evanston, Ill., 1956, p. 7.
12 'A five-year plan of research', *Africa*, 1932, p. 1.
13 Ibid., p. 3.
14 W. M. Hailey, *An African Survey*, London, 1938 (ref. to 1950 edn, p. 51).
15 Ibid., pp. 59–60.
16 H. J. Braunholtz, 'Anthropology in theory and practice', *Journal of the Royal Anthropological Institute*, 1943, p. 8.
17 G. G. Brown and A. B. Hutt, *Anthropology in Action*, London, 1935.
18 Godfrey and Monica Wilson, *The Analysis of Social Change*, Cambridge, 1945.
19 A. I. Richards, 'Practical anthropology in the lifetime of the International African Institute', *Africa*, 1944, p. 295.
20 H. G. Barnett, *Anthropology in Administration*, p. 49.
21 Joyce Cary, *An American Visitor*, London, 1952.
22 A. I. Richards, 'Practical anthropology', pp. 293–4.
23 M. Fortes, 'An anthropologist's point of view', in Rita Hinden (ed.), *Fabian Colonial Essays*, London, 1945, p. 223.
24 Jacques Maquet, 'Objectivity in anthropology', *Current Anthropology*, 1964, p. 50.

Chapter 5   From charisma to routine

1 R. R. Marett, *A Jerseyman at Oxford*, London, 1941, p. 169.
2 See *Research in Social Anthropology*, Social Science Research Council, London, 1968. For many of these figures I am indebted to Dr K. Garbett, secretary of the ASA.
3 E. and S. Ardener, 'A directory study of social anthropologists', *British Journal of Sociology*, 1965, pp. 300–2.
4 E. E. Evans-Pritchard, 'Anthropology and the social sciences', in J. E. Dugdale (ed.), *Further Papers on the Social Sciences*, London, 1937, p. 73.
5 Reprinted in E. E. Evans-Pritchard, *Essays in Social Anthropology*, London, 1962, reference to p. 26.
6 E. E. Evans-Pritchard, Letter in *Man*, 1970, p. 704.
7 Godfrey Lienhardt, 'E-P: a personal view', *Man*, 1974, pp. 299–304, citation from p. 301.
8 S. F. Nadel, *The Theory of Social Structure*, London, 1957, p. 158.
9 R. Firth, *Elements of Social Organization*, London, 1951, p. 36.

10 G. P. Murdock, 'British social anthropology', *American Anthropologist*, 1951, pp. 466–7.

Chapter 6   Leach and Gluckman

 1 B. Malinowski, *Crime and Custom in Savage Society*, London, 1926, p. 123.
 2 E. R. Leach, introductory note to the 1964 reprint, *Political Systems of Highland Burma*, London, p. ix.
 3 E. R. Leach, *Lévi-Strauss*, London, 1970, p. 9.
 4 M. Gluckman, 'The kingdom of the Zulu of South Africa', in M. Fortes and E. E. Evans-Pritchard (eds), *African Political Systems*, London, 1940.
 5 M. Gluckman, *Analysis of a Social Situation in Modern Zululand*, Rhodes–Livingstone paper no. 28, 1958 (reprinted from *Bantu Studies*).
 6 Elizabeth Colson and Max Gluckman (eds), *Seven Tribes of British Central Africa*, Manchester, 1951.
 7 M. Gluckman, *Order and Rebellion in Tribal Africa*, London, 1963, p. 18.
 8 E. E. Evans-Pritchard, 'The divine kingship of the Shilluk of the Nilotic Sudan' (1948 Frazer Lecture), reprinted in *Essays in Social Anthropology*, London, 1962, quotation p. 83.
 9 D. F. Pocock, *Social Anthropology*, London, 1961, pp. 77–82.
10 M. Gluckman, *Order and Rebellion in Tribal Africa*, p. 20.
11 Ibid., p. 28.
12 M. Gluckman, 'Seven-year research plan of the Rhodes–Livingstone Institute . . . ', *Human Problems in British Central Africa*, 1945, p. 9.
13 V. W. Turner, *Schism and Continuity in an African Society*, Manchester, 1957, p. xix.
14 Ibid., p. 129.
15 E. R. Leach, *Social and Economic Organisation of the Rowanduz Kurds*, London, 1940, p. 9.
16 Ibid., p. 62.
17 Ibid., p. 9.
18 E. R. Leach, *Political Systems of Highland Burma*, London, 1954, p. 9.
19 Ibid., p. 16.
20 Ibid., p. 203.
21 Ibid., p. 204.
22 Ibid., p. 87.
23 Ibid., p. 263.
24 Ibid., p. 228.
25 Ibid., p. xii.
26 Ibid., p. 97.
27 E. R. Leach, *Pul Eliya*, Cambridge, 1961, p. 298.
28 Ibid., pp. 298–9.
29 Ibid., p. 7.
30 Ibid., pp. 300–1.
31 Ibid., p. 130.
32 M. Fortes, *Kinship and the Social Order*, London, 1969, pp. 221–8.

33 E. R. Leach, 'Jinghpaw kinship terminology', *Journal of the Royal Anthropological Institute*, 1945; reprinted in *Rethinking Anthropology*, London, 1961, quotation pp. 30–1.
34 E. R. Leach, *Rethinking Anthropology*, London, 1961, p. 2.

Chapter 7 Lévi-Strauss and British neo-structuralism

1 C. Lévi-Strauss, *Structural Anthropology*, New York and London, 1963, p. 21.
2 E. R. Leach, 'Introduction' to Leach (ed.), *The Structural Study of Myth and Totemism*, London, 1967, p. xv.
3 C. Lévi-Strauss, 'The future of kinship studies', *Proceedings of the Royal Anthropological Institute for 1965*, p. 18.
4 David Schneider, 'Some muddles in the models: or, how the system really works', in M. Banton (ed.), *The Relevance of Models for Social Anthropology*, London, 1965, p. 69.
5 E. R. Leach, 'Bridewealth and marriage stability', *Man*, 1957, reprinted in *Rethinking Anthropology*, 1961, quotation p. 122.
6 M. Fortes, 'Descent, filiation and affinity: a rejoinder to Dr. Leach', *Man*, 1959, p. 209.
7 I am quoting from the translation which appeared in a special 'structuralist' issue of *Yale French Studies*, nos. 36–7, 1966, pp. 41–65.
8 C. Lévi-Strauss, *Totemism*, London, 1962, p. 90.
9 C. Lévi-Strauss, 'The bear and the barber', *Journal of the Royal Anthropological Institute*, 1963, p. 9.
10 Introduction to the English edn of *The Elementary Structures of Kinship*, 1969, p. xxix.
11 C. Lévi-Strauss, *Structural Anthropology*, p. 230.
12 Mary Douglas, 'The healing rite', *Man*, 1970, p. 303.
13 E. R. Leach, *Lévi-Strauss*, London, 1970, pp. 7–8.
14 E. Ardener, 'The new anthropology and its critics', *Man*, 1971.

Chapter 8 An end and a beginning

1 See Anthony Jackson (ed.), *Anthropology at Home*, London, 1987.
2 A. R. Radcliffe-Brown, 'The comparative method in social anthropology', *Journal of the Royal Anthropological Institute*, 1951, p. 16.
3 E. R. Leach, *Rethinking Anthropology*, London, 1961, pp. 2 and 5.
4 A. R. Radcliffe-Brown, 'The comparative method', p. 16.
5 Henrietta Moore, *Feminism and Anthropology*, Cambridge, 1988; Shirley Ardener (ed.), *Defining Females*, Oxford, 1993; Carol MacCormack and Marilyn Strathern (eds), *Nature, Culture and Gender*, Cambridge, 1980.
6 See Maurice Bloch, *Marxism and Anthropology*, Oxford, 1983.
7 Marc Augé, *The Anthropological Circle*, Cambridge, 1982, p. 67. This book gives an interesting, insider's account of French social anthropology in the 1970s.
8 A. R. Radcliffe-Brown, 'On social structure', *Journal of the Royal Anthropological Institute*, 1940, vol. 70, p. 2.
9 E. E. Evans-Pritchard, *Social Anthropology*, London, 1951, pp. 17–18.

10 E. R. Leach, *Political Systems of Highland Burma*, London, 1954, pp. 16–17.
11 A. L. Kroeber and Clyde Kluckhohn, *Culture: A Critical Review of Concepts and Definitions*, Cambridge, Mass., 1952, p. 181.
12 Clifford Geertz, *The Interpretation of Cultures*, New York, 1973, p. 250.
13 For a historical review, see Roy D'Andrade, *The Development of Cognitive Anthropology*, Cambridge, 1995.
14 Clifford Geertz, *The Interpretation of Cultures*, p. 10.
15 Ibid., p. 5.
16 Ibid., p. 19.
17 J. Clifford and G. Marcus (eds), *Writing Culture*, Berkeley, Calif., 1986. This collection of papers was the most influential text of the post-modernist movement in American anthropology.
18 See, e.g., G. Marcus and M. Fischer, *Anthropology as Cultural Critique*, Chicago, 1986; Renat o Rosaldo, *Culture and Truth*, Boston, Mass., 1989.
19 See James Clifford, *The Predicament of Culture: Twentieth-Century Ethnography, Literature, and Art*, Cambridge, Mass., 1988.
20 See, e.g., Marilyn Strathern, *After Nature: English Kinship in the Late Twentieth Century*, Cambridge, 1992.
21 Marvin Harris, *The Rise of Anthropological Theory*, New York, 1968.
22 See, e.g., Marshall Sahlins, *The Use and Abuse of Biology*, Ann Arbor, Mich., 1976.
23 Jack Goody, *Production and Reproduction: A Comparative Study of the Domestic Domain*, Cambridge, 1976.
24 Ernest Gellner, *Plough, Sword and Book: The Structure of Human History*, London, 1988.
25 Tim Ingold, *Evolution and Social Life*, Cambridge, 1986.
26 The first volume of the Monograph Series of the EASA, *Conceptualizing Society* (1992, ed. Adam Kuper), includes general statements on theory by leading European social anthropologists.

Name index

Subject Index

Aborigines *see* Australian Aborigines
accident concept 74
aesthetic occupations 7
Africa: anthropology used mainly in the empire 96, 98; best regional ethnography coverage in 110; bitty work occasionally done on behalf of colonial governments 105–6; British colonial policy 99; cohesion of society 101; Copperbelt studies 142, 143, 146; descent theory might be helpful in much of 168; fine late Malinowskian studies of states 130; Fortes predominantly concerned with 122; highy-differentiated societies 92–3; historical materials in interpretation 126; Indirect Rule 103, 108, 111; justification for traditional focus on rural peoples 177; maladjustments in society 103; Malinowski's first student to do a study of 'culture change' 104–5; move of anthropologists from Pacific to 69; new historical anthropology 182; new wave of recruits found employment in 116; office of kingship in states 132; postmodern 189; proposals on orthography 100; relatively novel problems thrown up by new wave of research 81; social scientists competing for funds to do research in 176; stateless political systems 82; symposium on culture change (1938) 64; traditional values and culture 111; two types of polity 82; universities xi; virtually an academic monopoly of anthropologists 104; young men in armed forces had their first experience of 115; *see also* Central Africa; East Africa; International Institute; South Africa; West Africa; *also under various country names African Political Systems* (ed. Fortes and Evans-Pritchard) 69, 80, 82–3, 91, 94, 123, 130, 137, 138, 148
African Society 97
African Systems of Kinship and Marriage 91, 92, 129, 132, 133 (symposium, 1950)
Afrikaans ethnologists 98
agriculture 84
alliance theory 165–6, 167; opposed the idea of kinship systems providing solidarity through a series of exchanges of women 168; seemed to fit in many South-East Asian societies 168
alliances 55, 61, 190; cross-cutting 139; exchanges binding the segments in 162; marriage 150; people observed to pursue their interests in 159; prescriptive 166; range of possible forms 60; structurally prior politico-jural 168
Alur people 130–1

Malawi 131
Malaya 104, 134
Man (journal of Royal Anthropological Institute) ix, 6, 11, 124–5, 168, 190
Manchester School 143–7, 154, 157; conflict theory of 123
Manchester University 46, 116, 122, 124, 158, 181; close association with Rhodes–Livingstone Institute 134; Gluckman went as Professor to 118; major department 120; *see also* Manchester School
manners 21
marriage 27, 85; alliances 150; Aranda-type systems 43; choices adapted to political and economic circumstances 167; cross-cousin 164; customs 3; extremely complicated system 43; facts pertaining to four-class system 42; 'group' 11; incompatible 43; inherently unstable 144; Kariera-type systems 43; members of different lineages allied in 60; objective rate of certain choices 165; registration of 105; regulated 43; relationship 168; system is based on reciprocity 165; Tallensi law 101; *see also* exchange; marriage rules
marriage rules 56, 133, 150, 164, 169; customary, regulating 103; positive 162, 163, 166; prescriptive 166; specifying which women a man should marry 162
Marxism 122, 192; attempt to counter 29; cargo cult at University College London 183; colonial anthropology a target of 182; reduction to a sort of dietetics 29; refusal to consider theory 113; theory 190
mathematical models 127
matriarchal society 59
matrilineal societies/systems 26, 92, 131, 144, 145, 168; differing interests in 27; familial and politico-jural constraints upon

92; forms of social organization 172; moieties 55
meaning 183; analysis of culture in search of 187
media communication 172
mediation 87
medical anthropology xi, 191
Melanesia 5, 7, 31
mental universals 165, 167
metaphysics 29
methodology: innovation 142; structural 181–2
Mexico 18; growing schools of social anthropology 178
Middle East 103, 104, 134; potency of nationalist movements 116
mind 165, 172; basic structures 181; facts which are true about 175; imitating itself as an object 169; spiritual being without 186; unconscious 178
misbehaviour 70
misfortune 75–6; 'socially relevant cause' of 79; way of identifying a socially relevant cause of 131
missionaries 6, 21, 45, 94; anthropological research 99; Catholic 17; image of metropolitan scientist in correspondence with 32; mess made of traditional Tswana morality 71; missions and support of mission education 108; more sophisticated, interests of 100; social relations 30
moieties: endogamous 55; exogamous 55, 163; matrilineal 55; which exchange women 61
monogamy 11
morality 3, 112, 138; interpretive study of systems 183; order 48, 54
Moscow 192
Mozambique 58
multiculturalism 189
murder 105
museums 180, 188
musical typology 68
mutual dependence 48
mystical acts/forces 74, 78, 79; agents of harm 75, 77